LIVING CERAMICS, STORIED GROUND

UNIVERSITY PRESS OF FLORIDA

Florida A&M University, Tallahassee
Florida Atlantic University, Boca Raton
Florida Gulf Coast University, Ft. Myers
Florida International University, Miami
Florida State University, Tallahassee
New College of Florida, Sarasota
University of Central Florida, Orlando
University of Florida, Gainesville
University of North Florida, Jacksonville
University of South Florida, Tampa
University of West Florida, Pensacola

LIVING CERAMICS, STORIED GROUND

A History of African American Archaeology

Charles E. Orser Jr.

UNIVERSITY PRESS OF FLORIDA

Gainesville/Tallahassee/Tampa/Boca Raton
Pensacola/Orlando/Miami/Jacksonville/Ft. Myers/Sarasota

Publication of this work made possible by a Sustaining the Humanities through the American Rescue Plan grant from the National Endowment for the Humanities.

Copyright 2023 by Charles E. Orser Jr.
All rights reserved
Published in the United States of America.

28 27 26 25 24 23   6 5 4 3 2 1

Library of Congress Cataloging-in-Publication Data
Names: Orser, Charles E., author.
Title: Living ceramics, storied ground : a history of African American archaeology / Charles E. Orser Jr. .
Description: 1. | Gainesville : University Press of Florida, [2023] | Includes bibliographical references and index.
Identifiers: LCCN 2023005963 (print) | LCCN 2023005964 (ebook) | ISBN 9780813069791 (hardback) | ISBN 9780813080260 (paperback) | ISBN 9780813070575 (pdf) | ISBN 9780813072975 (ebook)
Subjects: LCSH: African Americans—Antiquities. | Africans—United States—Antiquities. | African Americans—Social life and customs. | Africans—United States—Social life and customs. | United States—Antiquities. | BISAC: SOCIAL SCIENCE / Archaeology | HISTORY / African American & Black
Classification: LCC E185.89.A58 O73 2023 (print) | LCC E185.89.A58 (ebook) | DDC 973/.0496073—dc23/eng/20230324
LC record available at https://lccn.loc.gov/2023005963
LC ebook record available at https://lccn.loc.gov/2023005964

The University Press of Florida is the scholarly publishing agency for the State University System of Florida, comprising Florida A&M University, Florida Atlantic University, Florida Gulf Coast University, Florida International University, Florida State University, New College of Florida, University of Central Florida, University of Florida, University of North Florida, University of South Florida, and University of West Florida.

University Press of Florida
2046 NE Waldo Road
Suite 2100
Gainesville, FL 32609
http://upress.ufl.edu

Contents

List of Figures vii
Preface ix

Introduction 1
1. Kingsley: African America and the Rise of Plantation Archaeology 5
2. Africanisms: Tylor, Franklin, Herskovits 21
3. Delay: White Blindness, Black Archaeology 39
4. Pots: Colonoware, African America, Native America 57
5. Cross-in-Circle: BaKongo in America 82
6. Pipes: Tobacco and Meaning 103
7. Pits: Cellars and Storerooms 127
8. Bundles: Hoodoo, Fear, Protection 151
9. Secrets: Henry Bibb and the World of Subterfuge 177
10. Kingsley and Beyond: The Transformative Future 199

References 207
Index 245

Figures

1. *Panorama of the Monumental Grandeur of the Mississippi Valley* 44
2. Colonoware pot seen by Ferguson 68
3. African American archaeologist 71
4. African American archaeologist 71
5. An X on colonoware identified by Ferguson 83
6. Dikenga symbol 92
7. White clay pipe 108
8. House excavated by Kenneth Brown at Jordan Plantation 157

Preface

This is a book about discovery. It tells a tale about matters that, although once overlooked, have proven unimaginably enlightening and significant. The story of how archaeologists first ignored and then encountered antebellum African American culture recounts how historical blinders were removed by a simple willingness to see.

Human life without physical objects is impossible. The inanimate and the animate have collaborated since the first cave dweller grabbed a stone and smashed it against the leg bone of a dead gazelle. That simple act led eventually, through an unsteady array of twists and turns, false starts, and blind alleys, to today's nanotechnological age. Archaeologists understand this often-haphazard evolution better than most. After all, they spend their entire professional lives immersed in the material possessions of men and women long deceased. Theirs is one of the small number of professions where trash truly is treasure.

We humans surround ourselves with objects that carry messages. We may not always hear the messages or understand them. We may not even be aware that such messages exist. For thousands of years, our ancestors used locally available materials to make just about everything they used. Living in our hyperconsumerist world, we select our material possessions from an enormous array of mass-produced things. Enslaved Africans and, later, emancipated African Americans stood astride a world that was both manufactured and handmade. They adopted and adapted to create their material world, and in doing so they bequeathed to all of us a richer cultural environment, even as they struggled against racism and injustice.

This book concentrates on the archaeology of the antebellum era, when thousands of African Americans were bound, beaten, and denigrated. I touch on the postbellum era only when it pertains to the archaeological discoveries of the hidden worlds inhabited by plantation-bound African Americans. In truth, another book should be written about the archaeology of the postbellum era because Black Americans during this period experienced the many of the same humiliations of the earlier era, although they also achieved significant triumphs as well (as did many self-emancipated men and women during slavery days).

Like all books, this one could never have been written without the gracious assistance of several individuals. Kenneth Brown, Matthew Emerson, Leland Ferguson, Garrett Fesler, Mark Leone, Patricia Samford, and Kathryn Sikes all kindly read first drafts. Their advice helped make this book much stronger and more accurate. I apologize for any misinterpretations I may have made. Others who assisted in various ways were Anna Agbe-Davies, Bruce Baker, Elizabeth Bollwerk, Ann S. Cordell, James Davidson, Chris Espenshade, Charles Ewen, Christopher Fennell, Daniel L. Fountain, Maria Franklin, William Graham, Jason Gray, Barbara Heath, J. W. Joseph, Rochelle Marrinan, Akinwumi Ogundiran, Steven D. Smith, and Gifford Waters. Tina Ross kindly drew Figures 5 and 7, and Daisy Njoku diligently tracked down and provided the Smithsonian images. I greatly appreciate everyone's assistance. At the University of Florida Press, I wish to express my sincere thanks to former editor Meredith Babb for believing in this book from the beginning. I also thank Mary Puckett at UPF for her support and for shepherding this book through the process, and the three anonymous readers whose comments and suggestions significantly improved the text.

As always, Janice Orser acted as my companion, adviser, critic, editor, sounding board, and greatest supporter. It is not hyperbole to call her my muse.

Introduction

The capture, brutalization, enslavement, and transatlantic shipment of millions of African women and men stands as one of the bleakest episodes, if not the bleakest, in world history. Occurring for generations and involving numerous African cultures, the European rush to exploit the labor of innocent captives was rooted in a belief that Black Africans and their descendants were, as one historian observes, "stamped from the beginning" with an indelible mark of inferiority (Kendi 2017).

In the land that became the United States, all colonizing European powers were complicit in the enslavement of both African and Indigenous peoples. The French in the Mississippi Valley, the Dutch in today's New York, and the Spanish in the Southeast and Southwest were all guilty of perpetuating the enslavement of Africans. Europeans throughout North and South America and the Caribbean also enslaved Indigenous people, but they often spoke of Indigenous peoples as equal to White settlers, at least in theory (Newell 2015: 7–8). Africans were always set apart as innately inferior to Whites.

The British importation of Africans into the future United States began as a double theft. The "20 and odd Negroes" disembarked at Point Comfort, Virginia, in 1619 had originally been stolen by slavers from the Portuguese colonial post of Luanda in Angola. The English had stolen the captives from the Portuguese ship on its way to delivering the kidnapped Africans to the Spanish colony at Vera Cruz, Mexico (Thornton 1998: 421). It was these 20+ Black individuals who composed the African American "Charter Generation" and who laid the first bricks in the foundation of African American culture in the Americas (Berlin 1996: 253–254; Heywood and Thornton 2007: 236).

What began as a trickle of twice-stolen people taken to the United States eventually became a torrent. In 1790 estimates are that around 700,000 captive Black laborers were toiling in the country against their will. At the start of the Civil War, that number had ballooned to over 4 million (O'Neill 2021). The estimates are open to re-evaluation, but one thing is true regardless of the final tally: a huge number of people of African descent have lived in the United States since before the nation's birth. Most were held as enslaved chattel, destined to work with no pay for their captors' benefit.

When White historians first looked back on the era of enslavement, they were usually drawn to the lives of the White imprisoners rather than all those individuals who provided the wealth and lifestyle of the captors and their families. These scholars worked within "a profession overflowing with white racism," so many of their interpretations were biased toward life in the plantation "Big House" (Genovese 1970: 478). Even as late as 1970, it was the case that "despite a library full of books on slavery, we do not have more than a few fragmentary studies of slave life, of the activity of the quarters, of slave religion (understood as something other than the religion that masters thought they were imposing on slaves), or on slave folklore" (Genovese 1970: 483).

The blinders of White historians began to fall away when Black historians asserted their right to detail the history of their own people's experiences. John Hope Franklin's *From Slavery to Freedom* (1969), first published in 1947, led to John Blassingame's hugely influential *The Slave Community* (1979). Blassingame was one of the first American historians to explore the material world experienced by captive Africans in the United States. His overt interest in housing, banjo and drum design, and the content and meaning of spirituals and dances drew attention away from the written word and toward the expressive, tangible world. Innovative historians like Blassingame also recognized the wisdom to be found in the memories of Black Americans (see Blassingame 1977; Drew 1856; Rawick 1972–1978; Redpath 1859).

Blassingame, who possessed a deep understanding of African American enslavement, described American slavery as "intriguing, complex, and opaque" (Blassingame 1979: vii). Part of the cloudy character of enslavement in the United States derived from the reality that much about the captives' daily lives was not available in written records. Ledger-keeping captors, visiting journalists, traveling tourists, and inquisitive diarists usually provided the briefest mention of the Black captives they encountered. White eyewitnesses to brutality must have considered much of what they saw as too insignificant or unimportant to be committed to writing. Perhaps they failed to grasp the meaning of what they observed and, refusing to reveal their ignorance, simply decided not to mention it. When they did happen to mention captive laborers, their accounts were often colored by racist attitudes and elements of White superiority.

White outsiders may not have chosen to notice the African patterns of everyday life documented by Blassingame and remembered in the testimonies of the former captives. The silences imposed on the realities of African American enslavement would have remained steadfastly in place had numerous Black scholars not demanded that they be revealed.

Despite some historians' dedication to exposing the actualities of Black lives lived in bondage, much remained obstinately hidden from view. The most mundane aspects of everyday human existence involve thousands of little events and hundreds of objects. From the moment a person wakes up until they retire for the night, they use an almost-countless array of things. The same was true of enslaved women, children, and men. One prominent image of the Black captive laborer is someone who rises early, goes into the field from sunup to sundown to toil at cotton or sugar cultivation, and returns home exhausted. This image, although idealized, is not necessarily incorrect, but what about the person's actual life? What did they eat and what utensils did they use? Did they find time to make their own material possessions, things that may otherwise have been denied them, and, if so, what kinds of things were they? Did they practice religion? Did they alter their homes to make them more personal? These and many other questions remained unanswerable until the archaeology of the African Diaspora was created. Only archaeological researchers have the potential to dig under the surface to expose what is hidden.

The archaeology of African America developed slowly. It began in earnest with Professor Charles Fairbanks at the University of Florida in the late 1960s. The research of this traditionally trained American archaeologist would go on to inspire countless other archaeologists, both Black and White, men and women who accepted the challenges presented by the serious examination of African enslavement in the United States. With time, the archaeological inquiry into the daily lives of stolen, enslaved, and oppressed Africans would spread into the Caribbean, South America, Canada, and even into Africa itself. This research has provided unparalleled fresh understandings and wholly new perspectives on the trials, struggles, and triumphs faced by enslaved Africans in a world specifically designed for individuals having light-colored skin. Today's archaeology of the African Diaspora has advanced to the point of urging the entire archaeological profession to adopt an overtly anticolonialist, antiracist practice, one that includes equal partnerships with descendant communities. The archaeologist who started it all would not live to see how others would take his original idea and grow it into one of today's most important lines of archaeological inquiry.

The archaeological research detailed in this book describes some of the main avenues that archaeologists have followed in the search to understand the Black past. Not every line of inquiry is mentioned, partly because the research is proceeding at such a rapid pace that a full narration is impossible. This book, in detailing much of the research now available, will perhaps suggest additional directions of research. Archaeology, like most of the social sciences, reflects the time in which it occurs, and as the United States and the world continues to move toward greater inclusivity, the archaeology of the African Diaspora will undoubtedly reveal elements of the past that are today unimaginable. Included here is the past; the future awaits.

1

Kingsley

African America and the Rise of Plantation Archaeology

When the "Empress of the Blues," Chattanooga-born Bessie Smith, sang "Down Hearted Blues" on her first recording in 1923, she channeled the experience of enslaved and degraded African Americans, individuals who like her had faced hardship and "Trouble, trouble" (Sagee 2007). When she sang that she had "the world in a jug," she could not know that a jug would crack open a doorway into the material realities of African American enslavement. A series of discoveries beginning with a jug would change the telling of American history, but it would take over fifty years after she sang the song before archaeologists would even begin to appreciate her message.

When Professor Charles H. Fairbanks closed his office door at the University of Florida in Gainesville the summer of 1968, his destination was Fort George Island, a coastal sea island lying about a hundred miles northeast of the university, just to the north of Jacksonville. The island he sought, with its pine trees, white sand, and waving sea oats, is one of the low-lying barrier islands resting lazily along the Eastern Shore of the United States. Like many of the other islands, Fort George attracts its share of flip-flop-wearing tourists searching for dazzling sunsets, unhurried dinners, and quiet walks in the sand. But this island, for all its romantic appeal and undeniable beauty, holds a terrible secret. This was a place of brutal African enslavement.

Charles Fairbanks—or Chuck, as his peers knew him—is a near mythological figure to many American historical archaeologists. A dedicated smoker of Philip Morris cigarettes and an ardent believer in the thirst-quenching power of Coca-Cola, he had been trained, like all his contemporaries, in the archaeology of America's ancient Native inhabitants. The archaeology Fairbanks and his fellow students learned was a discipline steeped in the White supremacy that portrayed Indigenous Americans as a vanquished "race." Most archaeologists at the time viewed Native individuals, past and present, as belonging to cultures that were worthy objects of study, but few regarded Indigenous Americans as people who, having faced centuries of persecution, deserved dignity and a voice in archaeological research and the telling of their own histories. Even in 1968 historical archaeologists almost never mentioned African American history, preferring studies of famous historic properties and their elite, White occupants. With time, Indigenous and Black archaeologists would challenge archaeology's inequitable perspective (Blakey 2020; Flewellen et al. 2021; Franklin et al. 2020). But their call for the development of antiracist archaeology would come long after Fairbanks's death. So when Fairbanks decided to excavate the dwellings of the enslaved at Kingsley Plantation, he was stepping outside the bounds of conventional historical archaeology.

Born in upstate New York in 1913 and surrounded by the rich history and presence of the Onondaga Haudenosaunee (Iroquois), Fairbanks developed a keen interest in ancient Native American culture early in life. He spent many days traipsing through the lush valleys of the Upper Susquehanna River, scouring the ground for signs of ancient artifacts, what local people called "Indian relics." These clay potsherds and stone arrowheads intrigued Fairbanks for the rest of his life, even as he turned professionally to more recent history.

Fairbanks got his first experience as a professional archaeologist far from upstate New York at Ocmulgee National Monument in Macon, Georgia. Indigenous Americans had lived in the impressive village they built there for around 17,000 years (Hally 2009). The earthen mounds holding their dead still rise ever-silently from the landscape.

History records that the land on which the ancient village sits was home to the Muscogee (or Creek) culture during the era of British colonialism. During wars between them and the British, Muscogee people were regularly captured and sold into slavery. In 1836–1837, thousands of Muscogee were forcibly removed from their homes and made to walk over 800 miles to their government-allocated reservation land in unfamiliar Oklahoma. Hundreds of Muscogee continue to make annual visits to their ancestral homeland and the ancient village site (Haveman 2018; Vermillion 2021).

To stimulate the economy during the Great Depression, the US government instituted a massive archaeological program at the Ocmulgee site. The government employed over 800 men and women to excavate the site and catalog the collection of over two million potsherds, stone and bone tools, shells, and hundreds of other things extracted from the earth (Lyon 1996: 178–185). Part of Fairbanks's job at Ocmulgee was to establish an archaeology lab and to devise a way to finish cataloging the massive pile of objects left untouched when the government abandoned the project and moved on. It was at Ocmulgee that the embryo of Fairbanks's interest in historical archaeology developed, even though it would take many years before he thought to address African American history.

Returning to Georgia after a two-year stint in the Pacific Theater during the Second World War, Fairbanks and his wife, Evelyn, who had married in 1941, traveled north to Ann Arbor, Michigan. There Fairbanks enrolled in the University of Michigan's powerhouse archaeology program led by the redoubtable James B. Griffin and Albert C. Spaulding.

Jimmy Griffin and Al Spaulding were men of completely different cloth, but when stitched together they made a formidable duo. Few archaeology programs in North America could match their expertise, and in terms of eastern North American archaeology, the Michigan program they built was unparalleled. When Fairbanks entered the program in 1948, Griffin was only eight years his senior and Spaulding was actually one year younger than Fairbanks. Despite the similarity in their ages, Griffin had already established himself as the doyen of midwestern archaeology with his nearly 400-page study of what archaeologists call "the Fort Ancient Aspect," an Indigenous American culture that had existed for about 750 years beginning around the year 1000. This culture had constructed several villages and a series of extraordinary earthen mounds throughout the fertile Ohio Valley. One of their most astounding achievements was the Great Serpent Mound, an earthen construction in Adams County, Ohio, built in the shape of a writhing snake with an egg in its mouth. Griffin's meticulous study, first published by Michigan's Museum of Anthropology in 1943, described the sundry artifacts that composed the Fort Ancient culture. His attention was drawn to the clay pottery, and it was here that his unparalleled knowledge of museum collections would make the greatest contribution to American archaeology.

As Griffin's stature grew, he developed a fierce reputation for demanding the accurate identification of pre-Columbian Indian pottery. He considered ancient pottery as supremely important for revealing information about periods of the past for which no written records exist. He fervently believed that, with careful study, archaeologists could decipher the hidden meanings buried within ancient pottery because their makers had left visible clues on their pots' surfaces. The lines, dots, and swirls impressed onto the outside walls of clay pots, in addition to their different body shapes and rim forms, carried concealed messages. He trusted that archaeologists could learn to read the messages like historical documents. The problem, of course, was that the language the pots' makers had used was totally unknown. At the very least, Griffin thought archaeologists should be able to examine collections of sherds and create chronologies from them. Different designs should correlate with various eras of Indigenous history. The symbols on clay pots should also contain evidence about cultural difference because a culture's potters surely made their own styles of pots and used decorative symbols unique to them. These ideas and his vast knowledge of the pottery of the American Midwest made Griffin a giant in his field. With him in the audience at professional conferences, nervous graduate students delivering papers on Native American pottery would watch in terror for telltale signs of Griffin's reaction. A good sign was when he straightened up in his chair and leaned forward; the kiss of death was when he sat back and turned off his hearing aid (Anderson 1997: 129–130).

Spaulding's approach was different from Griffin's. Born in Montana, he had a broader geographic focus than Griffin, and he had gotten his doctorate degree from Columbia, not Michigan as had Griffin, who had been born on the Kansas prairie. Whereas Griffin was renowned for his encyclopedic knowledge of midwestern pottery styles and pre-Columbian cultural history, Spaulding's perspective was less historical and more scientific. He advocated for the creation of scientific models and the use of statistics to help archaeologists discover the hidden patterns in ancient artifacts. He held that science should lead the way. So while Griffin tended to stay wedded to a style of archaeology that relied on developing chronologies, Spaulding anticipated the scientific revolution that would transform archaeology in the late 1960s and 1970s (Cowgill 1977; Ford 2002; Voorhies 1992). Their differing perspectives complemented one another and gave their students, many of whom became major figures in the field, a well-developed appreciation for what archaeology as then designed could do.

Neither Griffin nor Spaulding had expressed the view that their research should be relevant to living Native Americans, that they should consult Indigenous Americans, or that they should collaborate equally with tribal members. Archaeologists at the time did not perceive their research as meaningful beyond the narrow limits of academic archaeology. They viewed their excavations of Native artifacts as scientific collecting, seldom pausing to consider whether Indigenous Americans might perceive archaeology as the simple theft of cultural property (Zimmerman 2006).

Thus, it was not unusual for archaeologists to believe that they alone should determine how the unwritten past would be presented. Those days are now gone because most archaeologists try to respect the wishes of America's tribal nations (Atalay 2006; Schneider and Panich 2022), but it was in the earlier environment that Fairbanks received his archaeological training.

Fairbanks knew of each man's achievements and stature in archaeology before he arrived in Ann Arbor. While still an undergraduate at Chicago, he had had the temerity to cite one of Griffin's pottery studies in his first professional publication on the coiled pottery he had collected in New York State (Fairbanks 1937). Fairbanks appreciated the difference between Griffin and Spaulding, but he understood their connection, later writing, "Spaulding's insistence on rigorous methodology and tactics was often in sharp contrast to Griffin's intuitive grasp of relationships and processes." Despite their differences, Fairbanks found the men to be profoundly committed to archaeology's then-understood role of exclusively focusing on the ancient history of Native North America to the exclusion of more recent history. He described his Michigan experience as a "great awakening" (Fairbanks 1994: 206–207).

Fairbanks received his doctorate in 1954 with "The Excavation of Mound C, Ocmulgee National Monument," a standard archaeological text and one that undoubtedly pleased his professors. With his freshly minted PhD in hand, Fairbanks and Evelyn set off for Tallahassee, Florida, where Chuck had accepted a teaching position at Florida State University. He quickly discovered that he liked teaching and, in an expression of his growing interest in historical archaeology, began to collaborate with John Goggin, the acknowledged master of Florida archaeology and professor at the University of Florida (Rouse 1964; Sturtevant 1964). Fairbanks and Goggin developed hands-on resources for students interested in historical archaeology, including a collection of specimens that scholars still consult.

Goggin, like Griffin and Spaulding, is a legend within archaeology. He is honored in historical archaeology for his study of colonial Spanish majolica, the heavy earthenware Spaniards took with them throughout their New World empire. His fourteen-year-long investigation of its dates of manufacture, styles, and points of origin has been influential for all further studies of this colonial ceramic. The world-renowned Middle American Research Institute at Tulane University in New Orleans had originally agreed to publish the work, but Goggin kept discovering new specimens and could not bring himself to submit a final manuscript. Goggin was still hard at work on the manuscript when he died, but given its well-recognized significance, Fairbanks collaborated with the Smithsonian's William C. Sturtevant, Yale's Irving Rouse, and Goggin's widow to prepare the unfinished manuscript for publication. The Department of Anthropology at Yale finally published the study in 1968 (Goggin 1968).

Goggin, like Fairbanks, grasped the inherent value of historical archaeology. In addition to his ceramic study and his work with Fairbanks to develop student-focused resources, he was instrumental in creating a forum for historical archaeologists to gather, exchange ideas, and compare artifact finds. At the time, the professional archaeology associations seldom included historical archaeology in their conferences or journals, so historical archaeologists were forced to create their own venues of interaction and debate. The Conference on Historic Site Archaeology, generally dedicated to the historical archaeology of the American Southeast, was one such body. When plans were under way for its first gathering, Goggin punned that archaeologists needed to "get down to brass tacks" and learn more about non-Indigenous, European artifacts (South 1964: 34). Learning about brass tacks, iron nails, mass-produced ceramics, glass bottles, and the thousands of other artifacts manufactured and used during the past five hundred years became one of the primary duties of historical archaeologists.

Readers will note that Griffin, Spaulding, Goggin, and Fairbanks were all men. The overrepresentation of men in archaeology was no accident because until quite recently the field was the almost-exclusive realm of White men, who were either straight or had to pretend to be. Men considered excavation to be a macho pursuit, and women, if they were present at all at an excavation site, were usually relegated to the laboratory where they were assigned the washing and inventorying of finds made by men. Despite archaeology's woman-at-home mentality, some women did defy the odds and force themselves into the field (Lurie 1966). The male domination of archaeology, however, did not begin to change until women archaeologists, many influenced by the feminist movement, demanded a voice (Claassen 1994; Conkey and Gero 1997; Gero 1985). The proper representation of women in archaeology and other underrepresented groups is an ongoing issue within the archaeological profession (Bardolph 2014; Overholtzer and Jalbert 2021; Voss 2021).

Fairbanks was successful at Florida State where he taught many students, including women, who would build their own successful careers in archaeology. After only eleven years he was enticed away to the University of Florida, just before Goggin's death in 1963. It was at the University of Florida that Fairbanks would begin his inquiry into the world of enslaved Africans. Among his many students was Theresa Singleton, one of the first archaeologists to advocate for the study of African American households and communities (Singleton 1980).

Fairbanks's path to American enslavement was a circuitous one. It was in this realm that he would inspire a revolution in American archaeology. What he started in northeastern Florida in the late 1960s would spread, by the second decade of the twenty-first century, across the entire African Diaspora to wherever captive Africans had been forced to labor for another's benefit. But to begin this journey, Fairbanks would have to do two things: learn about plantations and enter the strange world of Zephaniah Kingsley.

The roots of America's plantations extend back in time to the slave-operated Roman latifundia, but when English speakers first used the word "plantation" in the early fifteenth century, they simply meant "the placing of plants in the soil so that they might grow." With the decision by England's nobility to enter the high-stakes game of global exploration, colonization, and appropriation, the meaning of "plantation" was stretched to encompass "the settlement of persons in some locality." The plantation ideal many of us hold in our heads today did not come about until the early eighteenth century, when the term was expanded even further to mean "an estate or farm . . . on which cotton, tobacco, sugar-cane, coffee, or other crops are cultivated . . . by servile labour" (*Oxford English Dictionary*). A more sociological definition of more use to archaeologists is that the plantation is "a large landed estate, located in an area of open resources, in which the social relations between diverse racial or cultural groups are based on authority, involving the subordination of resident laborers to a planter" (Thompson 2010: 3). What was the role of this required subordination? Quite simply, to produce "an agricultural staple which is sold in a world market" (Thompson 2010: 3). Such definitions, although not technically incorrect, whitewash the reality of the hellscape the enslaved faced daily. Frederick Douglass, who had direct experience with chattel slavery, described the institution as "one of perpetual cruelty" where enslaved men, women, and children are "subjected to all the evils and horrors of slavery—to the lash, the chain, the thumb-screw" (Blassingame, ed. 1979: 37, 41). Black enslavement generated White personal and familial wealth. Over time, many plantation owners rose into an aristocracy they jealously guarded. Underpinning it all was White supremacy (Thompson 1940, 1959).

Learning about plantations is easier than understanding the puzzle that was Zephaniah Kingsley. From today's vantage point, Kingsley appears as an unusual character. He was even an enigma in the nineteenth-century American South, where most White southerners viewed him as out of step with those around him, a curious individual with unusual beliefs (see Fleszar 2012, 2013; Fountain 1996; May 1945; Schafer 2003, 2013; Stowell 2000; Tilford 1997; Walker 1988). Some viewed him as a visionary, but others saw him as a reckless and dangerous madman. When she met him in 1842, abolitionist Lydia Maria Child remarked that she had met "many strange characters" in her travels but that Kingsley was "one altogether unaccountable" (Child 1843: 141). Like many others, she was at a loss for words to explain or even to understand Kingsley.

Born in Scotland in 1765, Kingsley was one of eight children of an English merchant father and Scottish mother. In 1773, just when the political situation was heating up between the British Empire and its American colonies, Zephaniah Kingsley Sr. decided to uproot his family from their comfortable London home and transport them across the wide Atlantic to the bustling port city of Charleston, South Carolina. Charleston had already established itself as an important American port, one experiencing a brisk trade with the Mother Country. Twenty-two ships regularly transported commodities out of Charleston Harbor, receiving consumer goods in return. As tar, furs, rosin, rice, and indigo traveled east, everything from bolts of cloth to cases of beer and decks of playing cards moved west. At least 60 other ships also regularly made transatlantic voyages to and from the harbor, seldom leaving the docks free of men, ships, and commotion. When the Kingsleys arrived, the city boasted over a thousand "dwelling-Houses," many with graceful balconies and "a genteel Appearance." Guests invited inside beheld "decently, and often elegantly, furnished" rooms (Milling 1951: 141–142).

Charleston was a place of wealth and grace for the elite class of business owners, shippers, and merchants who inhabited its grand townhouses. But Charleston was also the dark heart of the American slave trade. Its hectic docks were the entry point for thousands of captive African men, women, and children, individuals who were brutalized, manacled, marched onto the city's auction block, and peddled like oxen. As the property of strangers, they would be led away to begin lifetimes of servitude, toil, and exploitation. The enormous funds generated by the lucrative trade in human flesh not only propped up the city's economy, it also supported the entire colony. Around 40 percent of all enslaved Africans who entered the United States came through Charleston, with about 93,000 arriving before 1775, just about when the Kingsleys first set foot on the dock (Hicks 2020; Morgan 1998; O'Malley 2017).

Kingsley the elder burrowed snuggly into Charleston's commercial scene and quickly established himself as a leading merchant. A broker of commodities from the Old World, including tea, in November 1774, Kingsley senior found himself crossways with the city's rebellious Committee of Observation. The British Parliament had passed the despised Tea Act in May of the previous year, and in places like Charleston, the citizens' emotions ran high against it. After all, they were being asked to use their taxes to bail out the heavily indebted, although immensely powerful, East India Company. Revolted by the Crown's insult, angry revolutionaries dumped Kingsley's seven crates of tea into Charleston Harbor, in a southern re-creation of the previous December's Boston Tea Party. Things went from bad to worse for Kingsley who, as a dedicated loyalist, found his estate confiscated in February 1782 and his family banished from the colony just as the Revolutionary War was winding down. With the war swirling around him, Kingsley had the nerve to request that Charleston's British commandant appoint him as the commander of a royalist militia. Kingsley not only attempted to import tea in the politically charged, tea-hating environment, he also had the gall to ask for an active role against the revolutionaries' cause.

Where the family went after being ejected from Charleston is a mystery, but by 1803, Zephaniah Kingsley Jr. had appeared further south in Spanish Florida. He had assumed his father's mantle as a commodities importer, but instead of trafficking in tea and other consumables, Kingsley junior found his source of wealth in the sale of human beings. His burgeoning maritime shipping empire ranged as far north as British Nova Scotia and as far south as Danish St. Croix. Being more committed to accumulation than to nationalism, and perhaps remembering where politics had gotten his father, the younger Kingsley acquired Danish citizenship on St. Croix and, after moving to Florida, obtained Spanish citizenship. Willing to flaunt national borders, he was not above smuggling captive Africans between Spanish Florida and English America.

Kingsley was optimistic but embittered, ruthless in business yet personally engaging, intelligent but susceptible to self-delusion. His most controversial views involved African Americans and enslavement. Kingsley defended African slavery while he evoked sentiments of comradeship with free people of color. He believed that Africans were "physically and morally" superior to Whites (Child 1843: 143), but he had no reservations about owning Black human beings and profiting from their suffering. Before 1810 he owned at least 74 captive Africans purchased in the Caribbean and along the coast of the southern United States, including in Charleston. Seeking to settle down, he established a home in St. Augustine and built a slave-laboring plantation (see Baptist 2016) called Laurel Grove south of Jacksonville. In 1813 he made his final move to Fort George Island, where Fairbanks found his plantation's remains 150 years later. Kingsley would eventually purchase thousands of acres in Florida and exploit the labor of around 300 captive Africans.

For an antebellum plantation owner who relied on others' labor for his sustenance, Kingsley's approach to African enslavement was at odds with most of his fellow enslavers. He appointed mixed-race Africans as plantation managers and generally appeared to believe in some degree of humane treatment. He freed a slave woman he had purchased in Havana and regarded her as his wife. He and this remarkable woman, the former daughter of an African chieftain, had four children, whom he emancipated and had properly educated.

As an emancipated Black woman, Anta Madgigine Jai, or Anna Kingsley, was able to petition and receive a land grant from the Spanish government. With the grant in hand, she gathered what she would need to operate her own slave-laboring plantation near Kingsley's home estate. Depredations by raiders from the United States destroyed her plantation as well as Kingsley's Laurel Grove, acts that precipitated Kingsley's removal to Fort George Island. When the United States finally acquired Florida in 1821, Kingsley, then a wealthy and powerful planter, was named to the territory's legislative council. Being what was then considered an enlightened slave owner, Kingsley tried to persuade his follow councillors to adopt Spain's somewhat liberal attitude toward civil rights for the region's free Black population. He was ultimately unable to persuade the councillors, and the territory adopted the much harsher, more American way of treating individuals of African heritage. Writing as "An Inhabitant of Florida" in his *Treatise on the Patriarchal or Co-operative System of Society . . . Under the Name of Slavery*, first published in 1828, Kingsley argued that agriculture is "the great foundation of the wealth and prosperity of our Southern States." He further proposed that Whites are unsuited to laboring in hot, humid climates, and that "the idea of slavery," when practiced in a cruel and unjust manner, "is revolting to every philanthropic mind; but when that idea is associated with justice, and benevolence, slavery . . . easily amalgamates with the ordinary conditions of life" (Kingsley 1828: i).

Kingsley had no reason to elaborate on his assertion about the importance of agriculture to the American South. This was one thing that just about every White American accepted. All one had to do was to consider the explosive growth of cotton culture and its commanding place in the United States and Great Britain, the world's two greatest economies (Baptist 2016: 114). Cotton, brutal plantations, transatlantic shipping, and enslaved Africans were an ensemble that defined the nineteenth century. The relationship between climate and race was less universally accepted, so Kingsley tried to explain it.

He began by observing that the nation's "white population extending from the Chesapeake Bay to the Mississippi" had a "sickly appearance." The unhealthy appearance of the average White American in the South, he claimed, was most evident among "the lower orders," those individuals who, because of their stations in life, usually worked outdoors. Kingsley noted that the reason for the Whites' frailty was not that they had a "natural indisposition" to work but simply that their "white complexions" rendered them unsuited to labor in the scorching sun. He believed that "the darkness of complexion" was more appropriate for the "endurance of labor" in sweltering environments (Kingsley 1828: 5). The White population of the South therefore could not be faulted for their failure as agricultural laborers; the defect was in their physical makeup, what we today would call their genes. Given Whites' innate weakness, the enslavement of people of color was the only reasonable option Kingsley could imagine. Because slave labor created "nearly all the springs of national and individual prosperity" (Kingsley 1829: 6), the South could not abandon it if it were to maintain its role as a major exporter of cotton and other agricultural money makers. Given the supreme importance of African enslavement to the South, the only reasonable option was to reform it, to treat enslaved individuals in "a just, conscientious and humane" manner. To his mind, a good master was one who provided "for the physical wants of his servants, his wife and children, in health, sickness and old age" (Kingsley 1828: 5). He overlooked, or simply refused to acknowledge, the inhumane cruelty that is the essence of human enslavement.

As proof of the efficacy of his approach, Kingsley offered a personal account of his Fort George plantation, begun "about twenty-five years ago" with "about fifty new African negroes, many of whom I brought from the coast [of Africa] myself." Adopting the paternal posture common among Southern slave owners, Kingsley noted that he "taught them nothing but what was useful, and what I thought would add to their physical and moral happiness." In addition, he claimed to have "encouraged as much as possible dancing, merriment and dress," and because his "punishment was quite light," his captive laborers were "perfectly honest and obedient, and appeared quite happy" (Kingsley 1828: 14).

Kingsley's climatic theory of race—and, hence, his justification for slavery—was not new. Apologists for enslavement had long used this argument to justify the capture and enslavement of Africans living in hot climates. The idea that inhabitants of such places have certain physical traits has its roots in the writings of Greek and Roman scholars. Hippocrates, the storied progenitor of Western medicine, provided the belief's foundation. Writing in 400 BCE, he directly linked a region's climate to its residents' general appearance and susceptibility to disease. Dividing the world into hot, cold, and moderate regions, he supposed that moderation is always to be preferred, a fact he thought observable in nature: in places with moderate temperatures, "the inhabitants are, for the most part, well coloured and blooming," and they "have clear voices and in temper and intellect are superior" to people from harsher climates, whether hot or cold (Burnell 1881: 18–19).

The link Hippocrates forged between physical appearance, personality, and climate held sway among Western scholars for centuries, including throughout Kingsley's lifetime. Authors often reargued Hippocrates's position by sprucing it up with modern language and more contemporary concepts. In the late eighteenth century, Englishman William Falconer, a medical doctor and Royal Society fellow, outlined the influence of climate and other variables on human nature. Falconer contended that hot climates induce human cowardice, timidity, indolence, and immorality and concluded that Hippocrates had been correct: moderate climates produce moderate temperaments and thus good citizens. Conversely, hot and cold extremes produce extreme temperaments. A place like Sub-Saharan Africa, said Falconer, could not produce even-tempered, cultured individuals because "although not absolute savages, [they] are still in a very imperfect state of civilization" (Falconer 1781: 6–14, 277). This kind of racist thinking, supported by the day's misguided science, made arguments like Kingsley's seem perfectly reasonable. Such beliefs, reinforced by structural racism, kept people of color outside the halls of power and denied them authority and social power.

Whereas Kingsley's views on the connection between climate and race were generally accepted, his other ideas were considerably more controversial. Not only did he openly live with a formerly enslaved African woman, he also readily acknowledged their children as his own, just as he did with children by another women. His views that people of African heritage were morally superior to Whites especially rankled his detractors because it attacked the shaky foundation of the slave regime. If Blacks were judged to be superior, what did their enslavement say about those who enslaved them?

Kingsley's unorthodox views made him a frequent target for abolitionists and enslavers alike. Ruffling feathers was one thing; assaulting the entire slave regime was something else entirely. Fearing retaliation from both neighbors and strangers, the headstrong Kingsley decided that proving his point on his Florida plantation was not enough. He had to adopt a more radical plan, one that would dramatically demonstrate the righteousness of his views. So beginning in 1835 and lasting until his death in 1843, Kingsley sought to create a viable community of African workers in Haiti. Sending around 60 of his enslaved laborers to the island to toil in the fields, he put his mixed-race son, George, in charge of the estate's day-to-day operation. Kingsley bound the people he sent to Haiti to nine-year terms of service, at the end of which he required them to pay for their freedom at the price he determined. While this experiment in "free, African labor" was under way, the African men and women living on his Florida plantation remained in the same state of bondage as ever (Kingsley 1838).

Fairbanks's association with Kingsley began serendipitously. The Florida State Park Service was planning to rebuild an enslaved person's house on the old Kingsley property, and they believed that an excavation would uncover the specific architectural details they would need to construct an accurate dwelling. Using archaeology to document architecture was a tried-and-true method that had been wildly successful at Williamsburg, Virginia. There archaeologists and historical architects had worked side by side since the 1930s to document and rebuild some of the most iconic colonial buildings in the United States (Yetter 1988). Surely the process would work again at Kingsley plantation, where the planned reconstruction involved only one small building.

Fairbanks saw a unique opportunity by helping the park service. He knew that giving them the architectural details they sought would be relatively straightforward. Buried foundations, and even their subtle traces if removed, are easy to locate, and nails and window glass can offer clues about a building's superstructure. But Fairbanks grasped that he could accomplish so much more. As he studied the story of the plantation's eccentric owner, his enthusiasm grew, and he became profoundly intrigued. Kingsley's unorthodox approach to African enslavement might open doors that had remained firmly shut to scholars. Archaeology might expose lost details about things captive Africans had made themselves, handcrafted items totally unrecorded in historical accounts. These objects would in turn provide new insights into the daily lives and survival strategies of America's enslaved African captives.

A nineteenth-century slave-labor plantation was a model place to provide the evidence Fairbanks sought. During the earliest years of the transportation of Africans to the United States, most future plantation owners operated only small farms, generally with one or two enslaved workers. Most owners believed that such a small workforce did not require its own living space, so they forced individual Black laborers to live in attics or lofts, or to sleep in kitchens, sheds, or other outbuildings. Only when plantations began to expand to eventually become the quintessential, Gone-with-the-Wind-type estates did owners determine that large numbers of individuals of African heritage should be segregated in their own living spaces. The owners' decisions may have been based on fear rather than their concern for the captives' well-being. Surveillance was easiest when all the workers were housed in the same general place (see Delle 1988: 155–161).

Fairbanks believed that Kingsley's actions—including the importation of men and women directly from Africa, his efforts to teach them "useful" skills, and his alleged permissive attitude—meshed to create a unique cultural environment. Fairbanks hoped that these decisions would have made it possible for Kingsley's captive Africans to express elements of their native cultures. These features of life in the Old World, termed "Africanisms," would constitute the physical, irrefutable evidence for the ways African men and women at Kingsley's Florida plantation had retained elements of their past homelands.

The general idea behind Africanisms was that such items should present an unvarnished view of an African lifestyle under enslavement, things that reveal hidden truths about daily lived reality. If he could discover material Africanisms in his excavation, Fairbanks believed he could crack a door into the material connections between Africa and Florida and perhaps even shed light on links between the African Diaspora and the Western Hemisphere (Fairbanks 1974: 63–64, 1984: 2).

Many nineteenth-century Southern planters arranged the homes of their enslaved laborers in neat "quarters," rows or straight lines of houses along narrow dirt roads. Being unorthodox in most things, Kingsley arranged the dwellings of the enslaved on his plantation in a semicircle located about a thousand feet south of his home. A road, bordered on both sides by palmettos, divided the arc into halves, leaving sixteen cabins on the east side and presumably the same number on the west side, although only a few remains were visible in 1968. Fairbanks chose the largest house next to the road on the west for his excavation. The cabin just east of the road, also the largest in that side of the semicircle and presumably a mirror image of the one to be excavated, was the one the park service planned to reconstruct.

The home, partially intact in 1968, had been built of poured tabby, a dense mixture of locally available sand, water, lime, and shells. Known locally as "coastal concrete," the mixture was extremely durable. Fairbanks could tell that the house's builders had harvested a nearby Native American midden for the tabby's shells because embedded in the walls were pieces of a colonial Spanish majolica of the sort Goggin had studied.

The building for the enslaved was around 16 × 25 feet on the outside, with two interior rooms divided by a thin wall. The smaller, eastern room measured about 16 × 8 feet, and the western room was about 16 × 12 feet. The smaller room had two windows, one each on the north and south walls. The larger room had the building's only door, on the north side. A large brick-and-tabby fireplace, measuring almost 9 feet wide, was situated on the western wall of the larger room.

Fairbanks's excavation of the cabin's interior produced an abundance of mass-produced glazed earthenware sherds, heavy pieces of stoneware from storage jugs, fragments of window and bottle glass, iron nails and other building hardware, buttons, tobacco pipes, and a few pieces of Native American pottery. As is true of many excavations at nineteenth-century domestic buildings, the glazed ceramics provided the most telling information.

When he studied the ceramics excavated from the Kingsley cabin, Fairbanks realized that the glazed pieces could be divided into two components, an early group, with an average date of 1819, and a late group, averaging about 1857. These findings puzzled Fairbanks because the first group dated before Kingsley developed the plantation, while the second group dated to after Kingsley's death. Explaining the second group was easy. Someone must have lived in the dwelling after Kingsley's death, but Fairbanks had no way of knowing whether they had been enslaved or free laborers. The earlier ceramic group was more difficult to interpret. Fairbanks reasoned that it must have been used by the enslaved individuals who lived in the house during Kingsley's lifetime. The problem was that the dishes were about ten years too early in date. Faced with this puzzle, Fairbanks drew the conclusion that the Kingsley family must have slowly discarded individual pieces of tableware and then passed them on to the enslaved laborers (Fairbanks 1974: 82).

The idea he proposed in 1968 was revolutionary. No one had ever given much thought to an enslaved person's material possessions, especially something as mundane as their dishes, and none of the anthropologists or folklorists who spoke with once-enslaved individuals had apparently ever thought to ask them about such a mundane matter. Fieldworkers collecting oral histories were usually more interested in folk tales and stories of life under enslavement. But the use of ceramic hand-me-downs created a new line of investigation. It suggested that individuals accorded no value in America's race-based society were given, or obtained by some means, objects of no value. This was a completely fresh insight into the day-to-day reality of what it meant to be a captive African imprisoned on a plantation. Considered no-account people, they were accorded no-account castoffs.

Despite the magnitude of this discovery, Fairbanks was disappointed. His quest to find Africanisms was unfulfilled. The puzzle remained. Why had his excavations revealed nothing that he could readily identify as having African characteristics? Reflecting on this question, Fairbanks later noted that "I felt that the special circumstances of Kingsley being a slave-importing station, and Kingsley's permissive attitude toward his charges, would assure that some elements of African material culture would have been recreated in the plantation situation." But in the end, "We found nothing, however, that could surely be identified as such" (Fairbanks 1974: 90).

Over twenty years after Fairbanks's death, archaeologists returned to Kingsley Plantation and conducted excavations in three houses located further along the western part of the semicircle of dwellings. These excavations mirrored Fairbanks's results. The excavators unearthed several fragments of mass-produced glazed earthenware dishes, most of which dated earlier than the cabins. The excavated collection also contained nothing that at the time was considered to have obvious African features (McIlvoy 2020). That view would eventually change.

Fairbanks's pathbreaking research at Kingsley's plantation raises two important questions: what was so intriguing about Africanisms, and what took archaeologists so long to decide to excavate sites associated with African Americans? Answers to both questions help us understand the nature of African American archaeology, how it came about, what it means today, and why it is so important.

2

Africanisms

Tylor, Franklin, Herskovits

Charles Fairbanks's effort to find tangible evidence of African culture in the soil—Africanisms—was not based solely on curiosity. No archaeologist knows exactly what might be uncovered during an excavation, and expectations for a surprise usually run high. Fairbanks was no exception. Because no one before him had thought to expend serious energy excavating sites known to have been inhabited by African Americans, Fairbanks had no way of knowing or even anticipating what he and his students might encounter at Kingsley's former plantation. Hope for discovering the new and unusual is always in each excavator's mind as they scrape through the earth. But Fairbanks had deeper, more profound thoughts beyond the finds themselves. His mission, what ran beneath his interest like an underground stream, was to determine the meanings of tangible African cultural survivals—provided, of course, that he could find them. What might they say about African American life during enslavement? What might they reveal about our own time?

Fairbanks was certainly not the first person to think about Africanisms, or, as they were more broadly termed, cultural survivals. In fact, the genesis of the idea is ancient. The first person who is recorded to have thought about them was the ancient Greek historian Thucydides. An insightful thinker, he wondered about the persistence of older ideas and practices in the Greece of his day (M'Lennan 1896: 24–26). If every feature of Greek life could not be accounted for solely within Greece itself, then where had peculiar beliefs and practices come from, and what did their presence mean to Greek culture? Given the limitations of his era, many of the issues he pondered remained unanswerable and mysterious.

Thucydides's musings about cultural survivals were largely forgotten until the late nineteenth century. Interest in cultural survivals was ignited when an inquisitive Englishman named Edward B. Tylor began to examine them. For Tylor, the world's first professional anthropologist, survivals seemed to offer a perfect explanation for cultural characteristics that had no other explanation. If a practice, belief, or behavior seemed out of place, why was it out of place, and how had it developed?

Tylor was born in London to a prosperous Quaker family in 1832. He was one of those privileged, White, nineteenth-century scholars, like Charles Darwin, who harbored an unbounded curiosity about the world around them. Under the tutelage of his scientifically minded brother, Tylor was first drawn to geology, a field in which he developed into an above-average amateur. Although firmly within the middle class, Tylor was not a member of the state-sanctioned Anglican Church. Thus, his religion barred him from receiving the university education that would legitimate him as a geologist. The religious bias directed against him, although undoubtedly personally distressing, was not the insurmountable hurdle the establishment had hoped. Not only would Tylor be remembered as the first professional anthropologist, he would also have a long association with Oxford University, one of the institutions that had once so cruelly denied him admission (Lowie 1917; Wingfield 2009).

After a brief career in business, Tylor, at the age of 24, developed an impulse to travel. Setting off from London infused with youthful exuberance, he headed into the wild Atlantic. During a stopover in Havana in 1856, he met and came under the influence of a wealthy London banker named Henry Christy. Like Tylor, Christy harbored an infinite curiosity, but unlike Tylor, he had already made a name for himself as an authoritative but self-trained anthropologist and geologist. He was also an inveterate collector of ancient exotica. Even the catalog of his stone tool collection fills over 90 tightly printed pages (Steinbauer 1862).

Tylor deeply respected Christy and, admiring his many achievements, decided to accompany him on a trek through Mexico. It was this expedition that started Tylor on his lifelong journey to chart the intricacies of humanity's infinite cultures. In his first book, published in 1861, Tylor recounted the four months he spent with Christy rambling through Mexico on horseback. While Christy was busy haggling with weavers and potters for the product of their labors, Tylor was discovering everything he could about ancient Aztec irrigation systems and ancient temples as well as contemporary Mexican rites and festivals.

Unable to shake his English ethnocentrism, Tylor viewed rural Mexico through jaundiced eyes. He fell prey to the same biases expressed by White

Englishmen who were disgusted by the dark-skinned people they encountered in India, the Middle East, and South Africa. Tylor accepted the scientific wisdom of the era by believing that Hippocrates had been right to link physical appearance with the ability to labor in hot climates. Considering men and women of African heritage to be inherently lazy, he therefore accepted that enslavement was the only way to induce them to work. Tylor's words also suggest that he accepted the dubious link between ability and skin color.

The origin of the alleged tie between personal characteristics and skin color is difficult to pinpoint, but one element of it undoubtedly came to Spain through the Islamic world. As early as the ninth century, Muslims differentiated between White and Black captive workers. At the time, captors drew distinctions between enslaved White Europeans, who they viewed as investments worthy of protection, and enslaved Black Africans, who they considered expendable (Sweet 1997: 145). Ibn Khaldun, the influential fourteenth-century Muslim scholar, agreed with Hippocrates on the connection between environment and human ability but specifically added skin color to the equation. Ibn Khaldun maintained that people living in temperate climates are "well-proportioned" and live in well-built houses "embellished by craftsmanship." "Negroes," living in zones that "are far from temperate," dwell "in caves and thickets, eat herbs, live in savage isolations and do not congregate, and eat each other" (Ibn Khaldun 1958: 168).

The direct contact between Muslim North Africans and Christian Europeans began in earnest with the Muslim conquest of Iberia beginning in 711 (Thackeray and Findling 2001: 1–7). Spain's Reconquista took almost 800 years and, given the duration of the interaction between Muslim and Spanish scholars, it was perhaps inevitable that ideas such as Ibn Khaldun's would remain fresh in many people's minds. Such ideas undoubtedly played a significant role in the Spanish capture and enslavement of the over 1.5 million Africans they sent to their American colonies. The Spanish passed along their views to other European colonizers (Borucki et al. 2015: 434). The English, for example, adopted the term "white moor" to refer to light-skinned North Africans, but the term "Blackamoor" indicated "a black More, or a man of Ethiope" (Das et al. 2021: 403; Orser 2018: 258–260). The difference that early scholars perceived between individuals of light and dark skin evolved into the scientific racism Tylor so easily accepted.

Tylor's prejudice was not limited to people different from him. He also entertained ideas that exist solely within the realm of pseudo-archaeology. His comparison of Egyptian pyramids with those in Mexico, his belief that ancient Mexican cultures originated in the Old World, and his acceptance of the similarities between the language of the Aztecs and Sanskrit all showed that he was not always a discerning scholar (Tylor 1861: 11, 80, 103–104, 141–142, 333–335). Oddly, however, these prejudices led him to develop the concept of survivals.

As Tylor looked around at the Mexican world and pondered what he saw, he began to wonder why certain practices and beliefs appeared to have no purpose. As a Victorian scientist who accepted the concept of progress as a matter of faith, he marveled that the Mexican people had not adopted some of the advances made by modern, nineteenth-century, Western culture, things that he viewed as useful and efficient. Why did rural Mexicans continue using old and inefficient tools when they could use modern ones? Why did they accept outmoded ideas and beliefs? He found it curious that in Mexico, "the old types descend, almost unchanged, from generation to generation. Everything that is really Mexican is either Aztec or Spanish." He was amazed that the Mexicans, "who rose in three centuries from the condition of wandering savages to a height of civilization that has no equal in history . . . have remained since the [Spanish] Conquest, without making one step in advance." As he thought about it, he could understand how evolution had led to the greatness of the Aztecs, but he could not account for why Mexican culture had apparently stalled at that level. His conclusion went straight to the concept of survivals: "They hardly understand any reason for what they do, except that their ancestors did things so—they therefore must be right" (Tylor 1861: 50–51, 85).

As Tylor thought about the concept of survivals more deeply, especially in his more famous book, *Primitive Culture,* first published in 1871, he offered several more examples of cultural retentions. By this point he had begun to refer to the concept in a broader, more scientific way, defining survivals as "processes, customs, opinions, and so forth, which have been carried on by force of habit into a new state of society different from that in which they had their original home, and they thus remain as proofs and examples of an older condition of culture out of which a newer has been evolved" (Tylor 1871: 15). Cultural retentions, it seems, could take infinite forms.

One of Tylor's examples involved magic and witchcraft. As a well-heeled Englishman, Tylor viewed any acceptance of the occult as a throwback to an earlier, more pagan era. To show this, he made a broad survey of non-Western societies, just those places White Victorian readers could imagine as barbaric. Tylor even expanded his survey to Western societies, using sneezing as one example. Many of his English readers may have been primly aghast to learn that members of both Zulu and English societies said some form of "God bless you" after someone within earshot has sneezed. In both societies, the idea of offering a blessing is thought to protect the sneezer from evil.

Tylor's concept of survivals gave him a way to explain what he thought was otherwise unexplainable, to account for what he believed was illogical. He thought that human cultures became more complex and sophisticated over time, beginning when the first humans formed themselves into tiny bands. Having adopted this view of progressive cultural development, Tylor decided that incompatible practices and beliefs had to be holdovers from earlier ages. This was the only way he could explain the presence of "primitive" ideas among "civilized" peoples. For him, White Victorians would bless a sneezer only if the practice had ancient, long-forgotten roots (Hodgen 1931, 1936).

As the concept of progressive cultural evolution lost some of its luster among scholars over time, researchers still intrigued by survivals began to refer to them in terms of their history rather than their evolution. Many preferred this modification so they could add cultural interaction into the mix. They proposed that some survivals may be the result not simply of cultural evolution but also of "the blending of peoples." The "simple process of evolution" need not be the only reason why cultural retentions continue to exist in the world's cultures (Lowie 1918; Rivers 1913).

The move away from evolution as an explanation was important, but of more pressing concern was to determine what cultural retentions meant. Did their presence in society have any serious or lasting implications?

Tylor's examination of the meaning of sneezing, children's games, sun worship, and other practices and beliefs made it seem that survivals were simple curiosities, amusing anecdotes from long-gone pasts. Like holding one's buttons when passing a cemetery, they affected life in insignificant ways, if at all. But if cultural survivals were trivial, why would anyone other than a curious collector of folktales pay attention to them?

Hidden within what may have seemed inconsequential was a matter of great significance. Tylor had expressed this while he was in Mexico traveling with Christy and reaffirmed it during his library research. As he gathered his examples, Tylor discovered a curious survival then being practiced among Scottish, English, and French boatmen. They believed in letting a drowning man perish because saving him meant that the saved man was destined to eventually do the rescuer bodily harm. Better to let the unfortunate man drown now and be safe later. Tylor was indignant by this unfeeling belief and labeled it "inhuman" and a practice of "less civilized races" (Tylor 1871: 97–98).

Tylor's pejorative language for people who were, like him, of European heritage makes it easy to see how some people could use the existence of survivals to promote ideologies of inequality, persecution, and even genocide. The continuing expression or belief of something old fashioned, out of place, or, in the case of the boatmen, inhumane, could be used by demagogues to condemn and torment its practitioners.

Tylor's research, despite its inadequacies and nineteenth-century perspective, opened an important line of inquiry. Questions regarding the existence of survivals, their form, and ultimately their meaning held a universal appeal because, as Tylor had demonstrated, they continued to be practiced around the globe regardless of a culture's geographical location and supposed evolutionary stage.

In the United States, the question of survivals was intimately linked to the African American community. Although some respected early-twentieth-century academics had referred derisively to African Americans "the Negro Problem" (Odum 1910: 262–297), by the late nineteenth century several writers had already described some of the Africanisms they had observed in the American South. At this time in American history, memories of the antebellum era and the Civil War were still fresh in many minds, and the presence of thousands of African Americans, now freed but still subjected to withering racism, made them a subject of curiosity to many White academics and journalists. Dancing, singing, and drumming by African Americans wearing African clothing and performed in "exotic" places like New Orleans and the West Indies titillated White audiences and, if an account was written in a prejudiced way, could reinforce White stereotypes of African American simplicity and backwardness (Cable 1886a, 1886b). Renowned scholars were not immune to these impulses. As distinguished White sociologist Robert E. Park (1919: 112–113) mused, "Is the Negro's undoubted interest in music and taste for bright colors, commonly attributed to the race, to be regarded as an inherent and racial trait or is it merely the characteristic of primitive people?" African American scholars like Zora Neale Hurston (1930), Thomas W. Talley (1922), and Arthur Fauset (1927) toiled alongside such misguided views to document the richness and dignity of African American life through the medium of folklore. Long before Fairbanks became involved in the search for African survivals in the United States, others would work to either confirm Tylor's concept or demolish it entirely. One early researcher was W.E.B. Du Bois.

In 1897, with his Harvard PhD only two years old, W.E.B. Du Bois accepted a professorship at Atlanta University. Founded by Methodists shortly after the Confederate army had fired its last minié ball, the institution was the first historically Black university established in the South. The university had been lucky that Du Bois had decided to join them. A prolific scholar of rare insight and an activist of unusual commitment, Du Bois stands prominently among the greatest of the United States' most important thinkers. Never one to rest, the same year he arrived in Atlanta, Du Bois began an innovative project he titled the "Atlanta University Negro Conference." The conference's goal was to examine the realities of African American life as never before and to use empirical findings rather than innuendo and supposition. Du Bois conducted the project for the next several years, probing deeply into Black life in America. One of his most consuming interests was the African American family.

In his report on the family, Du Bois stressed the connection between the United States and Africa. He did this not simply because African Americans are of African descent "but because there is a distinct nexus between Africa and America which, though broken and perverted, is nevertheless not to be neglected by the careful student." He added the caveat that history made it "exceedingly difficult and puzzling to know just where to find the broken thread of African and American social history" (Du Bois 1908: 9). He understood that the answer began with the era of enslavement, but he was savvy enough to realize that the idealized Southern image of the happy slave was merely a disguise for the endless toil, cruelty, humiliation, and family disruption that enslavement carried with it. Du Bois and his team carefully amassed information from both Africa and the United States on marriage, the home, household economics, and the family. Du Bois accepted that the connection between Africa and the United States might be difficult to establish empirically, but he believed it was there; one simply had to be persistent enough to tease it out of the evidence.

The research Du Bois and his students conducted on the African American family laid the groundwork for one of the greatest debates in twentieth-century social science. Two intellectual giants would face off on opposite sides of the question, and their divergent views rippled across the academic world. The debate would ultimately intrigue Fairbanks and underpin his inquiry into the lives of enslaved African Americans. The men facing off were E. Franklin Frazier, sociologist, and Melville J. Herskovits, anthropologist.

Edward Franklin Frazier was born in Baltimore, Maryland, in 1894. His father, who had never attended school, taught himself to read and write. He taught Frazier and his four siblings the value of education as a path to social advancement.

As an adult, Edward Frazier sometimes signed his name as "Franklin," but he became famous as "E. Franklin," a slightly pudgy, bespectacled scholar of average height with an imposing mind. After graduating from Baltimore High School in 1912, Frazier went on to Howard University, where he received his bachelor's degree in 1916.

Frazier's first documented activism came during his first year at Howard. When Woodrow Wilson was to be inaugurated as the US president, several college and university presidents were asked to contribute students to a parade to be held in Wilson's honor. Howard University, being in Washington, DC, was asked to participate. At the time any parade permitting African American involvement required them to line up at the back of the parade, behind the White marchers. Wilson's academic parade was no different, and the Howard students were shuttled to the back of the Black section. Frazier found this situation intolerable and formed a committee to draft a petition to Wilson's inaugural headquarters with the simple request that the Howard group be placed along with the other institutions, White and Black, in alphabetical order. The inaugural committee made what in their minds was probably a generous concession: they would allow the Howard contingent to march immediately after the White section. Frazier was steadfast in refusing this compromise, but the members of his committee gave in and accepted the committee's offer. Frazier refused to march in the parade and watched from the sidelines (Davis 1962: 430–431).

Frazier had come by his militancy fairly. His father often sent letters to the editors of Baltimore's newspapers pointing out episodes of racial injustice. His father's letter-writing and his own experience with the inaugural parade stayed with Frazier for the rest of his life and helped provide the rationale for the FBI to compile a dossier on his activities and affiliations. In this regard, Frazier joined good company because the FBI also conducted surveillance on Du Bois and several other prominent African American scholars (Maxwell 2013).

After leaving Howard, Frazier led the life of a wandering scholar. When the United States was beginning to contemplate entering the First World

War, Frazier's life was still unsettled. In 1917 he took a job teaching English and history at Saint Paul's Normal and Industrial School (now Saint Paul's College), a historically Black institution in Lawrenceville, Virginia, founded in 1888. The next year Frazier returned to Baltimore, where he began teaching math at his old high school. During that school year he decided he had a higher calling than high school teaching, so he entered Clark University in Worcester, Massachusetts. There he received a master's degree in 1920. Founded only a year before Saint Paul's, Clark was quickly developing into a major research university, and it was an exciting place for someone with Frazier's energetic mind. After graduating he was able to obtain a year-long research fellowship in New York City at the New York School of Social Work, but when this ended he was forced into hourly labor at various steel mills in and around Worcester. For the next few years Frazier continued to take short-term academic posts, including a brief stint as an instructor of sociology at Morehouse College in Atlanta, another historically Black institution. By 1927 Frazier had decided to enter the University of Chicago for a doctorate degree in sociology. This degree would solidify his position within the scholarly world and make his name world renowned as a committed thinker and activist (Davis 1962; FBI File 2020).

Melville Jean Herskovits, born in 1895, was almost exactly one year younger than Frazier. The social worlds that spawned each man were wholly distinct, but each man held an abiding interest in African American culture and history. It was this shared concern that caused them to clash in the academic world.

Herskovits was born in central Ohio in a small town northwest of Columbus. This midwestern town was a far cry from the rush and hustle Frazier encountered in urban Baltimore. Like thousands of others in the late nineteenth century, Herskovits's father had arrived on the shores of the United States as an Austro-Hungarian immigrant. Life in central Ohio went reasonably well until Herskovits's mother's poor health forced the family to relocate to a sunnier and warmer part of the United States. They chose El Paso, Texas. Over 1,600 miles southwest of Columbus, El Paso was like another world, but at least it lacked the bitter winds of a midwestern winter.

Herskovits spent a large part of his youth in El Paso, where he undoubtedly developed his long-held confidence in multiculturalism long before the term had obtained today's currency. When his mother died in 1911, the family uprooted once again and moved back north, this time to Erie, Pennsylvania, where Herskovits graduated from high school in 1912, the same year as Frazier. In 1915 Herskovits enrolled in the University of Cincinnati and Hebrew Union College, but the First World War intervened, and he found that he was wanted elsewhere. Until his discharge in 1919, Herskovits spent his days in the uniform of a private in the US Army Medical Corps. Finding himself in western France after the armistice, Herskovits decided to enroll in the University of Poitiers. Founded in 1431, luminaries such as René Descartes and Francis Bacon had once also called its medieval buildings their academic home. But France was not home to Herskovits, so he returned to the United States and enrolled in the University of Chicago. He graduated with a bachelor's degree in history in 1920 (Dorson 1963; Merriam 1964; Wolf 1963).

The 1920s were a heady time for American anthropology. The excitement swirling around the discipline blossomed into a frenzy after Margaret Mead published her renowned but controversial *Coming of Age in Samoa* (1928). The book made Mead a household name and propelled her to anthropological sainthood. Herskovits shared with Mead a profound interest in the human condition, and while working toward his bachelor's degree, he discovered that history and anthropology shared many of the same concerns. In the early twentieth century, as anthropology was just being formulated as a stand-alone discipline, anthropologists and historians were not afraid to peer across disciplinary fences to see whether anything interesting was happening on the other side. It seemed to Herskovits that all the energy and excitement was in anthropology, so in 1920 he moved to Columbia University to study with Mead's mentor, the world-renowned master of American anthropology, Franz Boas. Herskovits received a master's in 1921 and a doctorate in 1924.

Under Boas's tutelage, Herskovits was first drawn to the study of human variability. Ever since 1882, when Boas first encountered the Native peoples of Baffin Island as a young scientist, an event that focused his attention away from physics and toward anthropology, he had been intrigued by human variation. His interest in head shape and nose structure appear today as terribly misguided, but at the time eugenics and the relationship between appearance and behavior were topics of great interest to scholars and the public alike. At Columbia, Boas built an impressive anthropometry lab. Consisting of eight rooms, he divided the lab into three sections. One area was dedicated to displaying the physical characteristics of Native Americans and so-called half bloods, a second area to the growth and development of children, and a third area to a working lab concentrating on collecting body measurements from living populations (King 2019: 68–69).

Despite the questionable use of body measurements to understand human variation, Boas was sympathetic to racial equality, including when it came to African Americans. In 1905 Du Bois wrote to Boas inviting him to one of Du Bois's Atlanta University conferences. He also asked Boas to deliver the commencement address to the class of 1906. Boas accepted the invitations, and in his address to the university graduates he pressed upon them something they undoubtedly already knew: that the shiftlessness, licentiousness, and lack of initiative Whites often attributed to Black people were not innate traits but were "the result of social conditions." He also spoke about Africa's cultural achievements, noting that some cultures had learned to smelt iron while Europeans were still knocking rocks together to make stone tools. Du Bois was profoundly moved by Boas's brief history lesson about Sub-Saharan Africa, and as he looked back on the experience later in life, he viewed it as a personal turning point. Boas had left him "too astonished to speak" (Du Bois 1939: vii; also see Baker 1998: 121–122; King 2019: 204).

Herskovits had absorbed Boas's interest in African Americans at Columbia. While running Boas's anthropometry lab, Herskovits received a hard-won three-year grant from the National Research Council. The grant provided funds to carry forward his earlier research on the physical anthropology of African Americans. While engaged in the grant research, Herskovits lectured at Columbia, and in 1925 he accepted a teaching position at Howard University. In 1927 Herskovits moved west to Evanston, Illinois, taking a job teaching anthropology at Northwestern University.

One year later, in 1928, Frazier published his first journal article on the African American family while serving as the director of the Chicago Urban League's Research Department. His goal was to advance the research Du Bois had begun at Atlanta University and to solidify it with additional evidence. In the first sentence of the article, Frazier was unequivocal about the origin of the African American family: "The first fact which should be made clear about the Negro family as it exists in America today is that it has developed out of the American environment." Continuing, he added, "When the Negro was introduced into America the break with African culture was well nigh complete" (Frazier 1928: 44). As clear and concise as could possibly be, Frazier had fired the first salvo in the debate over Africanisms in North America. He would never change his mind.

One of the authorities Frazier referenced was the sociologist Robert E. Park. Park had worked with Booker T. Washington at Tuskegee Institute and was a professor at the University of Chicago during Frazier's time there. A few years after Du Bois had published his family study, Park, by then world-renowned, had acknowledged that many people thought that "a considerable fund of African tradition and African superstition" had been transferred to the United States. He believed this was merely an assumption. He claimed, and Frazier agreed, that "the amount of African tradition which the Negro brought to the United States was very small." Park thought that when African men and women were forced from their homelands and shoved onboard transatlantic ships, they left almost everything behind except their dark skin and "tropical temperament" (Park 1919: 115–116).

Having accepted Park's view that the African American family had no roots in Africa and that the family's structure was entirely American, Frazier was forced to identify the family's point of origin. If the family was 100 percent American, then where had it sunk its first roots? Frazier reasoned that it had two points of origin. The first was to be found among the free Black families who inhabited the cities of the east and south coasts, from New York to New Orleans. These families, many headed by prosperous entrepreneurs and a few slave owners who had somehow come to terms with the system, had built successful families, even amid racist restrictions. In voicing this idea, Frazier may have been channeling his own upbringing in Baltimore. Frazier's second, more surprising origin of the Black family was "within the slave institution itself." Relying on historical information, Frazier read the evidence in a way that implied that liberal plantation masters permitted enslaved men and women to form and maintain "family groups in the slave quarters" (Frazier 1928: 45–46).

Frazier repeated much the same argument in his study of the African American family in Chicago. Relying again on Park, he observed that "when the Negro was introduced into the strange world of the white man, memories of Africa soon faded and lost their meaning in his new environment" (Frazier 1932: 224). He again attributed much of the development of the African American family to plantation life, saying that small groups of enslaved families formed nuclei that eventually became twentieth-century families.

In this most well-read book on the African American family, *The Negro Family in the United States,* first published in 1939, Frazier devoted considerably more space to the question of African survivals. As was true in his other writings, he confronted the matter overtly and right from the start.

In the first chapter, Frazier once again boldly acknowledged his long-standing view that African traditions had no place in the United States.

Dismissing them outright, he called them "Forgotten Memories." Since he began studying the African American family, several anthropologists, often encouraged by Boas, had begun fieldwork among peoples of African heritage in the Americas and the Caribbean. Knowing that this body of evidence existed, Frazier was forced to concede that some African cultural expressions were indeed present outside Africa, but only in places like the West Indies. But, being forgotten fragments of the mind, these expressions were like dreams, "but dim memories of Africa." To further his argument, Frazier drew upon Herskovits's then-available research, noting that African descendants in the West Indies, Suriname, and Brazil use many words with African derivations. In some of these same places he conceded that "African culture still survives in the religious practices, funeral festivals, folklore, and dances of the transplanted Negroes." Frazier even acknowledged that anthropologists have found African elements within family structure in parts of the West Indies. Having made all these concessions, Frazier once again threw down the challenge: "In contrast to the situation in the West Indies, African traditions and practices did not take root and survive in the United States." Perhaps to sharpen the contest, Frazier added a provocative footnote: "Even Professor Herskovits, who thinks that research would reveal African survivals among the Negroes of the United States, makes the following admission: 'Yet to point to a Senegambian name, an Ashanti deity, a Congo belief among Negroes of the United States, recognizable as such, is almost impossible'" (Frazier 1939: 5–8). Case closed. There are no Africanism in the United States, and those in the Caribbean are merely dim shadows of Africa.

The Herskovits quote Frazier chose came from an article Herskovits had published in 1930. In it Herskovits argued that social scientists, like him and Frazier, simply did not know enough to say with certainty whether "African cultural survivals," what he termed "Africanisms," were or were not present in the United States. Revealing his emersion in the theory of measurement inherent in anthropometry, Herskovits proposed that even with the amassed knowledge available in the late 1920s, it would still be possible to construct a chart showing "the intensity of African cultural element in the various regions" of the Americas (Herskovits 1930: 149). Using what was then available, he believed that a chart could be constructed extending from Suriname, as the most African region in the Americas, with Haiti and the rest of the Caribbean appearing next. The chart would terminate with peoples who have African physical traits but no African cultural expressions. Herskovits thought that African Americans in the American South would fall just above those with no obvious African cultural characteristics (Herskovits 1930: 149–150). What Herskovits was implying was that more research was needed before social scientists could accept Frazier's claim about the total absence of African cultural traits in the United States. The big question was, How could one amass the right information to prove or deny the claims of either Frazier or Herskovits?

Only three years after Frazier's article appeared, Herskovits published an answer. Rather than eliminate Africa from the analysis, as Frazier had done, Herskovits forged an explicit link between the Americas and Africa. Drawing on his own background with the discipline of history, Herskovits proposed a research method that combined historical and ethnological evidence. Ethnographers would identify "the beliefs and behavior of New World Negroes" in the present while historians would seek to find the same traits in Africa during the time of the slave trade. Using this approach, Herskovits believed it would be possible to pinpoint the African origin of African cultures in the New World (Herskovits 1933: 247–248). Herskovits proceeded to demonstrate how this detective work might be accomplished and in the process proved Du Bois correct: the task would not be easy. But Herskovits was undeterred and argued that what exists in the United States is probably a "generalized" expression of West Africa. He added that this tradition of belief and behavior was stronger in Brazil, Haiti, Cuba, and Jamaica than in the United States, but it existed nonetheless.

Herskovits cemented his argument in *The Myth of the Negro Past* published in 1941. Du Bois called the book "epoch-making," adding that anyone interested in African Americans past or present and who remained "ignorant of its content and conclusions" did so at their peril (Du Bois 1942: 226).

The book reports on the 20 years Herskovits spent compiling information to ensure that the myths surrounding African Americans were finally dispelled with empirical information gathered using his anthropology/history research method. The myths Herskovits reacted most strongly against were ideas that African Americans were happily enslaved because of their supposed childlike nature and that the commingling of enslaved Africans on New World plantations caused individuals from different cultures to lose their cultural identity. Both myths, he believed, robbed African Americans of their histories. Herskovits also reacted against the biased perceptions that African cultures were inferior to the cultures of their European captors and that the most perceptive captives eagerly abandoned their cultural norms in favor of the "apparent superiority of European customs" (Herskovits 1941: 2).

Having made his argument against the myths of African American inferiority, Herskovits's next task was to establish that Africanisms exist and can be identified in the United States. He observed that some Whites, men like George Cable when writing about New Orleans, readily accepted the "savage and exotic nature of the presumed carry-overs" from Africa. Herskovits proposed that despite "a long line of trained specialists" like folklorists, who had demonstrated the presence of Africanism in the Americas, no one had drawn together all the evidence. Herskovits viewed the job of collation as vitally important because most scholars—not trained specifically to look for them—harbored the belief that Africanisms, if they existed at all, were things of the past (Herskovits 1941: 2–4).

Herskovits used the entire first chapter to explain the importance of Africanisms to African American life. For him, the failure to accept their presence in the United States was one of the principal joists in the edifice of American racial prejudice. If you can successfully deny the persistence of African beliefs and behavior in present-day African America, then you can destroy African history and reaffirm the myth of Black infantilism and savagery. As a practical matter, he observed that studying African cultures immediately immerses the student in an intricate cultural world, one as infinitely complex as any European royal dynasty. Herskovits knew that because Africa is a massive place with enormous cultural diversity, the study of Africanisms would be challenging. Students would face many intellectual blind alleys and experience frustration. Students of Africanisms, Herskovits said, must steel themselves for difficulty, agree to conceptually join Africa to the New World, and adopt a unique research method. Given the inherent complexities of the research, Herskovits fully expected the findings to be fragmentary, scattered, and possibly confusing.

Herskovits believed that one of the things that kept many scholars from recognizing the presence of Africanisms in the United States was their failure to conduct face-to-face ethnographic fieldwork among African peoples. Without this transformative, personal experience, he believed it was easy to underestimate, and thus undervalue, the complexity of African culture.

As early as 1928 Herskovits had begun ethnographic fieldwork in Suriname. In the following years he conducted research in Dahomey, Ghana, Nigeria, Haiti, Trinidad, and what was then the Belgian Congo. Following Boas's logic, Herskovits believed that the ethnographer's job is to document culture by being there, watching, and taking part. The lack of anthropological fieldwork both in Africa and the United States, he thought, created intellectual blind spots that could only be made visible with dedication and perseverance. He therefore urged others to begin field research as a tangible way to destroy the myths White scholars had built up around Africans and African Americans.

Herskovits's perspective is easy to comprehend. He was an anthropologist doing fieldwork and encouraging others to follow his lead. Frazier's reluctance to accept the presence of Africanisms in the United States is more difficult to explain.

Frazier's FBI file reveals that he traveled to many of the same places visited by Herskovits, but only after he had published his family study and had already formed his negative view of Africanisms. His FBI file also reveals that he was no apologist for White society and that he was unwilling to blithely look the other way in the face of racial inequality and discrimination. In 1921 he was arrested in New York City for picketing the showing of *Birth of a Nation,* the racist film extolling the virtues of the Ku Klux Klan (FBI File 2020). Frazier had also served as the president of a Washington, DC–based AFL–CIO chapter, but what really interested the FBI was a report that Frazier had allegedly attended a meeting of the Communist Party. In the 1930s and 1940s, Frazier was involved in Black activism and never regretted his association with leftists. Throughout his life he remained steadfastly outraged by the social inequality pressed forward by White supremacists, and he abhorred the Jim Crow laws intended to keep people like him in a state of servitude and fear. He contended that racist beliefs and practices were designed to deny individual personalities to African Americans. As a scholar, he was discomfited that academic sociology had pigeonholed him as "an expert on the Negro family" because he had far greater interests, including the political critique of sociology. Frazier was also a victim of McCarthyism, regularly being hauled before the House Unamerican Activities Committee to answer leading questions. He was even quizzed by the Senate Internal Security Committee. Near the end of his life the FBI collaborated with the US State Department to deny Frazier his dream job with UNESCO. As a final act of defiance, Frazier left his academic library to the University of Ghana.

Frazier never abandoned his disagreement with Herskovits over the presence of Africanisms in the United States. He was as steadfast about this as he was about racial injustice. As he matured, however, he did distance himself from his devoted attachment to Park's assimilationist perspective. The rise of the Black Power movement encouraged him to view assimilation as misguided. Why attempt to fit into a White society that rejected African

Americans as equals? Frazier's travels into the developing world undoubtedly helped change his mind. He was particularly influenced by the writings of African and West Indian intellectuals and came to believe that the plan to integrate the American public school system was a cynical move on the part of the US government. He thought they would use desegregation as a cover to continue turning a blind eye to segregation and inequality. He was especially distressed that the US government would use *Brown v. Board of Education* as a political weapon. When the Soviet Union criticized how unfairly the United States treated its minorities, the government simply pointed to *Brown* to prove otherwise. Frazier despised this kind of hypocrisy. But despite his modified views, as late as 1962 he continued to argue that "the process by which the Negroes were captured and enslaved in the United States stripped them of their African culture and destroyed their personality" (Frazier 1962: 35). He may have altered his opinion on assimilation, but admitting that African survivals existed in the United States was just a bit too far to go (Gaines 2005; Platt 1989; Thompson 1982).

Herskovits was also not immune from intellectual myopia. A notable blank spot of Herskovits's project to find clear evidence of Africanisms was buried within his training. As a cultural anthropologist, he exhibited the same blindness toward material objects common among many ethnographers. Archaeologists have long complained about the failure of ethnographers to report some of the most basic facts of daily life, actions and practices that could not be performed without physical objects. Archaeologists understand that human life itself is impossible in the absence of material things, but ethnographers, both professional and amateur, immersed in the activities around them, have typically ignored the material world—just the things archaeologists use to interpret the past. The failures of ethnographers, including Herskovits, meant that archaeologists have had to become ethnographers of the material world themselves (Castañeda and Matthews 2008).

True to form as an ethnographer, Herskovits only briefly mentioned African material culture. Even in *The Myth of the Negro Past*, he only referred to physical objects in passing by commenting on the Ashantis' skill in wood carving and weaving and the Dahomeans' expert abilities in brass and iron working. He glossed over these tantalizing clues to the possible origin of physical Africanisms and failed to pursue them. In the same short paragraph in which he mentioned African craftworking, he unwittingly dropped an archaeological bombshell: that the Yoruba and the Dahomeans "produce minor art forms in basketry, pottery, and other media" (Herskovits 1941: 77).

There it is: pottery, something all archaeologists know well. From this, could it be inferred the Yorubas and Dahomeans held captive on the plantations and cities of the Americas may have also made pottery? Fairbanks wanted an answer to this fascinating question.

3

Delay

White Blindness, Black Archaeology

In 1968 archaeology was a relatively new discipline. Self-taught amateurs and peripatetic dilettantes, usually well-off White men with expendable funds and abundant leisure time, had been snooping around in the Near East, Egypt, and on the European continent for about 200 years, but professional archaeologists in the United States, those few individuals who received paychecks for their sojourns into the past, could count less than 100 years of their discipline's history. Equally surprisingly, historical archaeologists had created their own professional organization only the year before Fairbanks first stepped onto Kingsley's soil.

Running independently alongside this history was the saga of African America. The kidnapping and enslavement of men, women, and even children from Africa had been a horrendous fact on the American continent for generations. One can be forgiven for supposing that this long and tortured chronicle of enslavement in the United States would have been hard to ignore, especially by those scholars whose profession it was to unravel the enigmas of the past. But at least one group of scholars—American archaeologists—were able to blithely ignore the African American past until 1968. Why had it taken so long for archaeologists to acknowledge African American culture and history? Why had Black voices been silenced for so long?

An awful secret of American archaeology is that it has its own long and troubling association with race. One major reason that African Americans were invisible to White American archaeologists was because, from the beginning, archaeology provided a reflection of the nation's racial politics. For most of their discipline's history, American archaeologists had adopted a generally conservative view of the past, one that promoted the rightness of whiteness and neglected or downplayed the contributions of others. It began with the bewildering mound builders.

As American settlers pushed west from the continent's east coast and beyond the Appalachians, many of the verdant landscapes they encountered were dotted with mysterious earthen mounds. Some of the mounds were small and conical, but others were much larger and flat-topped. Still others were elongated like military defenses, and some had even been fashioned into geometrical enclosures. Some were formed into indecipherable shapes, but the most curious were shaped like birds and mammals and sometimes even people.

Most of what was known about the mounds was at first pure speculation, interpretations of White surveyors who had stumbled upon them while traipsing through the woods or of pioneers who had found unusual mounds on their small plots of land. The discovery of odd-shaped pieces of chipped stone only deepened the mystery.

Early Americans could imagine only two interpretations for the mounds' origins: either the ancient ancestors of the local American Indians had built them or else they had been raised by someone else. Most American pioneers of European descent could not fathom that the ancestors of the local Indigenous cultures possessed the intelligence, the engineering skills, or the diligence to construct the often-intricate mounds. In 1820 Caleb Atwater, a postmaster by trade but a passionate amateur archaeologist by choice, agreed that the idea of the mounds' Indian origin was preposterous because, as he wrote, the achievements of "the North American Indians, are neither numerous nor very interesting" (Atwater 1820: 111). In his mind, the mound builders must have been someone else.

The ninth president of the United States, William Henry Harrison, who also holds the record for being the shortest-serving chief executive at just thirty-one days, agreed with Atwater. After examining the mounds around Cincinnati, Ohio, before ascending to the White House, he declared that the mounds must have been designed by the "engineers" of an advanced people, skilled designers who knew "the importance of flank defenses." As the victor of the Battle of Fallen Timbers against American Indian nations struggling to preserve their homelands, Harrison understood military fortifications. In his view, the "remains of pottery, pipes, stone hatchets, and other articles" found across the eastern states were "of inferior workmanship to those of the former people." Harrison believed that the higher civilization who had built the mounds had asserted their power in the "conquest of the half-civilized nation which once inhabited Ohio," just as he had done (Harrison 1839: 225–226, 236). Furthermore, the mounds, many of which were awesome in height and girth, could not be the product of the average Native American mind, he said. Harrison's conclusion? The mound builders must have been "the Astecks." They were the most famous, advanced Indigenous American culture capable of fielding the large labor force needed for such grand works. They must have erected the mounds in ancient times and then fled south to build their even grander capital at Mexico City.

Most Americans were less certain than Harrison about the mound builders' identity. Most men and women who pondered the subject wondered, if the Native Americans could not have been capable of making the mounds, then who was capable? The written word was silent on the subject, so the curious did the next best thing: they simply named their own contenders. Favorite candidates were the Lost Tribes of Israel, Phoenicians, Malays, Irish monks, Vikings, "Pre-Adamites," and Chinese seafarers. Some thinkers were at a loss for a suitable contender and simply decided that the builders were "a separate race of men," whom they dubbed "The Mound Builders" (Adair 1775: 11; Bieder 1986: 108–114; Silverberg 1970).

Years earlier, another president had also expressed an interest in the mound builders. That president was Thomas Jefferson, slave owner, agriculturalist, and amateur scientist (Willey and Sabloff 1993: 39).

Jefferson was well read when it came to America's mounds. The mounds, after all, were one of the primary scientific puzzles of the day. But Jefferson's restless mind meant that he could never be like Harrison, content to simply think about the mounds in the abstract. As a man of purpose and action, Jefferson decided to find the answers for himself. All he need do, he reasoned, was to dig into a local mound, assess what was inside it, and decipher what it meant. Jefferson had heard a rumor that the first person to die in an Indian village was buried standing up and covered over with enough earth to make a mound. All subsequent dead were put in the same mound, leaning up against the first person. Jefferson wondered if this was true.

Writing in *Notes on the State of Virginia*, Jefferson's only published book, he recounted how he had a mound excavated near his Monticello estate. The mound was spherical in shape and about 40 feet in diameter. He estimated that it was once about 12 feet high, but because the landowner had been plowing it, it must have been reduced by about half. But even 6 feet was cover enough to hide a person standing upright. Around the base of the mound was a ditch about 5 feet deep, which Jefferson figured was probably the source of the mound's earth. Haphazardly digging around in the mound at different depths from 6 inches to 3 feet, Jefferson discovered several human bones of both adults and children. To determine whether someone had been buried standing up, he decided to dig a trench through the mound's center, in such a way as to open it "to the former surface of the earth." When he was finished, he had a cut "wide enough for a man to walk through and examine its sides." Jefferson concluded that perhaps 1,000 individuals had been buried in the mound, but he could find no one standing upright (Jefferson 1832: 100–103).

Jefferson believed that Native Americans, and only Native Americans, were responsible for heaving up the great piles of earth. His mound excavation had proved as much, and he saw no further controversy in the matter. But even he, reticent to completely leave the Old World behind, noted that "the custom of burying the dead in barrows was anciently very prevalent. Homer describes the ceremony of raising one by the Greeks. . . . And Herodotus . . . mentions an instance of the same practice in the army of Xerxes on the death of Artachæas [Achaemenes]" (Jefferson 1832: 106–107). So even Jefferson harbored a niggling doubt about the mounds' true origin; otherwise, why draw even the slightest connection between ancient Greeks and America's Indigenous peoples? Despite his brief foray into field archaeology, the mystery of the mound builders remained an unsolved topic of debate in America's taverns, drawing rooms, and state houses. Others would have to look for answers on the ground.

One person to accept the challenge was medical doctor Montroville Wilson Dickeson. In 1837 Dickeson left his home on Lombard Street in Philadelphia and headed west. Only 27 years old, he was infused with the spirit of adventure. Like Jefferson, he planned to resolve the riddle of the mound builders himself, not with armchair philosophizing but with field observation (Barnhart 1989: 52–54; Penn Museum 2020; Tax 1973: 100–101; Veit 1997, 1999).

Born in Philadelphia in 1810, Dickeson developed an early love of natural history that would stay with him throughout his life. Deciding that a life in science was not a realistic option, in 1828 he enrolled in Dr. Joseph Parrish's medical school. Parrish was one of the nation's top professors of medicine. After completing his rigorous studies, Dickeson's passion for natural history got the better of him, and so he decided to interrupt his fledgling medical career and enter the mound-builder fray with both feet.

Dickeson, privileged with having the funds and available time, spent the next eight years, from 1837 to 1844, on a personal quest to discover who had built America's mounds. All told, he may have studied somewhere around 200 individual mounds. In Mississippi and Louisiana, where he spent a large portion of his time, Dickeson had devised a fool-proof program of research. He would approach the owner of a slaveholding plantation, usually someone with a mound on their property, and ask whether he could have permission to explore the mound. Having gotten consent, he would then inquire as to whether he might borrow the services of a few captive Africans to do the actual digging. Most planters were happy to oblige, and Dickeson would then settle into the planter's guest room and stay until the excavation was finished. With the enslaved excavators hard at work, Dickeson would stand on the sidelines, sketching what they discovered as they slowly exposed the mound's interior. When he was satisfied with the excavation, he would move to the next plantation and repeat the process.

Dickeson called his field sketches "renderings." His plan was to use them to illustrate a series of public lectures he hoped to deliver at the Jefferson Institute back in Philadelphia. Buried beneath Dickeson's scientific veneer was the soul of a showman, dormant like a soil layer within one of the mounds, so he understood that his rough sketches would never convey the mounds' true majesty or adequately depict how the excavators had peeled back the layers of soil to discover the mounds' astonishing finds. To solve this problem, in 1850 he hired John J. Egan, a traveling Irish painter, to transform his renderings into vibrant colored images. When he was finished, Egan had produced 27 full-color images painted on a huge 9-foot tall by 400-foot-long roll of cotton muslin. Grandly titled *Panorama of the Monumental Grandeur of the Mississippi Valley*, this extraordinary sheet is a marvel. When Dickeson first unveiled it to the public in Memorial Hall during Philadelphia's Centennial Exhibition in 1876, he had his attendants slowly unroll it. The stunned spectators gawked in awe as the richly colored, dramatic scenes slowly unfurled before them (Figure 1).

Included in Egan's canvas is a painting of a burial mound under excavation in Louisiana. The image is a remarkable, although perhaps unintended, visual statement about the social and racial climate of the nineteenth-century United States, where individuals of the different social classes and perceived races are separated by dress and occupation.

On the far left of the image is an azure swamp, its tall cypress trees reaching toward the sky and terminating in tuffs of brilliant green. A small conical-shaped mound rises on the plain stretching out behind the marsh. In the foreground on the far right, four brightly dressed Native Americans stand before two tents, odd combinations of tepees and US military tents.

Figure 1. John J. Egan, American (born Ireland), active mid-nineteenth century; *Panorama of the Monumental Grandeur of the Mississippi Valley* (detail), c. 1850; distemper on cotton muslin; 90 inches × 348 feet; Saint Louis Art Museum, Eliza McMillan Trust 34: 1953.

Both are decorated with straight lines and circular swirls. A Native man, wearing a headdress composed of four feathers—one each of blue, red, yellow, and white—and donning what may be a decorated buckskin robe, speaks to a similarly dressed Native man. Between the two men sit two Native women. One wears a dress of vivid blue; the other, holding a tightly wrapped infant, wears a white dress decorated with yellow and red along the hem. Behind them in the middle distance are a group of four White Americans, one man and four brightly dressed, bonnet-wearing women. The man, dressed all in black and wearing a top hat, points to the right as if showing the ladies something. Further in the distance stands another couple who appear to embrace. Further in the distance are two more conical-shaped mounds, and in the far background is a range of purple mountains, of the sort that are nowhere to be seen along the southern Mississippi River except in an artist's imagination.

Despite the activity on the sides of the panorama, the painting's focal point is its center. Here a conical mound rises above the uniform flatness of the Mississippi River floodplain. The brown hues of the mound's individual soil layers contrast with the verdant shell of grass and scrub trees covering the mound's exterior. The excavators have sliced through the grass and by cutting the mound in half have exposed its ancient contents. Tucked into the nine soil layers are 10 human skeletons lying on their backs. Most of them are accompanied by pots and other artifacts. One skeleton crouches in the middle of the mound near the top, in a shaft cutting through the mound's top three horizontal layers. At the base of the mound are five excavators. All are African Americans and, being dressed identically in blue-striped white shirts and blue trousers, they are clearly enslaved laborers. Two wield pickaxes and three use shovels. Two White men stand in the middle of the image. The one on the left speaks to the man on the right, who is writing something on a notepad. The man on the left, wearing a long black coat and a pale straw hat, has clearly not been digging. His white trousers are far too clean. He must be the plantation owner come to witness the excavators' progress. The other man may be a reporter scouting out a scoop for the local newspaper. Dickeson appears on the far left, sketching one of his renderings on a large white board. In this artfully composed tableau, Egan has conveyed an inescapable fact: African Americans were probably the first field archaeologists in the United States. We can well suppose that enslaved Africans had, without attribution, also excavated the mound for Jefferson.

"Borrowing" enslaved men for their muscle must have been a common practice for White antiquarians not content with just thinking about ancient America. In 1834, before Dickeson had entered the field, the brother of a man named Dr. Durkee was traveling in Florida. On the St. John's River south of Jacksonville, roughly in the same locale as Fairbanks's revolutionary excavation, the man took "two young slaves, furnished by a friend, for the purpose of visiting an ancient Indian Mound." Dr. Durkee's brother described the circular mound in effusive, romantic terms, as "covered with trees and shrubbery from the largest live oak, which is an ever-green, to the beautiful hawthorn and the aromatic myrtle, all of which are filled in with moss pendant from the branches, and imparting a dark and melancholy air to this mausoleum of the dead." Excavation, undoubtedly conducted by the captive African American workers, revealed several well-preserved skeletons, "from the helpless infant to the strong warrior," and at least one stone ax (*Canadian Correspondent* 1834).

Dickeson's antiquarian peers noticed his use of captive African Americans as excavators. Edwin H. Davis, like Dickeson, a trained physician and an avid amateur archaeologist, disparaged Dickeson's approach on two grounds. He held that Dickeson was too quick to accept "hearsay facts" and that "the negroes dig and he sketches" (Barnhart 1989: 53). Davis was no rank amateur. Two years before Dickeson had hired Egan, Davis and his collaborator, journalist Ephraim G. Squier, had set the archaeological world abuzz with their publication of *Ancient Monuments of the Mississippi Valley*. Squier, too, thought that Dickeson did more damage than good (Barnhart 2005: 82).

Neither Davis nor Squier had formal archaeological training, but there was nothing unusual about educated White men studying earthworks. Jefferson had proved as much. But their book on the Ohio Valley's earthen mounds was not just another dense tome of interest to only a few stuffy, parlor-bound antiquarians. Rather, it was so monumental that the prestigious Smithsonian Institution published it as its first *Smithsonian Contributions to Knowledge*. Although founded only two years before by an act of Congress, the Smithsonian had already become a preeminent scientific establishment. The institution's imprimatur bestowed instant credibility upon Davis and Squier's book. To undertake their laborious, wide-ranging field surveys, Davis and Squier had received funding from the acclaimed American Antiquarian Society, founded in 1812. When they overspent their budget, Albert Gallatin came to their rescue. Gallatin had served as the secretary of the treasury for presidents Jefferson and James Madison, and he was a founder of the American Ethnological Society (Bieder 1986: 16–54; Kennedy 1996: 23–39; Meltzer 1998: 1). To demonstrate their gratitude, Squier and Davis dedicated their masterwork to Gallatin, lauding him for "his patriotic services and scientific achievements."

In transmitting their manuscript to the Smithsonian for consideration, Squier and Davis had given it the subtitle *Comprising the Results of Extensive Original Surveys and Exploration*. The words "extensive" and "original" helped to substantiate the importance of their research and quickly made the book an archaeological classic even outside the United States. The book was so influential that Adolphe von Morlot, an archaeologist living in Switzerland, proclaimed Squier and Davis's research to be an example of "American bravery" comparable to the defense of Bunker Hill (Morlot 1861).

To increase the impact of their findings, Squier and Davis drew the mounds as they might appear from the air. They believed that only this perspective would allow readers to fully appreciate the earthworks' stunning magnificence. Despite their care in documenting the mounds, they failed to acknowledge their true history by concluding that the mound builders had been a "separate race" and not America's Indigenous inhabitants.

It was no accident that at the height of the mound-builder controversy, the theory of Manifest Destiny was alive and well in the United States. Harrison's conclusion that the mound builders were the Aztecs, Squier and Davis's understanding that a mysterious culture was responsible for the mounds, or even Jefferson's view that ancient American Indians were the mounds' creators were all consistent with Manifest Destiny. In the view of many White Americans, providence had decreed that the United States was fated to expand across the entire continent despite all natural and cultural obstacles (O'Sullivan 1845: 7). They believed that the Indigenous cultures of North America represented clear-cut cultural obstacles.

In an uninhabited land, one without Indigenous cultures, America's continental expansion may have been a relatively straightforward process. White pioneers from the east, the foot soldiers of Manifest Destiny—many bringing captive African Americans with them—could simply have moved west and begun farming. The illusion of the continent as terra nullius may have comforted many, but the reality was far different. The land stretching from ocean to ocean was far from empty. Native peoples had lived in North America's "uninhabited wilderness" for thousands of years. To create living space for White America, the fledgling United States government decided to attack its so-called Indian problem with bigotry, forced dislocation, and open warfare against Indigenous nations (Talbot 1981: 93–100).

Eastern-dwelling White Americans generally believed that Native cultures, which they often denigrated as primitive and uncultured, could be easily overwhelmed and, once defeated, could be carelessly disregarded as an unwanted burden. The enslavement of African Americans presented a different problem. Prosperous White Americans, immune to ideas of equality and looking to develop large plantations west of the eastern mountains, knew they had to rely on captive laborers to ensure their economic success (Baptist 2016; Du Bois 1896: 151–167). One of their fears was that the acquisition of the Louisiana Purchase would mean that the enslavement of Black workers would be curtailed or even terminated within its boundaries (Hammond 2003).

The debate about the identity of the mound builders, some of it with an underlying racist theme, continued throughout the nineteenth century as various writers—some serious, some outrageous—put forth their ideas. John Wells Foster, a professional paleontologist, wrote in 1873 one of the most widely read books about the mound builders. Foster was no quack. When the book appeared, he was president of the highly regarded Chicago Academy of Science. Foster rigidly backed the cause of Manifest Destiny and believed that Native Americans could never have built the mounds, arguing that "a broad chasm is to be spanned before we can link the Mound-Builders to the North American Indians" (Foster 1873: 347). He figured that the mound builders were a distinct non-Indian culture because they were settled, had agriculture, and could muster the huge numbers needed to erect massive earthworks. He used an impressive array of arrowheads, axes, celts, pottery, shell objects, copper tools, and textiles to claim that the mound builders were unlike any other culture in the world, past or present. Citing numerous authorities such as Darwin, Foster pressed his case for the greatness of the mound builder's civilization. Using his prodigious imagination combined with fragmentary evidence taken out of context, Foster concluded that the mound builders worshipped the sun like ancient Mexicans, the Natchez, the Scythians, and the Babylonians; that they buried "the most useful and most highly-prized" artifacts with the dead, as did the Chinese, the Aryans of India, and the early Christians; and that they engaged in human sacrifice like the Scythians and the Stone Age Britons (Foster 1873: 310–317). He argued that the mound builders had a "national religion" and that they understood the curative power of salt. Most jarring, Foster proposed that the mound builders were Caucasians, stating: "The Negroid type is believed by many to be the primitive type of mankind, and has remained constant to this day; while the Caucasian type is the result of a more improved state of society, and of more favorable external influences" (Foster 1873: 336). Given their high state of civilization, what did Foster think happened to the mound builders? His answer was simple: they were "expelled from the Mississippi Valley by a fierce and barbarous race" and found refuge in Central America, visions once again of Harrison's Astecks (Foster 1873: 351). The "fierce and barbarous race"? The North American Indians Foster reviled.

The mound-builder debate continued to simmer until late in the century, when their identity was finally revealed. A man born in the mountains of eastern Tennessee who, like so many others in the nineteenth century were drawn to archaeology through a circuitous route, would solidify the opinions of Jefferson and many others that the mound builders were in fact ancient ancestors of Native Americans. This man, Cyrus Thomas, will forever be remembered as "the slayer of the Mound Builder myth" (Silverberg 1970: 131). Thomas began by believing that the mound builders were an unidentified, mysterious people, but following in the footsteps of Jefferson, Dickeson, and countless unnamed enslaved African American excavators, he undertook a series of meticulous excavations that changed his mind. In the process, he transformed the history of ancient North America.

Born in 1825, Thomas spent his formative years in the Appalachians, where he developed a lifelong interest in natural history. Like Dickeson, Thomas realized that the surest avenue into a life of science was through medicine. So, like many others at the time, Thomas began studying with a local physician. He also read law books and, at age 26, having abandoned his medical training, he resettled in Illinois, was admitted to the bar, and set himself up in private practice. The practice of law was unsatisfying, and itching to do more, Thomas abandoned his practice and took a job as the superintendent of the Jackson County, Illinois, school system. Equally unsettled in this profession, he decided on the life of a clergyman and was ordained as a Lutheran minister. Four years later he gave that up as well, claiming that his "intense independent thought" made it impossible for him to continue as a religious leader. His scientific leanings led him in 1859 to propose the creation of the Illinois Natural History Society. This led to his being hired as the entomologist on the Hayden Geological Survey, the first American exploration of the Yellowstone region. Upon his return to Illinois, he was appointed professor of natural history at Southern Illinois Normal University in Carbondale. Thomas had finally attained his long-dreamed-of career as a scientist. He was appointed to the post of Illinois State Entomologist and was then named to the US Entomological Commission. He soon left the commission to take a chance as an unpaid researcher with John Wesley Powell's Bureau of Ethnology at the Smithsonian Institution. It was there that the redoubtable Powell, the intrepid explorer of the Colorado River, decided in 1881 to name the 57-year-old Thomas as the director of the bureau's Division of Mound Excavation (Barnhart 2015; Keel 1970: 9–10; Kennedy 1996: 238–239). Thomas's final gamble had paid off, for he would stay in the director's position until his death in 1910.

What spurred Thomas to refocus his energetic mind from insects to ancient Americans is unknown. Southern Illinois is world-famous for its jaw-droppingly large Cahokia Mounds, and the region is studded with earthen mounds of all sorts. Thomas had probably stumbled across mounds while tracking down elusive insects; as a consumer of science, he was undoubtedly familiar with the prevailing views on the identity of the mounds' builders.

Thomas set to work immediately after Powell promoted him. Traveling throughout the eastern United States and excavating over 2,000 individual mounds stretching from southeastern Wisconsin to northern Florida, Thomas learned the answer to the mound-builder mystery. Having moved massive amounts of earth and discovering hundreds of ancient potsherds and other objects in the process, Thomas's conclusion left no room for doubt. When asked, "Who were the mound-builders?" he would answer without hesitation that the mound builders were the ancestors of "several of the tribes of modern or historic times" (Thomas 1884: 90, 1894: 17). No serious scientist would ever again question the mound builders' identity.

It was no coincidence that on December 14, 1893, one year before Thomas's report was published, that 32-year-old historian Frederick Jackson Turner appeared on the scene. Paraphrasing the superintendent of the US census, Turner observed that the frontier of the United States had ceased to exist only three years before, in 1890. This pivotal event was, in Turner's mind, "the closing of a great historic movement." As he expressed it, "the existence of an area of free land[!], its continuous recession, and the advance of American settlement westward explain American development" (Turner 1893: 79). The White American dream had come true: Manifest Destiny had been achieved. Allied to this conclusion was the belief that the so-called Indian Wars in the West had ceased in 1892 (Collier 1948: 143).

Understandings of race, inequality, and prejudice have been the researchers' quiet companions throughout the search for the elusive mound builders. Resting in the background, the specter of race in America knew it always had a seat at the table.

In 1890 Daniel G. Brinton, US Army doctor during the Civil War and professor of archaeology at the University of Pennsylvania, published a wildly popular book proclaiming scientific racism. Brinton accepted the pseudo-science that cranial structures and brain sizes were unique to each of the four human "races." He also thought that each race exhibits its own psychology, complete with unique social instincts, the strongest of which was "the sexual impulse." Brinton also promoted racial superiority by accepting a hierarchy that could be observed by measuring the shape of the skull, the wideness of the nose, the prominence of the jaw, and the length of the humerus. Brinton argued that "to our eyes all Chinamen look alike" and that "one cannot distinguish an Indian 'buck' from a 'squaw.'" For him and many like-minded White thinkers, determining the distinctions between the "races" was "the corner-stone of the science of Ethnography," by which he meant anthropology (Brinton 1890: 18).

At around the same time, Du Bois was meeting with Boas, thinking about race, and pondering the connections between the United States and Africa. In his first book, published in 1896, Du Bois had explored how morality, politics, and economics had meshed in the United States to put an end to the slave trade. In writing about the moral awakening the nation had allegedly experienced, Du Bois observed, "There is always a certain glamour about the idea of a nation rising up to crush an evil simply because it is wrong." Regrettably, the truth was something else entirely because "this can seldom be realized in real life; for the very existence of the evil usually argues a moral weakness in the very place where extraordinary moral strength is called for." Du Bois sorrowfully concluded that ridding a nation of evils like African bondage and discrimination requires "exceptional moral foresight and heroism." Lacking that, a nation simply needs "a certain hard common-sense in facing the complicated phenomena of political life." He was forced to concede that "in some respects we as a nation seem to lack this" (Du Bois 1896: 195, 198).

Excepting the rants of privileged men like Brinton, where was archaeology during America's supposed awakening? After Thomas had closed the book on the mound-builder mystery, American archaeologists kept their heads down and worked as historians of culture, content to use boxes of potsherds and piles of chipped-stone tools to create complex regional chronologies of ancient Native America. This program left no intellectual space for studying non–Native American cultures, African, European, or otherwise. Immersed so totally in the complexities of assembling the chronologies and accepting that any new excavation might require the time sequences to be completely rewritten, American archaeologists were able to pretend that archaeology was apolitical, that it was about the past and only the past. Leaving it to non-archaeologists like Boas and Du Bois to reflect on the social ills around them, American archaeologists tacitly accepted the status quo. Burrowed into their research, they could claim to ignore racist segregation, brutal immigration laws, and the eugenics movement being pressed forward by some of the nation's leading scientific bodies (Patterson 1995: 59). Thus, when the first historical archaeology began at Jamestown, Virginia, in the 1930s, it was easy for White archaeologists to accept the premise that the archaeology of "history" concentrates simply on sites deemed important within the dominant ideology of the American nation (Schuyler 1976). Inequality could be safely ignored.

Despite archaeologists' focus on building chronologies of ancient American Indian history, a handful of archaeologists had investigated sites associated with African Americans before 1968. These examples of African American archaeology occurred largely by accident and had no immediate impact on the discipline.

In 1934 the director of the Georgia Park Service in Atlanta instructed 23-year-old park employee James A. Ford to travel to Blythe Island and investigate two tabby ruins thought to be the remains of the Spanish colonial mission of Santo Domingo. Ford, born in Mississippi, was in a good position to undertake the work. Soon after graduating from high school in 1927, he had been hired by the Mississippi Department of Archives and History, and, with another boy, given the task of digging into the area's earthen mounds to search for "Indian relics" suitable for display. Once at work, Ford decided that, rather than digging willy-nilly as many had done, a more sensible approach would be to institute controls on the excavation and to keep accurate field notes. This experience was life changing, and by 1937 Ford was at the University of Michigan studying with James B. Griffin. Ford spent only one year with Griffin, and after the Second World War he obtained a doctorate degree from Columbia University. Ford's greatest triumph was untangling the astoundingly intricate pre-Columbian cultural sequence of the lower Mississippi Valley (Neuman 1984: 51; Willey 1969).

But in 1934 Ford had little in the way of guidance. Historical records offered meager information about the Santo Domingo ruins, and so excavation was the only way to answer whether the remains of the colonial mission could be found. After spending six weeks sifting through the soil, Ford could find no evidence of Spanish occupation. Instead, because the site was located on the grounds of Elizafield Plantation, he reasoned that the tabby remains were those of an early-nineteenth-century sugar mill complex. When Ford asked the African Americans still living on the estate for information, he learned that one room of the structure had been "destroyed and the shell from it was used to build a road." Once Ford determined that the ruins belonged to the nineteenth century and not to the colonial Spanish, he completed a series of measured drawings, left a record of his excavations, and considered the project over (Ford 1937).

Less than a decade later Adelaide K. Bullen and her husband, Ripley P. Bullen, were engaged in an excavation of a site in Andover, Massachusetts, where colonial European ceramic sherds had been found in association with Native American artifacts (Bullen and Bullen 1945). Ripley Bullen was an engineer who had spent the early years of his career with General Electric. On a trip to Massachusetts, he met Adelaide Kendall, and they were married in 1929. Ripley harbored an interest in archaeology, and he helped found the Massachusetts Archaeological Society in 1939. One year later, he left GE and began working with the Peabody Foundation for Archaeology at Phillips Academy in Andover. He also entered graduate school at Harvard, while Adelaide enrolled at Radcliffe as an undergraduate. In 1941 she and Ripley took part in the University of New Mexico's field school near Chaco Canyon. Like just about everyone of that generation, the Bullens focused on Native American cultural history, with one of their projects probing the settled Puebloans' interactions with nomadic Plains cultures (Marrinan 2001; Wilkerson 1978). Adelaide would soon enter graduate school at Harvard, and before long she was an expert in the analysis of human remains.

In 1945 she and Ripley were investigating the American Indian site in Andover. While surveying the ground surface, they noticed a cellar hole about 900 feet south of the Native American settlement. Near the cellar were two refuse piles, a well, and a small depression that may have been a vegetable cellar. Despite the presence of a lumbermen's shack near the depression, it appeared that the site was undisturbed, so the Bullens decided to excavate it. The ceramic, glass, nails, and other objects they discovered in the cellar told them that the house had probably deteriorated after being abandoned, sometime during the first half of the nineteenth century.

Adelaide and Ripley were enchanted by the story of this mysterious house, and after conducting research in local archives they learned that a woman named Lucy Foster had been the former house's occupant. Born enslaved probably in Boston, Lucy had been the unwilling property of Job and Hannah Foster. When Hannah died in 1812, she left an acre of land and a house to Lucy for "her natural life." The Bullens had found the house's cellar. In October 1845, Lucy, then 84 years old, entered the Andover Infirmary. By then an impoverished ward of the state, she died on November 1, 1845. She had lived in her small Andover house for about 30 years.

Adelaide and Ripley presented Lucy Foster's life in a manner considered sensitive for the time, but they failed to pursue the research further. It would be another 30 years, an entire generation, before someone would take a deeper look at the artifacts the Bullens had collected from Lucy's property and almost another 40 years after that when someone would reconsider the significance of Lucy's life (Baker 1978; Battle-Baptiste 2011: 109–133).

In January 1950 native Floridian John W. Griffin spent several days conducting preliminary fieldwork at an old fort in the Apalachicola National Forest in the Florida Panhandle just southwest of Tallahassee. In the years before visiting the fort, Griffin had followed a familiar path: he had developed an interest in nature and science as a youth, spent time at a state university, and went to the University of Chicago to study anthropology. After finding archaeology most interesting, Griffin returned to Florida to work for the state's park service. Like almost every other archaeologist at the time, his focus was strictly on ancient Native American history. In a state-wide survey of ancient sites, one of the first places Griffin located was a Timucuan village depicted on a Spanish colonial map drawn in 1605. This extraordinary find gave Griffin the idea that digging at the village would provide "an opportunity to define Timucuan material culture as of 1605," an era that was then an archaeological blank spot. Griffin's research at the site convinced him that archaeologists needed to learn all they could about "European-derived material culture." This decision is what eventually led him to Fort Gadsden (Griffin 1994: 67–72).

In 1814 the British Army had built a small unnamed fort overlooking the Apalachicola River. They placed it near a trading post that had been established ten years earlier. The traders had located their building to take advantage of the local Native American trade, and when their first clerk arrived, he brought with him five enslaved Africans. The trading post—really a fortified house—was surrounded by a 15-foot-high octagonal earthwork enclosing about seven acres. The British occupied their nearby fort until 1815, when they withdrew at the close of the War of 1812.

The disappearance of the British did not go unnoticed by the region's slave owners, who began referring to the fort as "Negro fort." The place made them nervous because when the British left, several Native Americans and African Americans had continued to live at the fort. The British had transported several of the fort's residents of African heritage to Nova Scotia and the West Indies, but too many had stayed behind to suit the local slaveholders. They saw the fort as a welcoming beacon for the still enslaved because if plantation escapees could reach the fort, they would be immediately freed by the fort's self-emancipated residents. Fearing this, the American plantation owners sent a party to the fort to convince the recalcitrant Blacks to return to enslavement, but their entreaties were rebuffed with threats of violence.

The slave owners attempted to remove the fort's occupants by force but failed. The US government labeled the African Americans and the American Indians in the fort "banditti," thereby transforming them into criminals. The Americans also tried to exert pressure on the Spanish governor to remove them, but in an act of international brinksmanship, he refused. It was then that Andrew Jackson—slave owner, Indian hater, and general of the US Army in the region—decided to destroy the fort. Under his command, a large force, complete with gunboats, attacked the fort in 1816. The Americans captured all the once-enslaved holdouts who had not already sought refuge with the nearby Seminoles. Two years later, Jackson ordered the construction of a new, larger fort on the site of the "Negro fort," which he christened Fort Gadsden (Boyd 1937). The Confederate Army occupied this fort during the Civil War, but the place was abandoned thereafter.

Griffin spent most of his time exploring the remains of Fort Gadsden, paying far less attention to the "Negro fort." He observed the presence of "Indian pottery, 'China,' unglazed European earthenware, lead balls and melted lead fragments," and many other objects but concluded that "Fort Gadsden, or more specifically the so-called Negro Fort area, has the potentiality of aiding in the unraveling of historical Indian archaeology in

Florida" (Griffin 1950: 261). Like Ford and the Bullens, Griffin missed an opportunity to be a pioneer in African American archaeology.

In the years between Cyrus Thomas's fieldwork and Fairbanks's first trip to Kingsley's plantation, it was clear that Black America had developed its own avenues of self-determination. Du Bois had helped found the NAACP in 1909; Marcus Garvey, a Jamaican immigrant, had founded the Universal Negro Improvement and Conservation Association and African Communities League in 1914; Booker T. Washington had instituted the National Negro Business League in 1900; and the Ligue universelle pour la défense de la race noire had been created in Paris in 1924 (Du Bois 1936: 119; Langley 1969: 70; Sundiata 1970: 9; Washington 1910: 130). Such organizations, promoting Black empowerment in the United States and throughout the world, were the progenitors of the civil rights groups that would develop in the 1950s and 1960s. These organizations were not always compatible, and fissures occurred within the African American community about the methods, means, and motives of each. Despite the differences in approach, their presence on the nation's intellectual and political landscapes signaled that change was under way.

At the same time, a transformation was under way in archaeology as well, undoubtedly as a reflection of changes in society at large. The first shot in the intellectual battle that would create historical archaeology as anthropology and make serious African American archaeology possible was put forward by archaeologist Walter Taylor in his controversial doctoral dissertation. Slated for publication after its completion in 1943 but delayed by the Second World War and not published until 1948, Taylor's unapologetic investigation into the design, methods, and intent of archaeology raised the hackles of many within the senior ranks of the archaeological establishment. In pointing accusatory fingers and calling out names, Taylor forced archaeologists to think about what it was they were attempting to accomplish. Were they simply historians piecing together ancient, unwritten history, or could they do more? Taylor believed that archaeologists should do more and brashly said as much. He claimed that archaeologists were historians if their goal was only to create cultural histories. Their objective, he said, should be to understand the process of being alive. Rather than simply building dead histories with dry facts, archaeologists should be revealing the realities of past lives. By arguing that it is irrelevant whether the "subject matter is 18th century England, Blackfoot Indians, or an industrial community in Indiana," Taylor provided the theoretical rationale for historical archaeology (Taylor 1948: 41).

Taylor's assertion that archaeologists could not justify confining themselves to the study of Native American cultural histories was explosive. When he wrote that archaeologists, if they chose to do so, could work like anthropologists and study "the nature of culture, of cultural constants, or processes, or regularities, and of chronological development," he was essentially giving the green light to the archaeology of African American life (Taylor 1948: 38). By mentioning "processes," Taylor opened a world of possibilities, and it was this idea that Fairbanks grasped with both hands. The transmission of cultural traits from Africa to the Americas was, after all, a process, one that had divided Frazier and Herskovits, but one that Fairbanks believed could be resolved with archaeology.

For the first 100 years of their discipline's history, White privileged American archaeologists had been focused on a racist question over the intellectual abilities of Native Americans. By disregarding living Indigenous nations and often stealing their cultural property, archaeologists had perpetuated a colonialist kind of archaeological practice (Trigger 1984). Taylor did not question the racialist assumptions of White archaeologists, but his proposal for a different kind of research made it clear that things could change if archaeologists chose to do so.

Fairbanks's initial project made it clear that change was possible. It all began in earnest with what archaeologists had always been comfortable studying: clay pottery.

4

Pots

Colonoware, African America, Native America

It was no accident that Fairbanks wrote his first professional article about Native American pottery, or that students like him, eager to know more about such things, flocked to Ann Arbor to study with James Griffin, the acclaimed expert on the rich varieties of ancient pottery styles found across the American Midwest. During the twentieth century, pockets of North American archaeologists, professional and avocational, met together to compare notes about pottery types, to discuss their latest discoveries, and to argue if a type of sherd found in one place was the same as that found in another. Throughout the century and continuing into the present, handmade clay pottery forms a primary source of information for archaeologists probing the cultural histories of the American Indians before, during, and after the arrival of Europeans among them. The shape of pots, their methods of manufacture, and the meaning of the scratches and indentations they carry on their surfaces have long fascinated archaeologists, even though potsherds and even whole pots can be infuriatingly reluctant to surrender their secrets.

Buried beneath the dry, analytical attributes archaeologists collect from clay pottery rests a quasi-magical quality. Even the smallest sherd sparks wonder, forcing us to contemplate that some incredibly clever persons in the long-forgotten past discovered how to transform the ground they walked on into usable bowls and jugs. Theirs was an awe-inspiring act of invention, one that eventually lead to the creation of our modern world. Without the first clay pot, human social development would have been stalled for who knows how long.

The nearly mystical quality encapsulated within the metamorphosis of a pile of earth into a usable pot rests in the clay's inherent tactility. The reason why so many museums allow visitors to handle potsherds is because turning them over in one's fingers is intrinsically pleasurable. Some might even say that the experience has spiritual qualities. Holding a clay potsherd puts us immediately in touch with its past maker and users, real human beings who once walked the earth as we do now. We may only imagine our connections with them, but they seem real nonetheless. We are practically as transformed as the clay itself; we only substitute the physical heat of the fire for the warmth of our passions.

When John Griffin was toiling away in the soils of Fort Gadsden, he was forced to recognize as a purely practical matter that he knew almost nothing about the trinkets and baubles that Europeans had bundled on board ships and sent to their New World. What Griffin was silently conceding was that he already had considerable knowledge about ancient American Indian potsherds, chipped-stone tools, and other ancient objects. Like the rest of his archaeological generation, he had attended numerous lectures about these things. He knew how to recognize them, and he was even conversant with their regional differences. Archaeologists had spent long years classifying these distinctions, organizing them by place of discovery, and arranging them in chronological order.

Before the creation of American historical archaeology, most archaeologists' introduction to European artifacts almost always happened at ancient Native American sites (Cotter 1993; Quimby 1938). Most archaeologists began, like Adelaide and Ripley Bullen in Massachusetts, looking for one thing and finding something else. Excavators often unearthed recognizable non-Indian artifacts—iron knife blades, tiny glass beads, and copper kettles—at villages whose residents had experienced contact with Europeans. The problem was that archaeologists knew painfully little about these objects: how they were made, where they came from, and how they had gotten to an Indian village. Until the late 1960s, few archaeologists had dedicated the same amount of time and attention to knives, beads, and kettles as they had to clay potsherds.

Given archaeologists' familiarity with clay pottery, it was no surprise that these were the first objects they identified as possibly having links to African individuals forced to live in the United States as enslaved laborers. The connection took years to recognize because archaeologists at first associated the pottery with Native Americans, the cultures with which they were most familiar. Remarkably, the story of how archaeologists finally recognized the pottery's true makers began not in the United States but in faraway London, England.

As large swathes of London lay in ruins at the close of the Second World War, 18-year-old Ivor Noël Hume was looking for a job. He tried his hand at writing plays while in school, and, enjoying the creative process, he decided to become a playwright. The best he could do in those unsettled times, though, was to land a job as an assistant stage manager at a London playhouse. He would stay in this position for the next four years, but finding playwriting and even minor acting jobs elusive—and even failing to scare up an agent to represent him—Noël Hume decided to give something else a try. While listening to a BBC radio program, he learned about a man who spent his free time "mudlarking," and he was intrigued.

Mudlarking is an unlikely but immensely addictive hobby. The second definition of "mudlark" in the *Oxford English Dictionary,* dating to the late eighteenth century, is "One who dabbles, works, or lives in mud." The first definition, dating to the same era, is "hog."

When Noël Hume first discovered it, the term's meaning had evolved, but it still involved mud, a lot of mud. The river Thames, being tidal, rises and falls as it snakes its way through London. It has performed this dance for centuries, even long before the Romans settled at what they called Londinium. Throughout these same centuries, people had decided that bodies of water, like the Thames, are good places to throw the unwanted and worn out. In response, the Thames, as it ebbs and flows, pushes the detritus of generations to the shoreline.

Mudlarks were originally poor or homeless children and adults who scoured the Thames waterfront in search of usable or salable objects. Today's mudlarking hobbyists lazily stroll along the water's edge, heads down, panning with their eyes for anything valuable or historically interesting. What seems like a harmless pastime can become an obsession, one replete with the feverish expectation of the next big find. But serious mudlarks are not chancers. They study tidal charts and accept that the river sets its own schedule. The most effective mudlarks can almost sense the tides in their sleep. To be the first on the shore requires alertness and commitment, not to mention a strong back and sturdy boots.

Mudlarking can also offer more than momentary excitement. The potential exhilaration it offers is one thing, but the time spent trolling along the rocky shoreline can be a time of peace and reflection. As mudlark Lara Maiklem confesses, "When I was by the river, I was somewhere else, disconnected from the city and a world away from my problems. It was my escape, from people, work, awkward situations, even sometimes from myself" (Maiklem 2019: 24).

The BBC broadcast compelled Noël Hume to decide to try his luck and join the other seekers on the shore. This decision ultimately led him to a man named Adrian Oswald, an English pioneer in the study of modern-era artifacts. Oswald is today largely remembered for his pathbreaking studies of mass-produced clay tobacco pipes, which were often found by mudlarks. Oswald was then Keeper of London's Guildhall Museum. As Noël Hume described him at their first meeting, Oswald was "short, balding, and round-faced with a somewhat untidy moustache." He was also "immensely engaging" (Noël Hume 2010: 141).

Fascinated by the finds on the Thames shore and intrigued by Oswald, Noël Hume spent his spare time during the final years of the 1940s volunteering on Oswald's excavations, cleaning mud-soaked artifacts, and doing all the minutiae required by the rigors of archaeological excavation and its aftermath. It was Oswald who taught Noël Hume the basics of archaeological excavation. One day Oswald, who was the de facto archaeologist for the City of London, asked if Noël Hume would be interested in forsaking the theater and accepting a position at the museum. His big break in the theatrical limelight still nowhere in sight, Noël Hume agreed, figuring he would take the job until something else came along. The following week, Oswald developed pneumonia and left the museum, leaving Noël Hume, the frustrated thespian, in charge of London's rich archaeological history. He may not have realized it at the time, but the theater was now behind him.

Thrust into the position in one of the world's most historically iconic cities, Noël Hume decided that he should have an archaeological specialty. Because the attention of almost every other archaeologist in London was riveted on the city's Roman occupation, Noël Hume decided that he would concentrate on something no one else seemed to care about: post-medieval artifacts, those things made and used in the years between around 1500 and 1750 or so. Oswald had burrowed deeply into the subject of clay pipes, so Noël Hume decided to focus on English wine bottles. His simple decision would change his life forever.

During his time at the Guildhall Museum, Noël Hume worked alongside a volunteer named Audrey Baines. She had a bachelor's degree in Roman history and archaeology and was working toward a master's degree in the same subjects. She had studied with Sir Mortimer Wheeler, the renowned British archaeologist, and when Noël Hume met her, she knew a good deal more about archaeology than he. Finding one another's company rewarding, they married in 1950.

One day while toiling away in the lab, a visiting archaeologist named J. C. Harrington, or "Pinky" to his friends, appeared. Having just completed his excavation of the Jamestown, Virginia, glassblowing house, he had traveled to Britain to learn more about English glass bottles. (He also intended to undertake a tasting survey of the nation's many malt whiskeys.) The chance meeting between Pinky Harrington and Audrey Baines, who was in the lab that day, was auspicious for Noël Hume. A few years later, in 1957, when Harrington learned that Colonial Williamsburg was searching for someone knowledgeable about the arcane world of British colonial artifacts, he suggested they hire Noël Hume, arguing that "half the artifacts you find in Williamsburg are broken bottles, and he is a specialist in broken bottles" (Noël Hume and Miller 2011: 15). The simple act of showing an interest in old English bottles led to one of the most cherished positions in American historical archaeology.

Harrington's offhand reference sent Ivor and Audrey across the Atlantic to a life in the Virginia Tidewater. There they each would become renowned for their expertise and commitment to colonial archaeology and its artifacts. Noël Hume became a prolific and powerful translator of archaeology to the public, a writer who could marshal the skills of the dramatist and make the past live as few could (Kelso 1992; Noël Hume 2010; Noël Hume and Miller 2011). Audrey became a widely recognized expert in colonial artifacts in her own right.

Once Noël Hume left the shores of the Thames behind and started digging up Virginia's colonial properties, he began to encounter Native American artifacts. He had not come across these while mudlarking, and the Guildhall Museum was not known as a repository of North American Indian antiquities. Noël Hume's experience, however, did tell him that the unglazed potsherds were not the products of European hands. Bronze Age Britons had made unglazed pottery, and the Anglo-Saxons had carried on the tradition. But glazed containers had entered England with the Romans in the first century CE, and by the thirteenth century glazed ceramics were commonplace within homes across the British Isles (Noël Hume 2001: 26–29).

On the sites Noël Hume excavated, Native American objects never outnumbered English-made objects, but they were present enough to demand attention. As he observed with some exasperation, "Indian pottery" appeared at British colonial sites "with disturbing regularity" (Noël Hume 1962: 3). He knew little about the Indigenous pottery traditions of Virginia, but luckily for him, only a couple of years before he and Audrey had arrived in the United States, Smithsonian archaeologist Clifford Evans (1955) had published a detailed study of the state's pre-Columbian pottery traditions.

Noël Hume became so perplexed by the "Indian pottery" that he decided to write about it. In an article published in 1962, he began what would become a multiyear conversation. He had mentioned the pottery at an archaeology conference five years earlier, but no one had paid particular attention. His published paper would put the pottery in the forefront of many archaeologists' minds.

Noël Hume began, using a traditional approach, by detailing the pottery's main characteristics. He noted that the sherds were unglazed and that the vessels had been made by forming the clay without benefit of a wheel. Being fired in a simple campfire meant that even a single pot could vary in color from yellow to buff to red to black. Some pieces showed signs of having been burnished with a stick or a stone, and many of their outer surfaces lacked the indentations and impressions present on much pre-European Indian pottery. Most curious was that some of the specimens had been made in shapes more common to mass-produced, glazed European ceramics, including three-legged cups with large handles, narrow-mouthed jugs, teacups, and porringers. These forms were decidedly non-Indigenous. Noël Hume further observed that the ware appeared in the late seventeenth century but was gone during the early nineteenth century.

The ware's unique characteristics meant that, as a newly recognized pottery tradition, it required a name, one that would distinguish it from the hordes of other names archaeologists had already bestowed on the hundreds of Native American pottery styles then known to exist. Falling back on his London training, Noël Hume decided to call it "Colono-Indian" ware. This term was akin to the hybrid pottery styles he knew from London. Sherds of Romano-British pottery adorned the storage shelves of the Guildhall Museum and occasionally washed up on the shores of the Thames.

Believing that the unglazed, hand-formed ware was made by Native Americans, he suggested that its creators must have produced it as a marketable commodity. Judging it inferior to European wares, he thought that perhaps the pottery was intended for use by captive African Americans. Noël Hume thus tacitly channeled the Park–Frazier assimilationist view that enslaved Africans "would have absorbed enough of the European way of life to desire the same kinds of cooking and table wares as their masters." For their part, he believed that slave owners "would have been loath" to purchase English blue-and-white delft dinnerware or even sturdy stoneware jugs and storage jars for captive African use. Viewing "the astute Indians" as rational economic actors, he imagined that Native potters "tailored their wares to styles acceptable to these customers." He reasoned further that slave owners may have purchased what he considered to be inferior pottery for distribution to their captive laborers, thinking it unlikely that the enslaved could have purchased the vessels for themselves (Noël Hume 1962: 5).

Noël Hume's inclusion of enslaved Africans was new for him. In his study of Rosewell Plantation, published in 1963 but perhaps written before his 1962 article, he ascribed the wares strictly to Native American potters, only mentioning enslaved captives in passing. In the case of Rosewell, he believed that Colono-Indian pottery was probably made by Native Americans who lived on the estate as either servants or hunters of "unwelcome beasts of prey" (Noël Hume 1963: 172). By 1966 Noël Hume once again affirmed that the "proto-European forms" of the pottery had probably been made by "Tidewater Indians and probably intended for the use of the slave population" (Noël Hume 1966: 45).

Noël Hume was correct in his assessment that the pots may have been made as marketable commodities. In his fancifully romantic nineteenth-century tale of the Old South, *Caloya: or, the Loves of the Driver,* Charlestonian William Gilmore Simms (1853: 127) mentioned how the Catawbas, "a pitiful remnant" of a once-glorious people, would periodically appear in Charleston, bringing "a little stock of earthen pots and pans . . . which they bartered in the city for such commodities as were craved by their tastes, or needed by their condition." In his ethnography of the Powhatan culture in Virginia, written for New York's prestigious Museum of the American Indian, then located in the Washington Heights area of northern Manhattan, Boas-trained anthropologist Frank G. Speck, speaking with an elderly Indigenous woman, learned "how the women constructed clay pots, milkpans, and stewing jars, and carried them to the trading stores in the country." She told him that they would carry "the crockery upon their backs in cloth sacks" and trade them for "small wares, groceries, or cash" (Speck 1928: 409; also see Spivey 2019: 2).

Noël Hume's stature in historical archaeology, in conjunction with the dominance of American Indian cultural history ingrained in most archaeologists' minds, meant that his views about the unglazed pottery, and especially his term for it, were quickly adopted. In fact, in 1962 Fairbanks was one of the first to use it, describing a nearly whole pitcher found in Florida as "Colono-Indian Ware." Ascribing the pitcher to the Seminoles, Fairbanks (1962: 104) thought it was not intended "for the use of slaves on the plantations."

The Charles Fairbanks of 1968 may not have been so quick to agree with Noël Hume's assessment and disregard the ware's possible African connections. Only six years after Noël Hume's article had appeared, and with the Frazier–Herskovits debate more prominent in his mind, Fairbanks undoubtedly would have thought more broadly and at least considered some sort of relationship between the pottery and enslaved Africans.

For the next decade, archaeologists in the American Southeast still hedged their bets about the origin of "Colono-Indian" pottery. In the early 1970s Stephen Baker, then a graduate student at the University of South Carolina, had decided to investigate the ware's roots. He had direct experience with the ware, having excavated alongside Stanley South, one of historical archaeology's leading figures and one of the most important archaeological thinkers of the late twentieth century (Baker 1972).

During an excavation in the town of Cambridge, South Carolina, archaeologists discovered sections of 13 pottery vessels, each of which had all the characteristics of Colono-Indian pottery. None of the over 20,000 other artifacts found in association with the sherds dated after 1820, so Baker knew that the pottery had to date before 1820. Ethnographic accounts convinced him that the pottery was most likely related to the Catawbas, the Indigenous South Carolinians maligned by William Gilmore Simms. Like Noël Hume before him, Baker figured that the Catawbas made the ware specifically for sale. The strongest direct historical evidence for this conclusion appears in a statement made by John Ferdinand Dalziel Smyth, a British traveler who had swung through the Catawba's territory in the late eighteenth century. Smyth observed that the Catawbas, whom he judged to be "simple, submissive, and obliging," made few of their own material possessions, having been swept up into the British colonial marketplace. Smyth said that the only objects the Catawbas continued to make were straw baskets, table mats, and "an ill-formed kind of a half-baked earthen ware" (Smyth 1784: 193, 194). Baker found other historical accounts indicating that Catawba potters sold their wares to a range of consumers, both White and Black. Disregarding Noël Hume's opinion that the wares were inferior to glazed European ceramics, Baker (1972: 16) supposed that the residents of "many Indian, Negro and White homes" all would have willingly used the wares.

Baker's evidence, although persuasive, did not mean that the Catawbas were the only potters who made what archaeologists were calling Colono-Indian ware. Instead, he concluded that "Colono-Indian pottery production is not to be treated as a peculiarity of any one tribal group or even cultural area." This means that specimens unearthed in South Carolina may be linked to the Catawbas, whereas pieces found in Virginia may be associated with the Pamunkeys. In each case, the wares might also be attributed to an entirely different culture. The central point was that archaeologists accepted that Native American potters had made Colono-Indian ware. They also acknowledged that regional variation could make it difficult to define which Native American culture was responsible for any individual collection of pottery.

The year after Baker's paper was published Stanley South was contracted to direct excavations at the first Fort Moultrie, a late-eighteenth-century fortification built to protect Charleston, South Carolina. Both British and American soldiers had garrisoned the three successive forts erected on the same spot, each of which they named Moultrie. As was true of many other excavations then being conducted across the American Southeast, South and his colleagues found numerous pieces of coarsely made pottery they immediately recognized as Colono-Indian ware. At Moultrie, sherds had turned up in both American and British deposits.

Like any good archaeologist, South separated the excavated unglazed pottery from the glazed ceramics based on the sherds' visible features. All the clay potsherds had characteristics pointing to Colono-Indian manufacture. Some were gray, others were buff to orange, and some were glossy black with burnished surfaces. The ware's potters had added sand or fine mica to some of the clay as they mixed it, understanding that these additives would strengthen the clay enough to increase its chances of not cracking during the firing process.

South accepted that the wares he found at Fort Moultrie had been fashioned by skilled Catawba artisans and claimed that "both American and British enlisted men" had acquired it during their tours of duty. He suggested that a "high degree of similarity" appeared to exist between the Colono-Indian wares and "pottery being made today in West Africa," but ultimately he rejected any connection between the two (South 1974: 181–188).

South's brief allusion to West Africa did not go unnoticed. Paying attention was Leland Ferguson, one of South's colleagues at the University of South Carolina. As a young boy growing up among the red-clay tobacco fields of North Carolina, Ferguson dreamed of becoming an archaeologist. Nonetheless, when he entered college in the early 1960s, he decided to shelve his archaeological dream and opt for the seemingly more stable career of an engineer. After obtaining bachelor's and master's degrees in science, Ferguson discovered, like Dickeson and Thomas before him, that the pull of archaeology was too strong. So Ferguson decided to trade in his slide rule for a trowel and to immerse himself in unraveling the past. After assisting with the excavation of a Native American mound, Ferguson decided to begin doctoral work at the University of North Carolina. His principal professor was Joffre Coe, the doyen of North Carolina pre-Columbian archaeology. Like Fairbanks, Coe was another of James Griffin's students who would go on to establish himself as a prominent figure in the field.

As a doctoral student, Ferguson attended lectures on the fine points of Native American pottery traditions and chipped-stone tools. He and his fellow students also ingested a good dose of American Indian cultural history. Ferguson decided to focus his doctoral research on the Mississippians, the enigmatic Native American culture that had created a complex, multilayered social system and had built many large communities, including the imposing Cahokia Mounds on the Mississippi River across from St. Louis. Ferguson's first teaching post was in Florida, but in 1972 he went to work with the South Carolina Institute of Archaeology and Anthropology at the University of South Carolina (Kelly 2017). His plan was to continue probing the secrets of the Mississippians' fascinating culture. In his doctoral dissertation he had studied the Mississippian's South Appalachian expression, so he knew that the culture had reached into North and South Carolina. Their villages and mounds were smaller in the South than along their namesake river, but each settlement had its own unique secrets to reveal, nonetheless (Ferguson and Green 1984: 139–143).

One thing that makes handmade earthen mounds so distinctive, as Dickeson so faithfully depicted in his renderings, is that they sit high above the surrounding countryside. Armies find such vantage points to be irresistible as defensive outposts, and, true to form, in 1780 British Revolutionary War soldiers in South Carolina built a fortification on an ancient mound and dubbed it Fort Watson in honor of their colonel. Ferguson's initial charge was to investigate the mound itself. Although his first love lay in a much earlier period of history, as a responsible archaeologist he knew it was unethical to ignore the eighteenth-century military deposits sitting atop the mound (Ferguson 1975: 2–28).

One of the dirty secrets of much American archaeology prior to the formal creation of historical archaeology in the late 1960s is that archaeologists looking for pre-Columbian Native American deposits often ignored and even destroyed the more recent occupations resting above earlier deposits. Many early American homesteads, built on mounds, have been lost because single-minded archaeologists have dug right through them to reach what interested them underneath. Thankfully, Ferguson understood the value of the past in its entirety and turned his attention to the fort. The time he spent in this endeavor convinced him of historical archaeology's alluring power to reveal history, even in the presence of written records. His experience at Fort Watson nudged him away from the ancient Mississippians and toward our more modern era.

One day Stanley South read to Ferguson a letter he had received from Richard Polhemus, an archaeologist then visiting West Africa. Polhemus recounted that the handmade clay pots he witnessed being made in Ghana looked much like the hundreds of clay potsherds he had washed, numbered, and boxed up in South Carolina. All of the South Carolina specimens had been classified as Colono-Indian ware, but he found them to be indistinguishable from those being made on the other side of the Atlantic in Africa. When South finished reading Polhemus's letter, he and Ferguson looked at one another, each silently wondering about the letter's implications. But falling back on archaeological convention, not to mention Noël Hume's formidable reputation, they decided the similarities were interesting but not terribly compelling. They let the matter drop. Who were they to argue with the famed excavator of Colonial Williamsburg? When he returned home, Polhemus presented his thoughts in an archaeological report, but, as had happened to Noël Hume in the late 1950s, no one paid much attention. Polhemus had planted the seed of an idea, but it had been fixed so deeply that it took time to push its way to the surface.

One day a sport diver appeared at the door of the South Carolina Institute of Archaeology and Anthropology with an object in his hands. It was a coarsely made jug he had scooped up from the bottom of the Combahee River in Colleton County, South Carolina. Its bulbous body tapered into a much smaller circular neck and rim, and it had a thick strap handle reaching from its neck to its body. Several blocks of impressed parallel striations, possibly made using a carved wooden paddle, were visible around the jug's body. The diver had discovered it near Bluff Plantation, a place where captive Africans had once produced bushels of rice for the benefit of the estate's White owner. Despite the proximity of the slave-labor plantation, no thoughts of African American potters sprang to anyone's mind when they first examined the jug. They all assumed that Native Americans had made it (Figure 2).

Figure 2. Colonoware pot seen by Ferguson. Now considered Catawba. Courtesy the South Carolina Institute of Archaeology and Anthropology.

Meanwhile, Ferguson, still intrigued by what he had learned while excavating Fort Watson, decided he wanted to focus his archaeological attention on his Scottish ancestors in North Carolina. One avenue of evidence often consulted by archaeologists is folklore. Oral tales, anecdotes, and even sometimes barely believable yarns handed down through the generations often contain historical nuggets worthy of deeper investigation. So while sitting in on a folklore class at the university, Ferguson learned that direct descendants of enslaved West Africans living in the South Carolina Lowcountry, that strip of watery land lying along the Atlantic coast, still made coiled grass baskets. The obvious African features displayed in the baskets made his mind return to the Combahee River jug, and he had a flash of insight: could "Colono-Indian" pottery be related to Africans? Fascinated by the prospect, he decided to dig deeper (Ferguson 1992: 9–16).

Ferguson's revelation, spurred onward by his support of the civil rights movement, transformed American historical archaeology. As he recalls, "The lid was cracked on a box of ideas that has sat covered with dust in the darkest corner of North American historic sites archaeology—the contribution of Afro-Americans to the pottery we call 'Colono-Indian'" (Ferguson 1978: 69). As his colleague Stanley South (1979: 216) put it, "This ware has been found to be more likely Colono-Afro than Colono-Indian, after 16 years of assumption by archaeologists that the ware was Indian made."

The conclusion was inescapable: the pottery's producers were most likely enslaved African Americans rather than market-minded Native Americans. Since the revelation came after Fairbanks's trip to Kingsley's plantation, Ferguson credited Fairbanks's leadership in promoting the idea that American history could be understood "from a non-Western point of view." In short, Fairbanks had invented "the idea of an archaeology of African American history" (Ferguson 1992: xv).

In his first full-length study of the pottery, Ferguson addressed the history of the ware's identification beginning with Noël Hume. He then set out to answer some key questions: who made the pottery, when did they make it, and who used it? Archaeologists had unearthed bag loads of sherds at seventeenth- to early-nineteenth-century sites once inhabited by Europeans or African Americans, or both. With Polhemus's letter possibly in the back of his mind, Ferguson next noted that many West African cultures had rich traditions of making clay pottery stretching back in time for centuries. Based on his amassed information, Ferguson made a startling claim: not only was "the early Colono-Indian ware reminiscent of African wares, but African ceramic styles may have influenced American Indian wares," at least in their decoration. This remarkable assertion turned Noël Hume's interpretation on its head. Ferguson was proposing that at least some of the influence visible in the pottery had gone from Africans to Native Americans, not the other way.

Ferguson believed that determining the users of Colono-Indian ware could be relatively straightforward. The houses where the pieces appeared should indicate who had used the vessels. With such evidence in hand, Ferguson concluded that the wares were most likely used primarily by poor people, Black and White. He added that some better-off families may have allowed a few pieces of Colono-Indian ware to be kept in their kitchens for cooking special dishes—in the same way, perhaps, that cooks today swear by their timeworn cast-iron pots for making chili and jambalaya.

Ferguson's assertion that "Afro-American slaves made much if not most of the Colono-Ware we see in the archaeological record" meant that the term "Colono-Indian ware" was no longer suitable (Ferguson 1978: 79). Influential archaeologist James Deetz, excavating in Virginia and also finding Colono-Ware (now written "colonoware") backed up Ferguson's assertion (Deetz 1993: 89–90; Ferguson 1978: 89–90). The vessel shapes in Virginia, being made into European forms, were different from those found in South Carolina, but the conclusion that Africans had played a role in the creation of the pottery was firmly established. The extent of their involvement was still a mystery, however.

The recognition that handmade clay pots might involve skilled African American hands dripped with irony. Archaeological research up until then, with the occasional accidental example, was almost completely centered on Native American history. At the time Ferguson made his interpretation, American archaeologists were all White and mostly men. Despite this reality, for many years it was true that African Americans, both men and women, had toiled alongside many White archaeologists excavating America's Indian mounds and villages, particularly in the segregated US South. Before the Second World War, excavations conducted under the umbrella of Franklin Roosevelt's New Deal programs saw thousands of excavators, draftspersons, lab assistants, and many other technicians descend on archaeological sites across the eastern United States. African Americans were among the poor and unemployed who found meaningful work on several of these projects. Contemporary images published in local newspapers and filed away in obscure excavation records are eerily reminiscent of Dickeson's sketches of nineteenth-century mound excavations because they show Black archaeologists diligently excavating ancient sites (Claassen 1993; Fagette 1996: 71). Black archaeologists also excavated at Jamestown and Williamsburg, both in Virginia, during the early years of these sites' exploration. Jim Crow laws ensured that they were good enough to unearth America's "cradle of democracy" but not good enough to visit the sites as tourists (Reid 2022). Many of the African American women and men who carefully cleaned out ancient storage pits, unearthed middens, and washed finds remain nameless and faceless, even though their labors assisted in some of the most iconic excavations in the history of North American archaeology (Figures 3 and 4).

Despite the long delay in recognizing the African American contribution to American history, it seemed by 1977 that archaeologists had made the discovery that Fairbanks had hoped to make a decade earlier. It seemed

Figure 3. African American archaeologist. Original caption reads: "Photograph No. 44Je°14. The red clay fill of the C level being removed from the ramp. Archaeological Investigations, Jefferson County, Alabama. Photograph by Steve Wimberly, April 24. 1940." Courtesy the National Anthropological Archives, Smithsonian Institution.

Figure 4. African American archaeologist. Original caption reads: "Photograph No. 9Lav47. A typical midden pit and contents. Archaeological Investigations, Lawrence County, Alabama. Photograph by Steve Wimberly, October 11, 1940." Courtesy the National Anthropological Archives, Smithsonian Institution.

as if the case on African retentions in the United States was finally closed. The newly recognized ware, colonoware, was an Africanism. Or was it?

The initial optimism over the apparent origin of colonoware quickly faded. Archaeologists, now aware of the deep cultural significance of the ware, fanned out across the Eastern Seaboard of the United States with a new mission: to discover buried samples of colonoware. The findings of these archaeologists would spin the research on the pottery in new directions, and it would quickly become apparent that the solution of the colonoware puzzle was not as straightforward as originally thought.

One stubborn question remained: did Native Americans fit into the colonoware picture? North American archaeologists knew without a doubt that American Indians had made clay pots since time immemorial, but had they played a role in the creation of colonoware?

Ferguson's revelation about the possible connection between West Africa and the Combahee River jug implied that the questions about colonoware remained unanswered. A troubling loose thread concerned the stamped-block design on the jug's surface. As he dug deeper into the region's Native American pottery traditions, his detective work revealed that the stamped design on the jug's surface had been given a name years earlier. Called San Marcos Stamped ware, archaeologists had dated it to the 1625–1702 era, a time when the Spanish Empire controlled Florida (Smith 1948: 314–315). Seeking verification of his inclination that the Combahee jug may have a Native American origin after all, Ferguson showed it to Fairbanks and Kathleen Deagan, a Fairbanks student who would become a leading figure in Spanish colonial archaeology. Both agreed that the jug's decoration conformed to the San Marcos tradition, but neither Fairbanks nor Deagan were familiar with the jug's shape. The design motif was correct, but the shape was wrong (Deagan 1978: 27–33; Ferguson 1992: 15–16).

Other evidence linking Native American potters to colonoware continued to pile up. Archaeologists soon discovered that early-seventeenth-century Apalachee Indians living in Florida's panhandle had made pottery somewhat like that discovered in South Carolina. This Indian-made pottery shared the characteristics of the South Carolina pieces, including being fashioned into European chamber pots, pitchers, and cups (Vernon 1988: 76–82).

As archaeologists added new collections to the storehouse of colonoware, new questions arose. The leading question remained: who was responsible for its manufacture?

Archaeologists decided to follow two lines of inquiry to address the question. One path, mostly led by those with long experience with Native American archaeology, followed the idea that colonoware represented a colonial-era expression of deep-rooted Native American pottery traditions, customs often extending back in time for generations. The San Marcos pottery made by historic Guale Indians of coastal Georgia and Florida offered a good example. Their tradition of pot making had grown out of the earlier Irene tradition, a local variant of the Lamar tradition, which began about 1350 and ended around 1660 (Saunders 2012: 95). In this case, the historic colonoware signified Native American cultural continuity over time (Cordell 2013: 80–99; Ferguson 1992: 40).

The situation in Virginia was murkier because many archaeologists had assumed that the Native peoples there were in disarray when colonoware made its first appearance. James Deetz, as part of his stalwart support of the African link to colonoware, had proposed, using Thomas Jefferson's *Notes on the State of Virginia* for support, that Native numbers were too small to account for the large quantities of colonoware showing up in archaeological excavations. His assessment was succinct and to the point: "As the native population declined, and the African population burgeoned, Colono ware became increasingly common" (Deetz 1996: 240–241). Native numbers go down, Black numbers increase and colonoware appears.

But was this truly the case in Virginia? Was it really that simple?

In 1877 Otis T. Mason, a prominent member of John Wesley Powell's Bureau of American Ethnology, noted that a Dr. Dalrymple of Baltimore had "made an exhaustive study of the Pamunkey and Mattapony Indians of Eastern Virginia." The Mattapony were closely allied to the Pamunkey—so close, in fact, that Mason referred to them as a single culture, one he did not like, calling them "a miserable half-breed remnant of the once powerful Virginia tribes." The element of their life he found "most interesting" was "their preservation of their ancient modes of making pottery" (Mason 1877: 627). In his study of Virginia's Powhatan Confederacy, to which the Pamunkey/Mattapony were adjoined, Frank Speck wrote specifically about Pamunkey pottery. Writing fifty years after Mason made his prejudiced evaluation, Speck spoke with Mattapony potters. The three women he interviewed could "remember well the details of the ceramic industry and are still able to fashion small pottery vessels and jars." With the passage of time, however, none of the women could make a pot "with the adroit hands of their grandmothers or even their mothers." Speck even included a photograph of two Pamunkey men excavating clay on the riverbank, adding that the spot was "one of the traditional clay-holes" used for pottery making

(Speck 1928: 401, 409). Noël Hume had relied on Speck's report when he wrote in the 1962 article that it was "logical . . . to assume" that colonoware "was manufactured by local Indians, presumably on the reservations of the Mattaponi, the Chickahominy or the Pamunky" (Noël Hume 1962: 4). At the very least, Native American potters living in Virginia could not be eliminated as producers of colonoware.

The alternative research path followed by archaeologists like Fairbanks and Ferguson explored the possibility that colonoware was evidence for the cultural contributions made by women and men of African heritage in the New World. They accordingly argued that potsherds collected from slave-labor plantations, rather than from colonial-era missions or even Native reservations, offered the clearest window into this world (Singleton and Bograd 2000: 6).

The two threads of colonoware research, one focused on Native Americans, the other on enslaved Africans, would intersect and collide over the next several years. They would finally intertwine.

Archaeologists were increasingly realizing that they could apply the term "colonoware" to any handmade, unglazed, low-fired-clay pottery dating to America's colonial era beginning with the late seventeenth century and extending to the early decades of the nineteenth century. Excavations exposed specimens from colonial American Indian villages, Spanish missions, the kitchens of American plantation owners, and the homes of enslaved Africans. As Ferguson (1992: 20) put it, an example "needs only to be found on a Colonial period site" to be labeled colonoware.

Colonoware, it seemed, was not a tradition belonging to just one culture. Ferguson's assertion that African Americans made "a substantial portion" of the coarse pottery did not negate Noël Hume's attribution to Native Americans; it simply broadened the interpretation to include both Native and African potters. It could also encompass European users because archaeologists in Florida had documented that San Marcos pottery had been found in colonial Spanish homes (Ferguson and Green 1983: 279). Archaeologists in the United States have now unearthed colonoware on slave-labor plantations as far north as Delaware and in American Indian villages as far north as Massachusetts (Sansevere 2017).

Archaeologists had received a jolt of reality when they realized the difficulty they faced when attempting to sort out who made every clay pot they unearthed. Colonial situations are by nature untidy because peoples with vastly different cultural customs meet, interact, borrow, and reject elements of one another's traditions, religions, worldviews, and even material objects. The outcomes and implications of such multicultural interactions, not being preordained, never tread the same historical path because the people involved—Africans, Europeans, and Native Americans—were never isolated from one another like separate streams running across a floodplain. Rather, North American cultures were more like the Mississippi River, an ever-rushing current fed by numerous small streams. Seventeenth- and eighteenth-century America was a place of daily multicultural interaction, with social meetings being commonplace. In South Carolina, and undoubtedly other places as well, captive Africans, enslaved and free Native Americans, and indentured Europeans had frequent contact throughout each day. Their associations meant that individuals could learn from one another, hear different languages spoken, learn new words, listen to unfamiliar stories, and create crossbred artifacts (Johnson 2018: 171–218).

Colonoware was teaching archaeologists about this complicated process, that the ware, when considered in its totality, was not the product of a single, static tradition locked in time. Instead, colonoware had been a fluid, evolving tradition, one depending upon a host of social environments. The various streams contributed by Africans, Native Americans, and Europeans—all of whom lived in the Americas with their own unique, tightly held cultural customs—were woven together in various ways at different times and places. The Mississippi River has a different character in St. Paul than it does in New Orleans, but it is the same river, nonetheless.

Colonoware by its very nature may incorporate multicultural elements. Given the caprices of culture, this means that examples of colonoware can differ regionally or even from one place to another within a relatively small area. Colonoware varies because the potters' social lives varied. But the identification of colonoware and the revelation of its secret messages have been so momentous because they reveal that Herskovits's thinking was far too simplistic. Colonoware is much too complicated to be grouped together as a single type and afforded one simple interpretation.

The union of Native American and African cultural streams was profound. Resting within a colonoware vessel was an elusive substance, one drawing strength from its inherently non-European character. Every colonoware bowl, pot, jug, or other object lacking any sign of European influence stresses that neither African nor Native American traditions require European approval or acceptance (Ferguson 1991: 28–39; Galke 2009: 320). Even vessels made to resemble European examples are different enough to be special. The presence of pottery vessels not of European manufacture within the homes of Native Americans and enslaved Africans raises the specter that pots could be disobedient objects, silent reminders that Africans and Indigenous Americans were unwilling to concede that Europeans were indisputably in charge of the world (Cobb and DePratter 2012; Ferguson 1991). As one archaeologist has noted, colonoware "is remarkable . . . not for being distinctively African, but for being distinctly non-European" (Hill 1987: 138).

The appearance of colonoware expresses the extreme stresses experienced by Native Americans, whose populations usually declined after Europeans arrived bearing unfamiliar diseases, the concept of White supremacy, and ideas of personal land ownership. Africans, ripped from their homelands and taken to a new continent against their will, experienced equal stresses. Viewed this way, colonoware is an artifact of adaptation, one emphasizing disruption on the parts of both Native American and African populations but also one of survival. The clearest clues for the adaptive nature of colonoware come from those pieces made in the form of European dishes. It is within these special wares that we can see most visibly that colonoware potters had the creativity and impertinence to mimic foreign shapes.

Accepting collaboration between Native American and African potters deepens the colonoware mystery. In the southeastern United States, Native American potters began making clay pots about 4,000 years before the first Europeans appeared on the continent. The slow refinement of potting technology took another 2,000 years in the Southeast, but it was a homegrown creation (Sassaman 1993: 6). Each generations' potters taught the next generation how to shape and fire clay pots. Clay-pot technology was widespread throughout Native America, but the decorations and vessel forms tended to be restricted to individual cultures. These special symbols mark the unique characteristics that Fairbanks, Griffin, and scores of other archaeologists have used for decades to construct Native American culture histories.

West Africans first made pottery before the end of the tenth millennium BCE (Huysecom et al. 2009: 906), but in the seventeenth century, it was the idea of an African clay pot, not the pots themselves, that traveled to the Western Hemisphere. Africans in America had no local African examples to use as models; they only had those they carried in their memories. African captives, brutally chained together and herded on board oceangoing slave ships, were not allowed to carry personal possessions with them. The most a chained person may have managed to smuggle onboard may have been one or two small glass beads (Handler 2009). The notion that a captive would have been allowed to carry a clay pot on board runs counter to the brutal regime established by traders in humanity.

Strikingly, archaeologists have yet to locate a single eyewitness account of African American pottery manufacture. Clay pots inspired comment when made by Native Americans, but not when made by African Americans. European Americans undoubtedly recognized clay jugs and bowls when they appeared in their kitchens, but such objects still occasioned no comment. History has silenced African-made pottery in the United States.

The paucity of information about the role of enslaved Africans in making colonoware is curious because making clay pottery is not a simple matter. One just does not simply walk into a field, gather up a pile of clay, and take it home and shape it into a usable pot. Not all clay is created equal. Some can be fashioned into objects, others cannot. And not everyone is equally skilled at making pots. Centuries of potters the world over have learned through hard-won experience that some clays require additives like sand, grit, shells, and other natural materials to make them more durable.

In his study of the Virginia Pamunkey published in 1894, John Garland Pollard, future governor of Virginia, learned about the process of preparing pottery clay by "Mr. Terrill Bradby, one of the best informed members of the tribe." Bradby said that the clay, once acquired from a "clay mine," was dried, vigorously kneaded, passed through a sieve, and pounded in a mortar. Potters would burn and grind up "Fresh-water mussels, flesh as well as shell" and add it to the clay during the kneading process (Pollard 1894: 18). Making this "shell-tempered" pottery added a level of difficulty to the process because it required local knowledge about shells: which kind to use, where to find them, and how many to knead into the clay. Thus, the production of colonoware using shell-tempering, something American Indian cultures had known about for generations, may indicate that enslaved Africans learned shell-tempering from local Native Americans (Neiman 1999: 146).

Firing the pots also required considerable knowledge and practical experience. Speck noted that the Pamunkeys and the Catawbas "burned" their pots in similar ways. Potters covered the still-malleable vessels with cornstalks and pieces of dried pine bark and set the entire mass on fire. Newspaper reporter-turned-ethnologist James Mooney told a colleague at the Bureau of American Ethnology how the historic Catawbas fired their black polished wares. He said that once a set of pots, bowls, and other vessels had been given their final shapes, the potter would rub their exterior surfaces with a smooth stone or mussel shell to give them a sheen. The potter would then cover these vessels with a pile of carefully selected pieces of oak bark. She (most American Indian potters were women) then placed a larger, unfired pot over the smaller vessels, and piled another heap of bark over the inverted pot. She then set the mound on fire. The fire baked the large, upside-down pot first. Its heat caused the bark stuffed under it to combust. Without oxygen, the fire inside the inverted pot, now burning like charcoal, blackened the smaller vessels underneath the large pot. Once the fire died out and the vessels had cooled, more polishing left the vessels with their captivating black sheen (Myer 1928: 522; Speck 1928: 411).

The difficulty involved in successfully making clay pottery highlights another mystery. No one today knows where colonoware was made, if not produced in Native American villages. Some vessels may have been fired in campfires or perhaps even within hearths, but the lack of direct observation makes any idea speculative. The primary factor in the construction of making colonoware by enslaved Africans—from searching out usable clay deposits to firing whole vessels—undoubtedly rested with the creativity and secretiveness of African American potters.

Just when archaeologists thought they had finally begun to understand colonoware as the example par excellence of cultural mixing, excavations at two eighteenth-century English estates in South Carolina have again turned the spotlight on enslaved Africans.

Two properties in the South Carolina Lowcountry were owned by members of the English elite, families who had amassed considerable wealth from the forced labor of rice-producing enslaved Africans. Excavated sherds from these sites exhibit a surface decoration called "folded strip rouletting." The pattern is composed of almond-shaped elements linked together in parallel rows. After a series of experiments, archaeologists discovered they could replicate the pattern by twisting together two palm leaves. To give the experiment greater reliability, they used leaves growing at one of the properties where the sherds had been found. The pattern produced by pressing the twisted leaves onto the outer surface of an unfired pot resembles a design found on pottery in western Africa, particularly the "maize cob rouletting" used by the Yoruba (Soper 1985: 32). There the pottery dates to the era of the transatlantic slave trade, just when thousands of captive Africans were uprooted and forcibly taken to coastal South Carolina (Sattes et al. 2020).

No one is certain why potters stopped making colonoware in the United States. Similar potting traditions continue today in parts of the Caribbean and Latin America, but not in the United States. Numerous possibilities may explain the pottery's disappearance. Perhaps potters died out before passing on the tradition to others, or maybe British and, later, American mass-produced ceramics swamped the consumer market making colonoware unnecessary. Ferguson thought that the decline in colonoware might be related either to the cessation of the legal importation of captive Africans into the United States in 1808 or to the increasing availability of mass-produced iron kettles, cooking pots, and glazed dishes as the nineteenth century progressed. Plantation owners, facing pressure from abolitionists, may have also felt compelled to provide glazed dishes to their captives (Ferguson 1992: 107). Each of these possibilities, alone or in combination, or even none of them, may account for colonoware's enigmatic vanishing act in the early nineteenth century.

Without doubt, colonoware had significance within the many cultural contexts of the colonial and immediate postcolonial worlds. But it would be a mistake to assume that the impact of the pottery ends there, in the past, safely buried in history—meaningful, yes, but only in the remote past. The significance of colonoware is considerably more profound.

In 1924 Du Bois published *The Gift of Black Folk*, spelling out his goal in its subtitle: *The Negroes in the Making of America*. But 1924 was not a year to inspire nostalgia in the United States. In May the US Congress had passed, and President Calvin Coolidge had signed, the Immigration Act of 1924. The law established immigration quotas unfairly slanted toward light-skinned northern Europeans and against darker southern Europeans and mandated that Asians were ineligible for citizenship. The law also defined and codified biased concepts of race and nationality that would have implications for decades (Ngai 1999). Lynchings by frenzied mobs continued throughout the year, although their number had declined since the dark days of the 1890s (Seguin and Rigby 2019). In 1924 Coolidge also signed a bill giving Native Americans citizenship, even though huge numbers continued to be disenfranchised, and after the national election in November, the Ku Klux Klan, which had infiltrated both major political parties, claimed to hold 11 governorships, 75 House seats, and one-third of the Senate (Kleinfeld and Dickas 2020). In 1924 eugenics was still enjoying a heyday among scientists and the public at large. That year eugenicist and Harvard zoologist William E. Castle published the second edition of his popular textbook. Ostensibly about the successful breeding of plants and animals, Castle dedicated an inordinately large amount of space to the breeding of human beings. As a committed eugenicist and Social Darwinist, Castle expressed (1924: 343) his anxiety about intermarriages between individuals with different skin colors, especially between "a negro and a white person." Jim Crow was also in full swing.

Faced with all this, Du Bois sought to document what African Americans had contributed to America's national project. He began by erroneously identifying pre-Columbian Africans as the mound builders. In his view, the earthen mounds scattered across the American Midwest were "replicas" of the forts they knew from Africa. Du Bois was on much firmer ground when he turned to consider the roles of individuals of African descent in the expeditions of American exploration and discovery. He further demonstrated that for generations African American women and men had been laborers, soldiers, artists, and writers and had been outspoken proponents of freedom and willing donors to the spiritual quality of the country's ethos (Du Bois 1924: 343). Du Bois observed that the dominant society has been blind to the achievements of its men and women of African heritage, that "the glory of the world is the possibilities of the commonplace," and that much that has been possible has been due to "the common, ordinary, unlovely man" (Du Bois 1924: 33). Du Bois's crucial point was that Black women and men often toiled in the shadows like the unheralded Black archaeologists engaged in excavations before the Second World War.

The story of colonoware intersects with Du Bois because of his views on the relationship between African Americans and material things (Paynter 1992). Concentrating on inventions, he observed that during the existence of slavery, African American inventors were allowed neither to take credit for their inventions nor to apply for patents. Citing information from the antebellum era, Du Bois highlighted the large number of Black mechanics, coopers, carpenters, and others who were responsible for improving the physical machinery that made cotton king and solidified the prominent place of American-grown sugar and rice on the international stage. Even before the Revolutionary War, Black miners, ironworkers, millwrights, sawmill operators, marine carpenters, wheelwrights, and others lived and labored within Britain's American colonies (Du Bois 1924: 70–71; Johnson and Watson 2005: 86).

Colonoware constitutes one of the gifts African America has helped to bestow upon the American people even though the Black contributors to America's colonoware production remain unnamed. Nonetheless, their gift was finally recognized for what it is, not as an Africanism in its purist sense but as a tangible reminder of the African presence in American history.

Colonoware may have been revealed as a multicultural artifact, one with varying degrees of African involvement, but it was not finished revealing its secrets. A feature Ferguson spotted on some of the pots from the South Carolina Lowcountry, something that at first seemed insignificant, turned out to have immense importance.

5

Cross-in-Circle

BaKongo in America

In his letter to Stanley South, Richard Polhemus mentioned that in Ghana some of the handmade clay pots had an X incised on their bases. He remembered seeing this sign before. Far away from the stifling, equatorial heat of Ghana, other sherds with Xs were lying quietly in the air-conditioned archaeology lab at the University of South Carolina (Ferguson 1992: 10) (Figure 5). The presence of sherds with Xs on them in Africa and South Carolina raised a tantalizing question: Was this sign some kind of transatlantic message or was it merely a coincidence?

Intrigued by Polhemus's eye for detail, Leland Ferguson decided to dig deeper to see whether he could determine a possible meaning for the simple mark (Ferguson 1999). Combing through the archaeological collections at the university, he soon had 28 potsherds or nearly whole vessels having similar marks lying on the table before him. A full 18 specimens had been found underwater. Ferguson's sample, although extremely small by archaeological standards, deepened the colonoware mystery. What did the X mean, and why had so many clay objects bearing that symbol been found in water?

To discover what the specimens might be trying to reveal, Ferguson fell back on standard archaeological practice. Separating the objects into categories based on the marks themselves, he discerned three groups. In the first were three pieces with recognizable letters scratched onto their surfaces. One each had an MHD, a J, and an X. The second category included bowls with a large equilateral cross incised on their inside bottoms. Viewed from above, the effect was of two equal-sized, crossed lines resting inside the circle formed by the bowl's rim. In Ferguson's third category were vessels with the equilateral cross as in the second group, but in these objects

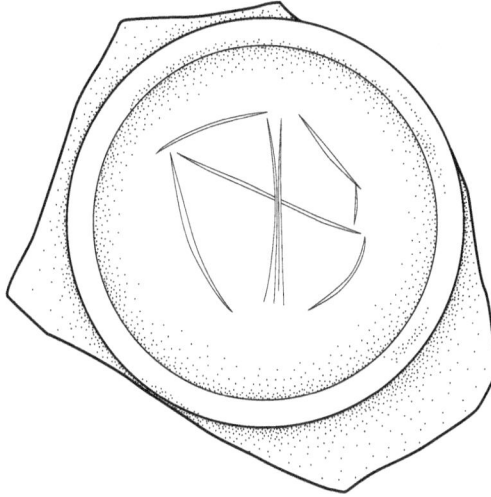

Figure 5. An X on colonoware identified by Ferguson. Drawing by Tina Ross.

a circle had been etched around the cross, effectively making two circles, a large one made by the bowl's rim and a smaller one inscribed inside it.

Ferguson's first thought was that some of the marks might be makers' marks. The bowls with the recognizable letters were the most likely examples. Potters and ceramic manufacturers have scratched and impressed initials and symbols on their wares as marks of identification for centuries. As far back as the Iron Age, potters in the Aegean had identified their pieces with Xs, and archaeologists have found alphabetical makers' marks on pottery pulled from the ashes of Pompeii, destroyed in 79 CE (Papadopoulos 1994: 441–445; Peña and McCallum 2009: 176). In the early fifteenth century, Ming Dynasty Chinese porcelain manufacturers placed Imperial reign marks on the bowls and cups they sent into the homes of the aristocracy (Pavan et al. 2018: 224). Native American potters have also used makers' marks, and the mass production in Europe ushered in by the Industrial Revolution motivated factory owners to put their factories' names on their mass-produced cups, bowls, saucers, and every other dish that rolled out of their massive kilns. In a world quickly falling under the thrall of consumerism and awash with rampant product imitation, makers' marks allowed mindful consumers to distinguish the authentic from the knockoff (provided, of course, that the forger had not also included the makers' mark on the fake). Makers' marks are the reason why, if you invite a historical archaeologist to dinner, he or she is likely to discreetly turn over the dinner plate looking for a maker's mark.

So potters have used marks for centuries to identify their wares, but could there be a much simpler explanation to account for the marks on some of the colonoware vessels? Was it possible that some owners of colonoware bowls may have marked them to distinguish their bowls from those of others? Ferguson considered this idea but discarded it as unlikely. The bowls themselves provided the evidence. Every colonoware bowl wears a distinctive pattern of tans, buffs, grays, reds, and even black. The patches of color indicate that the bowls were fired in a way that made it impossible to regulate the temperature. Firing a pot in a campfire rather than in a kiln would leave the telltale splashes of color, making each pot wholly distinctive and easily distinguishable from every other one.

The bowl marked MHD especially intrigued Ferguson. Archaeologists had unearthed the sherd at a grand, eighteenth-century captive-labor plantation in the South Carolina Lowcountry called Drayton Hall. Perched above the Ashley River just west of Charleston's International Airport, the plantation's exquisite Palladian mansion still proclaims the wealth the enslaved were able to wrest from its soil. What is so remarkable about the marked sherd is that a woman named Mary Henrietta Drayton, or MHD, lived on the estate from the 1780s to the 1840s. Ferguson deemed it entirely possible that one of Mary's Black playmates may have etched the initials into the clay before firing the pot (Ferguson 1992: 87–89). This unique discovery unlocked at least one mystery: African American potters must have made colonoware at the plantation during Mary Drayton's lifetime.

Moving on from the initials, Ferguson turned to the more enigmatic large Xs or crosses placed inside circles. Many of the scratches and marks found on Lowcountry colonoware sherds, including the initials, seemed to be idiosyncratic or incidental. Some may have been simple cut marks made by knives. Taken as a group, they formed no discernible pattern. But the cross-in-circle symbols were of an entirely different character (Ferguson and Goldberg 2019: 178). Ferguson wondered whether they might have had a special meaning. Since they have no practical function, could they have had a more profound significance, perhaps a spiritual one?

The idea of investigating the possible spiritual or religious nature of the marks was well worth pursuing, but Ferguson accepted that it would be difficult. Archaeologists have long acknowledged that religious views and spiritual ideas are the most puzzling elements of culture to decipher using excavation. Many archaeologists long discounted studying beliefs because such ideas exist in the mind alone. An excavator unearthing a religious medal might conclude that someone once living at the property was a believer in the religion associated with the medal, but does it necessarily mean that its former owner accepted the medal's intended meaning or that the person was even a believer? Interpretations are even more difficult to make when an object's meanings are more obscure. In a much-referenced article published in 1954, distinguished British archaeologist Christopher Hawkes (1954: 161–162) expressed the rationale behind the principle that deciphering past beliefs may be beyond the archaeologist's grasp.

Most archaeologists today think of culture as an intricate network, a meshwork of interconnected parts that work together to sustain human life. Some of the components plugged into each culture's web concern economics, some relate to social behavior, and others involve the sacred world. The number of constituent parts depends upon a culture's complexity and population size, but all cultural systems are complicated in their own special ways.

The network concept is easy for us to grasp today because so much of our daily lives revolve around networks and networking. Christopher Hawkes and most of his colleagues then living in a pre–computer age tended to view culture more like a layer cake than an interacting network. On the bottom layer were techniques, the processes and skills humans needed to master life on earth. Research on this layer meant that an archaeologist's main task involved figuring out how chipped-stone axes and clay pots had helped humans survive during different periods of history. Hawkes (1954: 161) viewed this research as "relatively easy" but "often tedious." Research often meant spending long hours of boredom measuring the thicknesses of clay potsherds or calculating the cutting angles of sharpened stone knives. Even today such painstaking analysis lies at the heart of most archaeological research regardless of one's theoretical views. Audrey Noël Hume at London's Guildhall Museum was probably engaged in this kind of activity and lost in thought when Pinky Harrington appeared at the museum's door in search of old English bottles.

Hawkes's next level of research concerned the connection between subsistence and economics. He said that on this level an archaeologist seeks to tie the "tedious" information obtained from the stone tools, pottery, and other objects to "the economic purposes implied by them." This research might include collaborating with geologists and wildlife biologists because of the natural environment's marquee role in most economic activities. Hawkes thought this process of discovery was "straightforward" and "rewarding." Sitting metaphorically above the economic layer were the sociopolitical institutions that allowed societies to preserve equilibrium through time. Hawkes accepted that research on this level was "considerably harder" than the others but saw it as one that archaeologists could work out through careful analysis (Hawkes 1954: 161). His argument was that if an archaeologist excavated an ancient village and discovered that one hut was bigger than all the others, then it might stand to reason that the society had a social ranking system, one that equated house size with social authority, such that the bigger the house, the greater the residents' influence in society.

In the upper layer of cultural life were religious institutions and spiritual life. Hawkes believed that understanding this level might at first seem easy, but the more he thought about it the more he decided that figuring out abstract signs and symbols requires far too much speculation. As he summarized it, "unaided inference from material remains to spiritual life is the hardest inference of all" because the "unaided inferences" pile up the further back one goes in time (Hawkes 1954: 162).

Archaeologists in the Holy Land had been probing religious sites mentioned in the Christian Bible for years (Smith 1926), but American archaeologists usually did not take the study of religion seriously until ideas like those asserted by Hawkes had begun to fade from popularity in the late 1960s.

Walter Taylor's (1948) heated attack on the creation of culture histories as an end point of research had made a strong case for archaeologists to adopt a more holistic approach to the past, one that was open to seeing life as composed of a series of networks. By the late 1960s, when much of the Western world was in turmoil because of protests over the brutal war in Vietnam, racial inequality, and social injustice, a new generation of archaeologists were committed to transforming their discipline. The idea of thinking differently, of being skeptical of the older generation, meant writing a new archaeological playbook, one that included strategies and innovative ideas for plumbing difficult subjects such as the mysteries surrounding spiritual life and religious beliefs.

Accepting a more sweeping perspective on history allowed archaeologists to think broadly, to move beyond the mechanical aspects of human survival. The new thinking unlocked the freedom for archaeologists to ponder past peoples' spiritual lives. The subject of religious and spiritual belief transported archaeologists to the existential side of humanity. Ferguson was to enter this realm when he began to ponder the meaning of the marks on the colonoware bowls.

But where to begin?

The first problem Ferguson faced was that cultures around the globe have drawn circles for millennia. Artisans in Neolithic China had made them, and ancient Europe abounds in stone circles and earthworks, Stonehenge being a notable example. The global usage of circles throughout human history raises a significant question: why do circles go hand in hand with humanity?

We may easily imagine that the sun, the greatest of circles, must have inspired awe in the preindustrial world when people's lives depended upon lush plants and healthy animals. And once the sun had retreated for the day and the world was awash in primordial darkness, the full moon must have inspired a similar but still different kind of wonder. As celestial spheres, the sun and the moon, in the sky for all the world's peoples to behold, shared, as author Toni Morrison (2015: 78) observed, "a distant friendship, each unfazed by the other." Of the two, the sun's power to create and nurture life gave it prominence. It was a genuine gift to humanity.

Among the peoples using circles symbolically in what became the United States were many Native American cultures. The circular earthen mounds Squier and Davis mapped in America's midcontinental valleys testify to the circle's deep antiquity in the region. Far from the Ohio Valley is Wyoming's ancient Medicine Wheel. Measuring about 80 feet in diameter and made up of hundreds of purposefully placed white limestone rocks, the circle rests on the earth and resembles a many-spoked wagon wheel. Native Americans still regard this National Historic Landmark as a sacred space. In the American Southwest, Puebloan peoples constructed subterranean, circular kivas for sacred purposes, and on the Plains, Native Americans lived in circular tipis and earth lodges (Brown 1997; Grinnell 1922; Hall 1985). In the eighteenth century the Chickasaws, who called the Upland South their ancestral home, used circles to represent the sun, which they venerated as "the great holy fire above" and "the sole author of warmth, light, and of all animal and vegetable life" (St. Jean 2003: 767). Even the original flag of the United States, the so-called Betsy Ross flag, had its 13 stars arranged in a circle.

One of the most remarkable examples of ancient circles was expressed in the pre-Columbian American Southeast, parts of which would later see the creation of colonoware. Archaeologists have termed this unique cultural expression "the Southeastern Ceremonial Complex."

First identified in 1945 at ancient villages once housing large, socially layered societies, the complex was deemed to have gained expression across a huge region stretching from Oklahoma and Arkansas and to Georgia and Florida. Additional excavations have revealed that southeastern complex-type artifacts also appear in central Illinois, southwestern Wisconsin, and eastern Missouri. When the complex was first identified, archaeologists were still deeply involved with identifying precolonial Native cultures by listing their distinctive traits. Some of the traits of the complex were stone and copper celts, delicate clay figurines, and intricately engraved shell ornaments and pottery. One of its most extraordinary features was its unique artistic motifs, including an array of circles, stars, human faces, and human hands, palms up, with a single staring eye on the palm (Waring and Holder 1945). One prominent design was the "Sun Circle," a figure depicted as an equilateral cross inside a circle. This symbol bears an astonishing similarity to the design present on some of Ferguson's colonoware.

The existence of a sprawling, complicated network of ancient villages sharing a special set of symbols stunned archaeologists. Because the complex had flourished for generations before the first Europeans arrived on the scene, no contemporary written records exist to explain it. All that is left to signal the one-time presence of this network are objects buried at ancient villages. After decades of pouring over the perplexing symbols of the complex, archaeologists followed the same path trod by scholars of colonoware: they abandoned their initial, simplistic perspective and accepted that all human cultures are infinitely complex by nature. Whereas archaeologists first imagined the complex as an organized, homogeneous subculture, they now saw it as multifaceted and varied. Some archaeologists had originally labeled the complex a "cult," and the use of this loaded term may have blinded some of them to a more nuanced, skeptical view, one that rejected uniformity throughout the eastern United States. This is the same thing that had occurred when archaeologists added "Indian" to "Colono-Indian ware"; the term temporarily blinded them to other interpretations. With time, it became clear that the Southeastern Ceremonial Complex "(1) is not [just] Southeastern, (2) is not ceremonial, and (3) is not a complex" (Knight 2006: 1–5; see also Brown 1976; Emerson and Pauketat 2008). Today's view is that various places in the south and central United States had interacting networks sharing artistic motifs and probably also certain rituals. The bond that tied the webs together, like the stitches in a crazy quilt, was not a static cultural sameness but a unique artistic style, one that included the equilateral cross-in-circle.

Archaeologists have found artifacts with the network's symbolic motifs at sites along the coast of Florida and Georgia. One such place was the now-destroyed Irene Mounds, near Savannah, Georgia. This once-vibrant community, occupied for about five hundred years beginning around 1100 CE, once included scores of square mud houses, a flat-topped ceremonial mound, and a mound for the dead. Excavations conducted by a crew composed of African American women unearthed several circular etched shells, some with designs that looked suspiciously like Sun Circles (Caldwell and McCann 1941: 47). The existence of the interacting network in ancient American history, including the presence of the symbolic motif in the same region as colonoware, raised an intriguing question. Could the cross-in-circle Ferguson saw on colonoware be a Native American design?

The idea that the symbol found on some Lowcountry colonoware bowls is an ancient North American Indian design is tantalizing but difficult to sustain. Archaeologists on the southeastern coast of the United States have learned that shell ornaments etched with network-style artistic symbols belong to pre-European history, an era ending in this region around 1565 when Spanish intruders first arrived (Larson 1958: 426). For the ancient Native American design to be present on colonoware would have required several generations of Indigenous potters to have remembered it but not used it until colonial times. Another possibility is that a creative colonial-era Native American reinvented the symbol and scratched it onto her pots with no knowledge of its ancient use. In this case, the similarity between the ancient design and its more modern cousin would be mere coincidence, a remarkable case of independent invention. Alternatively, perhaps a Native American potter found an ancient potsherd, saw its cross-in-circle design, and decided to mimic it on her colonoware. Or maybe a Christianized Native American marked the colonoware pieces as a sign of devotion (Steen 2011). From about 1500, the idea of taking Christianity to the Indigenous peoples of the Americas was a primary justification for Europe's grand vision of conquest and colonization (Stanwood 2006: 438). The religious conversion of Native Americans occurred in the same places that archaeologists find colonoware.

The main problem with the interpretation involving Christianity is that the designs etched onto the colonoware vessels do not resemble Latin crosses. The circle around the cross is an added problem. Celtic crosses have a circle around the spot where the arms of the cross meet, but the arms of the cross always extend beyond the circle.

Each of these interpretations is intriguing, but each requires a leap of faith. We must accept that the cross-in-circle hopped from precolonial times to the late seventeenth century, or we must be willing to acknowledge that the individuals who scratched the symbols onto their pots were incapable of properly forming a Christian cross. No one can know whether a colonial-era potter found an old potsherd inscribed with an age-old Sun Circle and decided to mimic it on her pottery. This interpretation seems unlikely but not impossible.

Given the alternative explanations to the presence of the cross-in-circle on the Lowcountry bowls, it seems more plausible that the cross-in-circle design on some colonoware bowls found in the South Carolina Lowcountry came from a non–Native American source. The most obvious alternative source in colonial America are individuals of African heritage (Ferguson 2011: 163). So if the cross-in-circles had something to do with Africa, where should Ferguson start to look for answers?

Du Bois often wrote about the importance of religion and belief to African Americans, beginning with the enslaved. He wondered about the average enslaved African's "attitude toward the World and Life. . . . What seemed to him good and evil—God and Devil?" Du Bois puzzled over the captives' "longings and strivings, and wherefore were his heart-burnings and disappointments." Du Bois maintained that appreciating the religious and spiritual nature of African American life is central to comprehending the entire history of African America, including during the dark days of enslavement. As he concluded, "The importance of spirituality to African slaves . . . should not be undervalued" (Du Bois 1903: 192).

Africa is so gargantuan that its size can be difficult to grasp. At almost 12 million square miles, it dwarfs the United States. Africa is even 2 million square miles larger than the United States and Canada combined. During colonoware's eighteenth-century heyday, over 3,000 separate cultures inhabited the continent, divided into a surfeit of traditional religions that had been practiced for generations. Filling out the portrait of African religious life were converted Muslims.

The huge number of religious expressions in Africa during the age of the transatlantic slave trade means that archaeologists must approach African American religion like cold-case detectives. They must steel themselves for innumerable hours spent shifting through yellowed reports and contradictory or vague eyewitness accounts and running down and rechecking what may seem to be trifling clues in pursuit of that one explosive tip that will provide the solution to the puzzle or at least illuminate other paths with more clues.

Christopher Hawkes (1954: 157–158) had suggested the way forward in 1954 when he drew a contrast between what he called the two "modes of archaeology." He termed one mode "text-free" archaeology, and the other he labeled "text-aided." By "text-free" archaeology Hawkes meant the study of that vast segment of history that was played out before the invention of writing. This was the archaeology that Jimmy Griffin and Al Spaulding taught Fairbanks, Coe, and classrooms of other students. In North America, this was the archaeology of pre-Columbian American Indian life, the cultural life of the continent before the arrival of land-hungry Europeans. By "text-aided" archaeology Hawkes meant classical and biblical archaeologies, which at the time was archaeology in the Holy Land and among the ruins of the ancient Greek and Roman civilizations. These text-aided archaeologists were as conversant with the contemporary accounts as they were with the eras' potsherds. When Hawkes enumerated the text-aided archaeologies, American historical archaeology was a mere blip on the archaeological radar, so he may not have been aware of the excavations at Jamestown and other colonial sites.

Since Ferguson was researching African American life, a subject that eyewitnesses and historians had written about for decades, he practiced Hawkes's text-aided archaeology. Having the advantage of being able to tap into a rich storehouse of information, he turned to the huge mass of historical and ethnographic information available for Africa to see whether he could find someone responsible for the cross-in-circle design.

After having reviewed the sources, Ferguson found a symbol that appeared remarkably similar to what he saw on some of the colonoware bowls from the South Carolina Lowcountry. This symbol has several elements: a simple equilateral cross like a plus sign with small circles on the end of each of the four, outstretched arms of the cross; a small oval or circle surrounding the spot where the arms of the cross meet; and four counterclockwise arrows positioned between each of the small circles on the ends of the cross pieces. The arrows give the impression of a cycle endlessly rotating counterclockwise (Thompson 1983: 108–109). The symbol, although not a perfect fit with what appears on the colonoware bowls, is similar enough to be suggestive (Figure 6).

The symbol Ferguson identified was used by the BaKongo, a culture who lived in the Kingdom of Kongo, in what is today parts of Angola, the Republic of Congo, and the Democratic Republic of Congo. During the time of European colonialism beginning in the early 1500s, the Kingdom of Kongo controlled a huge swath of west-central Africa, including the coast, where they first encountered European buyers and sellers of humanity.

The people of Angola first came into direct, long-term contact with the

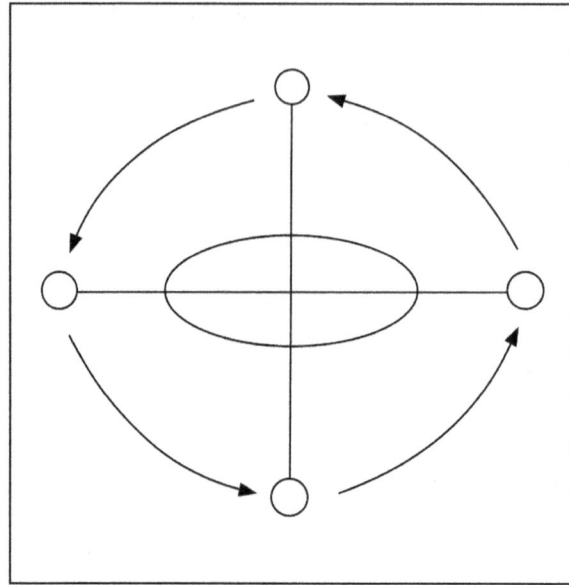

Figure 6. Dikenga symbol. Drawing by author.

European world through the presence of the Portuguese in the fifteenth century. Portuguese sailors were the first Europeans to create the transatlantic slave trade, a cruel market in humanity that would take root and flourish over the next three centuries. When they arrived along the African coast, the region surrounding the mouth of the Congo River and extending into the interior was home to the kingdoms of Ndongo to the north and Kongo to the south. The people of Ndongo bestowed on its kings the title of Ngola, which is where the Portuguese got the name Angola. With the arrival of the Portuguese, Ndongo and Kongo, each seeking its own political ascendency in the region, became entangled with the trade in human beings. Embroiled in a tragic competition, the kingdoms' rulers struck deals and forged alliances with enthusiastic European enslavers. In 1600 John Leo, or "Leo Africanus," reported that "every yeere" the "Portugals" take "about five thousand slaves" and other commodities from "Congo and Angola" (Leo 1600: 40).

The Portuguese formally established an Angolan colony in 1575, almost 100 years after their first caravels had raised their sails and slipped back home. The region spreading outward from the colonial capital of Luanda was composed of several provinces stretching inland from the coast to the dry backcountry. The estimated Indigenous population in 1650 was around half a million people (Thornton 1977: 519, 522).

West-central Africa was a land of mystery to Europeans. To wedge Catholicism into the region and thus to further their control, in 1591 Pope Innocent IX commissioned the Italian mathematician Filippo Pigafetta to transcribe an account of a Portuguese trader named Duarte Lopez who had spent 12 years among the Angolans. Eyewitness information, no matter how skewed, would help missionaries decide how best to convert African individuals to Christianity. Lopez described the people of Angola not as bloodthirsty savages but as people living in a complex, stratified social system. He was astute enough to notice that the people's social order was reflected in their dress. He saw that "men of the lower class" were "naked above the waist" and wore their hair "long and wavy." The women of the same class were "covered from head to foot," and the poorest among them wore "garments from the waist downwards." None of the poor owned footwear. Noblemen distinguished themselves by their "silk and other garments," and by their "small red and black caps" and their "velvet caps from Portugal." The noblewomen wore "certain mantles" that were "wrapped round the head, leaving the face free." Unlike the poorest among them, better-off women wore shoes (Hutchinson 1881: 29).

The social and political leaders and influencers were accompanied by skilled magicians whose realm was the supernatural world (MacGaffey 1970: 28). Individuals with special knowledge or unique spiritual gifts were valued among the BaKongo because ghosts were known to travel the earth. These beings were witches who had been turned away from the village of the ancestors because of the bad acts they had committed while alive (MacGaffey 1986: 73–74). As bad actors, they were dangerous because some of them might be able to cause disease. Humanity has been plagued by the threat of disease since time immemorial, and the BaKongo felt the terror no less than anyone.

As each African kingdom struggled for supremacy, the region became the stage for a prolonged drama with shifting alliances, large-scale migrations, and armed uprisings. The situation was made more challenging by the presence of the Portuguese intruders. The sociopolitics were so tense and confused that when the Kingdom of Kongo attacked the Kingdom of Ndongo in the middle of the sixteenth century, Portuguese soldiers fought on both sides (Henderson 1979: 82; Heywood and Thornton 2019: 207–208).

One reason for the ever-shifting political picture of the region was partly internal because kings were not chosen by heredity. Underneath the king in the social hierarchy was a cadre of powerful nobles. Upon the death of a sitting king, the nobles selected his successor. Their power was rooted in the revenue they extracted from their province, and as ambitious noblemen sought to climb onto the throne, they were not above engaging in the age-old intrigues and deceptions that have characterized kingly succession the world over. In the most extreme cases, scuffles among the nobles' factions could lead to disruptive civil wars (Thornton 2006, 2016). The king's overwhelming power and authority coursed through his network of connections like an electrical current. It ran through his extended kin and clients but also included his wives and elder female relatives, who could exert pressure via the king's lineage members.

The political structure of the kingdoms was mirrored by their settlement pattern. Long before the Portuguese first set foot on the Angolan shore, the kingdoms had begun a process of centralizing their authority into large villages. Gathering the elements of social and political life in one central place strengthened the king's influence. The capital cities of the various provinces were both ceremonial and symbolic centers surrounded by smaller agricultural settlements (Clist et al. 2015: 467).

Religion was an important facet within colonial-era intercultural relations. Many African cultures had experienced religious conversion long before the first Portuguese Christians had hauled their boats up on the Angolan shore. Muslims had migrated into Africa as early as the seventh century CE, first encountering the sedentary peoples living along the southern shore of the Mediterranean. Many cultures living in this region had already been Christianized by colonizing Romans, but neither Romans nor Muslims had penetrated into the sub-Saharan region to any great extent. Muslims referred to the region south of the Sahara as the "Bilad es Sudan," or the Land of the Blacks. That they had not settled south of the Sahara did not mean that Muslims had no influence in the region. Muslim merchants managed a vibrant trade in enslaved captives from the south. Once rounded up, the unfortunates journeyed northward along the well-trod caravan routes that snaked into the sub-Sahara (Alexander 2001).

The Portuguese were confident in their ability to promote the Christian faith in Angola, and their first goal was to convert the Angolan royalty. Accordingly, in 1491 King Nzinga, a Nkuwa of Ndongo, was baptized King João I of Kongo. His adoption of Christianity was a way for him to acquire more power, believing that the Portuguese would assist him in the region's complex political situation (Balandier 1968: 47). By the early 1500s many others had followed his lead. The first full-time Christian missionaries, Jesuits from Portugal, arrived in 1560. As they stayed and established missions, baptisms increased accordingly. To accomplish their goals, however, Christian missionaries had to adapt to the peoples' practices, in effect fulfilling the traditional role of healers, witch-finders, and magicians, who Africans in the region called *nganga* (Thornton 1977: 512–513). The Christian priests thought they were converting the people to Christianity, but the truth was that the people were forcing the European priests to conform to traditional African social positions.

Once it appeared to outsiders that Angolans had openly accepted Christianity, Europeans of all stripes—traders, settlers, missionaries, and diplomats—flooded into the region seeking alliances, converts, economic advantages, and land. Despite the influx of foreigners, the daily lives of most African people did not greatly change. Most Angolan cultures did not completely abandon their long-standing beliefs, and the outcome of the admixture was Kongo Christianity. It was entirely possible for an individual man or woman to be baptized as a Christian but still believe in certain aspects of long-established religious worldviews (Brinkman 2016: 258; Fennell 2007: 53–54; Thornton 2013).

The creation of Kongo Christianity affected the design of some villages in Angola, especially those with European missions. A drawing of a Capuchin mission village in the mid-eighteenth century shows it surrounded by a palisade. In the spacious, open plaza is a tall wooden cross set upon a pedestal of stones. A white-washed church, shining against the verdant foliage like the promise of salvation, stands directly behind the cross, while the church's brass bell, whose dull clang was used to summon the faithful, is fixed to a wooden frame beside the church. Five attached white-washed houses, each having only one small room, stand like sentinels along the edge of the plaza. These undoubtedly are the homes of the optimistic missionaries. Some distance from the brightly washed houses is a cluster of thatched-roofed, conical houses, the dwellings probably belonging to the Kongo converts living at the mission (Clist et al. 2015: 493).

Even the modification of the traditional village did not imply what most Europeans assumed. As was true of Christian beliefs in general, the presence of the Christian cross did not mean that Angolans had surrendered all their traditional beliefs. Rather, something much more profound was under way.

One feature of BaKongo life involved the creation of *minkisi* (*nkisi*, singular), or charms. The ritual specialists who interacted with the supernatural world, called *banganga* (*nganga*, singular) typically created these charms and used them for various reasons, including prediction, healing, protection, and retribution. Most *minkisi* were associated with crossed lines, either drawn on the ground or incorporated into the charm itself. The charms were enclosed in a container, ranging in form from a cloth bag to a ceramic bowl, all of which contained the powerful substance imbued by the *nganga*. Some *nkisi*, being wooden statues, were considered particularly powerful (Fennell 2007: 56–57; Jordán 1998: 30–31; MacGaffey and Janzen 1974: 87–89; Thompson 1978).

When Christian priests appeared in BaKongo villages and erected wooden crosses, the Angolans simply adopted the crosses as a *minkisi* and viewed the priests as *nganga* (Fennell 2007: 63). The missionaries mistook a new form of traditional Angolan belief as Christian conversion.

In the earliest years of the slave trade, English traffickers, like those sailing into Charleston Harbor, were content to steal human cargo from passing Spanish or Portuguese ships. When these acts of piracy failed, they had no hesitation about sailing straight into Iberian ports and doing face-to-face business. Profit-conscious English shippers and merchants adopted this business plan when it became increasingly clear that enslaving and selling captive Africans would yield undreamed of riches. By 1631 the English monarchy had granted exclusive rights to African trading companies three times, but each time they failed. With the reappearance of the English monarchy with the Restoration in 1660, the recently enthroned Charles II granted a charter that forever altered the faces of the African Diaspora and colonial America. His royal decree was originally bestowed upon the "Governor and Company of the Royal Adventurers of England trading into Africa" in 1662. This joint-stock company, later known as the Royal African Company, was given the king's expressed permission to extract African captives, like golden nuggets from a stream, from villages all along the unimaginably long strip of the west coast of Africa, the thousands of miles stretching from Salé in Morocco to the Cape of Good Hope. Charles II proclaimed that it was necessary to provide "a constant supply of Negro-servants" to "the English Plantations in America" (Hatfield 2011: 407; Pettigrew 2016; Royal Adventurers 1667).

By the eighteenth century the English were heavily committed to commerce in human cargo. British-owned ships accounted for 78 percent of the ships sailing into South Carolina's primary port of Charleston. Several of the colony's enslaved men and women had been ripped from villages in and around Angola (Domingues da Silva 2013; Littlefield 2000).

Despite the riches being amassed in London through the traffic in humanity, most English men and women were remarkably ignorant about Africa and Africans. In 1759, after about 200 of involvement with the theft and sale of African women, children, and men, English mathematician John Barrow was still able to confess that "the greater part of Africa continues unknown to us . . . our knowledge extends little farther than the regions lying along the coasts, especially those of the Mediterranean." Exasperated, he admitted that "with regard to the inland parts, as they were long believed to be inaccessible and uninhabited by reason of their intolerable heat, lying mostly under the Torrid zone; so they have . . . been little visited by any strangers" (Barrow 1759: 37).

England's unfamiliarity with Africa and Africans during the era of colonoware contributed to the development of racist views and the perpetuation of devastating cruelty. Many of the South's educated merchants and plantation owners, families like the Draytons living outside Charleston, were undoubtedly familiar with the works of David Hume, a preeminent member of the Scottish Enlightenment. In his essay "On National Characters," Hume expressed his view that "I am apt to suspect the negroes to be naturally inferior to the whites." Knowing nothing about the ancient iron-smelting accomplishments of some African cultures, or perhaps simply refusing to acknowledge them, Hume proposed that Africans had "no ingenious manufacturers amongst them, no arts, no sciences." He believed that even "the most rude and barbarous of the whites" were superior to every native African. He conceded that in Jamaica "they talk of one negroe as a man of parts [meaning well-traveled] and learning," but he disputed that such a Black person was possible, contending that the man must have made "slender accomplishments, like a parrot who speaks a few words plainly" (Hume 1799: 550–551).

The full-blown commitment of English slavers to removing Africans from their homeland against their will had a domino effect. As the profits of those complicit in the theft skyrocketed, the families of the largest slave-labor plantations ate fine meals and hosted lavish balls. Elsewhere on the same estates, men and women held in perpetual bondage, consigned to cramped homes, marked their clay creations with images that variously struck outsiders as mysterious, infantile, or meaningless gibberish.

The BaKongo, although only one culture, hold a central place in the cultural history of African America. Their influence derives from their early presence in the English Tidewater, where, constituting a large portion of the America's Black Charter Generation, they were the first to come to grips with their situation (Joseph 2011).

The Charter Generation concept was originally invented to help explain the Canadian social system (Porter 1965: xiii, 57–58). Studies showed that there individuals of British and sometimes French heritage occupied special social positions because they were the first European settlers in the country. The idea was adopted 20 years later to help account for the various cultural adaptations in colonial British America. Today the idea provides a useful way to think about African captives in the Americas and to account for their cultural influences (Berlin 1996, 1998).

One of the most important characteristics of the Charter Generation stems from their spatial proximity within Africa. Most members of the Charter Generation originated in a relatively small region of west-central Africa, what is today largely Angola. Members of the Charter Generation thus not only shared similar religious and cultural worldviews but they also spoke two related Bantu languages, Kikongo and Kimbundu. The general homogeneity among the region's cultures means that the Charter Generation practiced cultural patterns that distinguish them from the more heterogeneous Plantation Generations, those individuals who were transported to the United States after them. Despite, or perhaps because of, their relatively small numbers, the Charter Generation was likely to have retained many of their common cultural traditions (Breen 1984: 204–205; Kelley and Lovejoy 2016).

Members of the Charter Generation were unique in several ways. For one thing, they shared with their European captors the curious situation of being foreigners in an unfamiliar land. This meant that both Africans and Europeans had to work out how to live in the Americas, albeit on wholly unequal terms and with two entirely different mindsets. The social relations between them were asymmetrically unfair, but both Africans and Europeans had entered an environment previously unknown to them. The members of the Planation Generation did not have to learn the environment in the same way. Their lives were every bit as mentally stressful and physically painful as those of the Charter Generation, but by the time they had arrived, slave-plantation owners, their politically powerful allies, and the pliable White public had already enacted and accepted the racist, proscriptive rules and regulations governing Black behavior (Heywood and Thornton 2007: 236–267).

The BaKongo, as members of the Charter Generation, contributed their fair share to the cultural mix being assembled in colonial America. Religion was an essential aspect of their culture, as it had been in Africa.

The BaKongo believed in a supreme being called Nzambi Mpungu who created two worlds: the land of the living and the land of the dead. Nzambi also created the natural world and gave it its cyclical nature. The BaKongo world was filled with spirits, some that Nzambi had created but others that existed throughout an individual's cycle of life, death, and rebirth. The cross-in-circle, called *yowa* (or *dikenga dia Kongo, tendwa nzá Kongo,* or simply *dikenga*), is meant to represent the recurrent nature of life and death such that a person's life does not end with death but is merely transformed. The sun signifies the never-ending cycle of existence by eternally rising and setting. Like the human soul, it travels along the boundary of the divided universe between the living and the dead (Berlin 1998: 12–13). The cross-in-circle, the *dikenga*, is considered to be the core symbol of the BaKongo culture (MacGaffey 1986: 44–45; Thompson 2005: 288–294).

Each element of the *dikenga* symbol has metaphorical significance. The horizontal arm of the cross divides the living world from the kingdom of the dead. The deity is imagined at the top of the cross and the dead at the bottom. Water separates them. The top of the cross can also symbolize noon, maleness, north, or the peak of an individual's strength on earth. The bottom of the cross can represent the converse: midnight, femaleness, south, and the topmost point of a person's otherworldly strength. The four small circles at the ends of the cross's arms represent the sun's passage, and the circumference of the cross with the arrows represents reincarnation (Fennell 2007: 31–33). A key feature of the *dikenga* is that it refers to the constancy of change, blending, and innovation, "that nothing ever survives 'intact' because nothing ever survives in a fixed form. Period. Ever. Anywhere" (Thompson 1983: 108–109). As a point of personal reference, the *dikenga* acts as a moral compass, providing guidance through life's ups and downs.

Water played an important role in BaKongo spiritualism beyond serving as a barrier between the realms of the living and the dead. Upon death, the deceased was still within reach as it first entered the spiral universe represented by the arrows in the *dikenga*. Being close to the point of transition, it could be summoned back for good or bad purposes. With time, the deceased, now fully considered an ancestor, spins further away from the land of the living, and is thus less influenced by them. Eventually, all dead ancestors transform into spirits and are forever associated with rivers, springs, the ocean, and even white, waterworn stones (Gundaker 2011: 176).

Water's role in the BaKongo's traditional belief system was significant because it provided a level of plausibility to Ferguson's having linked the *dikenga* to the marks scratched onto the colonoware bowls. Ferguson now had a plausible reason why so many etched bowls had been found in water and retrieved by sport divers. Equally profound is that the South Carolina Lowcountry is, as Ferguson noted, a "watery world" (Ferguson and Goldberg 2019: 183). One seventeenth-century visitor to the region described it as "so plaine & Levyll that it may be compared to a Bowling ally full of dainty brooks & Rivers of running Water" (Denbow 1999: 410; MacGaffey 1986: 75). By the eighteenth century, after grand plantation estates had been rooted into the Lowcountry soil, enslaved men and women spent their days calf deep in flooded rice fields. Water, being a constituent element of daily life in the Lowcountry, perfectly conformed to the traditional BaKongo worldview. As a conduit to the spirit world, relief from back-breaking toil and endless mental stress might await the enslaved man or woman once they had passed through the water barrier and entered the land of the ancestors (Cheves 1897: 308).

The interpretation that the cross-in-circle was intended to represent the BaKongo *dikenga* made sense because several captive Africans taken to South Carolina had originated in west-central Africa, including the region in and around what is today Angola. South Carolina functioned as a slave society rather than a society with slaves, meaning that White plantation owners, merchants, shippers, and citizens depended upon the labor of enslaved men and women to create and perpetuate the economy. Without Black labor, South Carolina and certainly Charleston would never have become economic powerhouses during the days of the transatlantic slave trade. A collector of statistics recorded in 1708 that South Carolina had a population of 4,080 free Whites, 4,100 enslaved Blacks, and 1,400 enslaved Native Americans. Never again would the ratio between Whites and Blacks be so equitable. Callous, profit-seeking traffickers in human flesh transported captive Africans to the Charleston docks as fast as the wind and the ocean currents would allow (Ferguson and Goldberg 2019: 182). A huge number of the Africans transported to Charleston came from the region of the BaKongo (Ferguson 1992: 59; Wood 1974: 144). By the 1730s, South Carolina's Black population had grown so large that it astonished Swiss tourist Samuel Dyssli. Writing home to his mother and brothers from Charleston, what he called "Carlestatt," in December 1737, he commented that "Carolina looks more like a negro country than like a country settled by white people." Dyssli calculated that enslaved Africans outnumbered Whites 20 to 1 because of the "large shiploads of these people from the African negro country" (Kelsey 1922: 90).

Throughout the eighteenth century at least some potters of African descent living in South Carolina continued to use a cross-in-circle to mark their handmade bowls. The presence of this curious design signaled that elements of the BaKongo religion were remarkably resilient. Du Bois had been right about the profound importance of religion and spiritual belief.

The *dikenga* motif remains prominent today as an African retention in the music of the blues, where it is represented as a crossroads. Its most well-known presence is arguably in Robert Johnson's "Cross Road Blues," recorded in 1936. In the song, Johnson sings:

I went to the cross road, fell down on my knees,
I went to the cross road, fell down on my knees,
Asked the Lord above, "Have mercy. Save poor Bob, if you please"
   (Brackett 2012: 113).

Johnson, considered by many to be the quintessential representative of the Delta blues, has retained a central place in the mythology of American music both for his artistic gifts and from the rumor that he sold his soul to the Devil at a crossroads in exchange for musical talent (Ford 1998; Schroeder 2015: 83).

In many West African cultures, the crossroad is a place that presents a dilemma. It offers freedom and movement, but it also requires important decision-making. Thus, it simultaneously offers opportunity and danger. The crossroad has ambiguous power because it is overseen by a trickster. Known by various names, the trickster's qualities include "individuality, satire, parody, irony, magic, indeterminacy, open-endedness, ambiguity, sexuality, chance, uncertainty, disruption and reconciliation, betrayal and loyalty, closure and disclosure, encasement and rupture." With all these qualities and others, the trickster constitutes the "classic figure of mediation and of the unity of opposed forces" (Gates 1988: 4–6). The trickster is also the messenger of the gods, the figure who interprets the will of the gods to humanity. Presiding over the crossroads, the trickster, who may be characterized as the Christian devil as in the Johnson myth, has supernatural power over the humans who enter it (Smith 2005: 184). In the 1960s several White British musical groups, including Cream, Led Zeppelin, and the Rolling Stones, appropriated the Delta blues, including with Eric Clapton and Cream singing Johnson's "Cross Road Blues" (Palmer 1981: 125; Schroeder 2015: 83).

The precise link between the cross-in-circle found on some Lowcountry pots and BaKongo cosmology is perhaps not yet as certain as it might be. The connection with African potters, however, seems most plausible. Part of the difficulty stems from the hidden nature of the symbol in African

American art and culture. In her analysis of the secretive nature of the cosmogram, artist Nettrice R. Gaskins (2020) notes that in the basement of the First African Baptist Church in Savannah, Georgia, constituted in 1777 and still in operation, the builders punched holes in the floor in the shape of the cosmogram. The placement of the symbol in the basement demonstrates that pictorial representation could be as concealed as the meaning of the crossroad in the blues, a genre of music "composed of old identities constantly transforming in motion" (Jackson 2020: 157). As Gaskins (2020: 140) observes, "cosmograms served as an emblematic representation of the Kongo people and summarized a broad array of ideas and metaphoric messages that comprised their sense of identity within the universe."

Ferguson's research into the spiritual world of enslaved Africans in the South Carolina Lowcountry transformed the archaeology of the African Diaspora in three lasting ways. By purposefully centering his research directly on the enslaved, he sought to imagine their world using their pottery as a window into it. Some colonoware reflects the influence of Native Americans and Europeans, but the pieces with the cross-in-circle seem to belong to the African Diaspora. When viewed in its totality, colonoware proclaims its cultural difference from Europe. Whether inspired by African or Native American traditions, or even some blend of them, colonoware's appearance, style, and method of production stands apart from every piece of mass-produced ceramic that made its way west from Europe's industrial workshops. Ferguson's efforts solidified the need for archaeologists to reach into the spiritual world to learn what they could about the nonmaterial universe. Respecting Hawkes's advice that the search would be difficult, archaeologists have learned to read the subtlest of signals. The marks found on some colonoware bowls may be mysterious, but they are not meaningless. All their secrets are yet to be known.

6

Pipes

Tobacco and Meaning

When Ivor Noël Hume made his life-changing decision to study old English ceramics, his mentor in London, Adrian Oswald, was already deeply immersed in his own investigation into old white clay tobacco pipes. At the time Oswald was one of a handful of professional archaeologists with even a passing interest in colonial-era objects, let alone clay pipes. But Oswald (1969) soldiered on, and today's smoking pipe aficionados regale his research notes as a unique and irreplaceable treasure trove. It took over 80 years for another person to display Oswald's level of devotion to English clay tobacco pipes, but since then interest in them has grown to the point that a National Pipe Archive now exists in Liverpool, and numerous websites, books, and journal articles are dedicated to this humble object (Noël Hume 2003–2004).

Beginning in the late sixteenth century and continuing until the late nineteenth century, white clay smoking pipes were as common in the English-speaking world as past participles. A few diehard smokers even remained stubbornly committed to clay pipes in the early years of the twentieth century. Today observant spectators might peer through the black-powder smoke of mock battles to see a clay pipe clenched between the teeth of an appropriately dressed Revolutionary War or Civil War reenactor. In the archaeological world, the immense number of clay pipe pieces unearthed from the remains of forts, house lots, workshops, and industrial yards has meant that the connection between clay pipes and enslaved Africans initially failed to reach the same level of fanfare that colonoware experienced when it was first brought to light. Clay tobacco pipes were so abundant in the past that they seemed too mundane to be important. A link between clay pipes and enslaved Africans in the United States thus appeared equally unremarkable. The realization that clay tobacco pipes were significant objects to enslaved Africans took longer to emerge, but it was no less important than colonoware.

Smoking pipes on archaeological sites would not exist without tobacco. And without Native Americans, there would be no tobacco. Despite how one feels about it, tobacco is a weed that has truly seduced the world (Gately 2003; Norton 2008).

Tobacco belongs to a genus of plants biologists call *Nicotiana*, a name bestowed in honor of Jean Nicot, the French ambassador to the Portuguese court who is believed to have introduced tobacco to royal Parisians in the mid-sixteenth century. In an ironic twist that would only become clear centuries later, Nicot had transported tobacco plants from the West Indies to study their properties as a possible cure for cancer (Koven 1996: 4). Despite the nod to Nicot, an unknown but obviously savvy entrepreneur took tobacco seeds to Spain in 1518, and only 20 years later farmers in the colonial Spanish Philippines were already cultivating the plant. By 1660 tobacco had attained the global reach it jealously guards to this day (Winter 2000: 3).

More than 95 species of *Nicotiana* exist in the world, with the majority being native to South America. A smaller number are indigenous to Mexico and Central America, and 15 species are native to islands of the South Pacific, including Australia. One species is even known to have grown in Africa (Bryant et al. 2012: 208). Ancient gardeners decided to cultivate only a few species, and in the Western Hemisphere, the two that flourished were a pink-flowering species native to the Caribbean, Mexico, and lands further south, and a yellow-flowering species indigenous to North America. Both species have mild consciousness-altering properties, with the yellow species having a higher concentration of nicotine (Fox 2015: 16; Godlaski 2013: 2).

Determining the precise beginning date of anything is a tricky business. A new discovery can demolish a well-accepted date of origin and push it backward in time several decades or even centuries. The best current thinking is that American Indians first used tobacco somewhere around 3,000 years ago after it had filtered into the American Southwest from Mexico. The plant probably reached the eastern United States many years later. What is known with certainty is that when the first Europeans visited the islands of the Caribbean, the Indigenous peoples there made frequent use of the plant, often employing it as a key part of rituals and spiritual practices. Native individuals smoked, chewed, inhaled, and drank tobacco in various forms and concoctions, and used it medicinally to treat diarrhea, pain, and other maladies. Some even used tobacco as toothpaste (Kohrman and Benson 2011: 331).

One thing Europeans noticed in many of their encounters with Native American tobacco consumers is that they often used it with an unfamiliar object. Having no prior experience with smoking pipes, Europeans' earliest attempts to describe them were clumsy. In the early 1500s French explorer Jacques Cartier (1580: 60) portrayed the smoking pipe as "a hollow peece of stone or wood like a pipe." By "pipe" Cartier meant a musical instrument. Continuing, he reported that Native users of the "pouder" put "one of the endes of the sayd Cornet or pipe" in their mouths and suck so long that smoke "commeth out of their mouth and nostrils, euen as out of the Tonnel of a Chimny." About 30 years later, in 1565, John Sparke, sailing with Sir John Hawkins to the West Indies, was equally hazy about smoking pipes. He declared that the "Floridians" traveled with a "kinde of herbe dryed" and used "a cane, and an earthen cup in the end" to "sucke thoro the cane the smoke thereof" (Markham 1878: 57). Not long afterward Englishman William Harrison (Furnivall 1877: lv) observed that "the Indians" smoked an "herb" using "an instrument formed like a little ladell," and in 1590 Thomas Hariot (1590: 16), a protégé of Sir Walter Raleigh, observed that Native Indians drew smoke into their bodies with "pipes made of claie." By 1600, then, the English had finally settled on a common term for the implement needed to smoke tobacco; they called them pipes.

America's Native peoples offered tobacco to European explorers, and the newcomers readily accepted it, even though Cartier had remarked that when he tried it, it made his mouth feel as if it was filled "with Pepper dust, it is so hote." Despite Cartier's initial discomfort, the idea of taking tobacco appealed to Europeans partly because the Natives swore that tobacco "kepe them warm and in health" (Cartier 1580: 60).

Tobacco was controversial almost from the minute the first hogsheads touched the docks in England. Commentators, even in the seventeenth century, could not agree on who had introduced the plant to the island. A common belief is that Sir Walter Raleigh was the responsible party, but several Elizabethan writers disagreed, naming Captain Richard Greenfield, Sir Francis Drake, Sir John Hawkins, or even Ralph Lane, a settler from the doomed colony at Roanoke, as the introducers of tobacco (Orser 2018: 96). As the debate raged on, early seventeenth-century English observers acknowledged two things about tobacco: that it had come from the Americas—sometimes they even called it "Indian tobacco"—and that it had arrived sometime in the 1550s. Of considerably more consequence was that they could not agree whether tobacco was a gift from America's Native peoples or a curse sent from below.

As tobacco became more common on the streets of London, the opinionated lined up for and against it. The most illustrious opponent was King James I (1604), who famously opposed the "vile custome of Tobacco taking." Ben Agar (1643: 5), another English onlooker, argued that tobacco was the "image and patterne of hell" because "it is a stinking loathsome thing, so is hell." An anonymous woman in 1675 spread a thought-provoking report about tobacco and its effects on her husband, "a great Smoaker." After fourteen years of marriage, she had "never got with child by him but once, and that was so feebly done" (Anonymous 1675: 1). Countering this damning tale, others lauded the effects of tobacco, with one writer (Anonymous 1700) grandly claiming in 1700 that "this Rich Leafe . . . will cure ye All," meaning all the body's ailments, including those of the spirit. As late as 1773, a cure for drowning recommended in Amsterdam and known in parts of England included forcing "the Vapour of Tobacco" into the victim's lungs because it was deemed "more Stimulating than common Air" (Anonymous 1773).

Despite the heated arguments for and against tobacco, English consumers were not to be put off, and interest in the plant continued to grow. But regardless of the great demand, shippers and merchants captivated by the prospects of importing and selling tobacco had a significant problem, one extending far beyond the opinions of tobacco's promoters and naysayers. European adventurers had shown that it was relatively easy to cart a few tobacco leaves across the ocean, but when they arrived, they were virtually useless without the objects needed for smoking it. Snuff and chewing tobacco were always options, but smoking was the most popular by far. Thus, the English smoking world was confronted with two choices: either they could convince Native Americans to craft enough smoking pipes to sell to eager European consumers, or Europeans could create their own smoking pipe industry from the ground up. The first option would be incredibly difficult to begin and maintain. Indigenous Americans were unlikely to allow themselves to be turned en masse into unpaid indentured or enslaved laborers or even into mass-producing paid artisans. Even if a large-scale system of forced or waged labor could be developed and successfully run, it would still require massive costs to transport the finished products across the Atlantic. Once safely unloaded in port cities, the pipes still had to be stored and marketed, activities laying on more time and money. Faced with these obstacles, the most advantageous way forward was for Europeans to develop a new industry to mass manufacture clay smoking pipes. The English, who were the first to act, dove into clay pipe production like it was a tech company's IPO. The Dutch would soon follow, as would others seeking to elbow their way into the lucrative trade.

The smoking pipe, at first a curiosity, had become a common and much-desired item by the turn of the seventeenth century. No one is absolutely certain when the first English-made clay tobacco pipe was pulled out of the kiln, but sometime around 1580 is a most likely date (Noël Hume 1972: 303).

English pipe makers only had Native American examples to use as models. Indigenous Americans made recreational and sacred pipes in several forms extending from simple straight tubes to expertly sculptured pipes fashioned in the shape of humans, animals, and fantastic beasts (Steinmetz 1984). The sacred pipes of some American Indian cultures were made so that the bowl and the stem, both powerfully charged objects, could be kept separate until needed for special ceremonies (Paper 1987; Rafferty 2006: 455; Steponaitis and Dockery 2011).

European pipe makers never attached spiritual significance to tobacco or smoking. In their world, tobacco and tobacco pipes were merely commodities meant for sale. Zealous English entrepreneurs jumped on the opportunities presented by the new market, created a pipe-making guild, and in 1619 received their first royal charter from James I. The king, still an opponent to tobacco, must have thrown up his hands in exasperation when he was forced to accept that English men and women, committed to tobacco smoking in increasing numbers, needed tobacco pipes. At first the pipe makers were titled the "Tobacco-pipe Makers of Westminster in the County of Middlesex," but less than 20 years later they were reincorporated as the "Tobacco-pipe Makers of London and Westminster and England and Wales." King James I (1619) had proclaimed, upon issuing the original charter, that his royal permission had been necessary because "making Tobacco Pipes is easily learned." The pipe makers' charter was his way of attempting to instill order on a new but swiftly growing industry (Walker 1977: 247).

Seeing no need for the Indian-style separate stem and bowl, English pipe makers adopted a one-piece model, one with a small bowl and a long stem. Their initial, late-sixteenth-century creations had tiny bowls, about a quarter of an inch in size with stems measuring four to six inches long. Workshop owners chose a fine-grained clay they called "ball clay" or "pipe-clay" for their products. By the 1660s the first generation of English geologists were already scouring the countryside in search of good pipe-making clay deposits, like the "Grey or blewish Tobacco Pipe clay" found in west Yorkshire (Lister 1684: 746). Since usable clay deposits occurred naturally

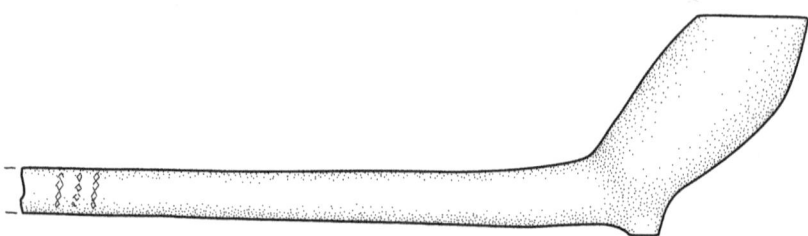

Figure 7. White clay pipe. Drawing by Tina Ross.

throughout England, pipe makers often found a treasured, favorite source for their pipes even if it was located miles from their workshops (Vince and Peacey 2006). The transportation costs were deemed worth the trouble (Figure 7).

As King James I had wryly observed, making clay pipes was not difficult. The process was so straightforward and the tools so low-tech that they have essentially remained the same today for the few small-scale artisans who produce clay tobacco pipes for historical reenactors or as tourist mementos. To begin, the pipe maker rolls a ball of clay into a long, solid tube called a "roll," leaving a large bulb at one end. Once prepared, the roll is placed in a two-piece, metal mold, and a piece of wire is run through the long stem to create the hole, or bore. Pipe makers originally formed the bowl by pushing a device looking something like an acorn with a handle on it into the bulb of clay. After around 1700, most producers had replaced the handheld tool with a bench, called a "bench-vice" or "gin-press." This simple bench was outfitted with a lever with a nob that was pushed down into the bulb of clay to fashion the bowl. Once fully formed, the still moist, fully formed pipes went into the kiln to be fired, thousands at a time.

The simple implements needed to make clay pipes reinforced James's opinion that pipe manufacturing was relatively easy, even though considerable skill and experience was required to calculate the kiln's proper firing temperature and to stabilize it throughout the entire firing process (Ayto 1990: 19, 20–21). Because pipes were made in molds, decorations were easy to apply onto the bowls and stems. Over time, pipe makers produced pipes having all manner of shapes and sizes. Some of the most creative artisans advertised their creativity and skill with examples having intricately twisted stems and multiple bowls. Different styles of white clay smoking pipes soon acquired unique names. In the eighteenth century, pipes with stems between 18 and 24 inches long were called "aldermen" or "straws," and later in the century, pipes with even longer stems, reaching as much as 3 feet in length, were known as "churchwardens." Pipes with short stems were variously known as "short churchwardens," or even "nose warmers" (Ayto 1990: 9–10; Noël Hume 1972: 296–297).

White clay pipes became so commonplace that by the late seventeenth century people in England used them as frames of reference and expanded the range of their uses. One man described a dental tool as "about a foot long, as big as a Tobacco-pipe," and a traveler who had visited Africa explained that there the Indigenous peoples' "brass, copper, and iron rings" were "about the bigness of the smallest end of a Tobacco pipe." More than one late-seventeenth-century English writer claimed that tobacco pipes could be used for murder, cataloging them as "one kind of Weapon, as by a Sword, Dagger, Stilletto, Stick, Tobacco-pipe, Knife, Sheers, or other like Weapon." The stabbing power of a clay pipe was proven by a strange story related by late-seventeenth-century surgeon John Muys. On an otherwise ordinary day, a man presented himself at Muys's London office complaining of an abscess in his jaw. When Muys lanced the man's painful red swelling, he was amazed to withdraw from it "a piece of a Tobacco-pipe equalizing the length of the Middle-finger." Astonished Londoners who had heard about the peculiar case immediately accused "the Devil and his Inchantments" for the unfortunate man's affliction, but the truth was far more mundane. It seemed that about six months earlier the man had fallen in the street while "taking Tobacco." The fall had jammed his pipe into his jaw, causing the abscess. Rising to his feet, battered and with a newly broken pipe, the hapless man must have assumed that his pipe had simply broken in the fall. Oddly, the man must not have noticed the uncomfortable sensation in his jaw (Muys 1686: 130–133; Orser 2018: 101).

White clay pipes could also acquire additional, considerably less traumatic uses. In the early 1970s archaeologists excavating at the site of Fort Orange in Albany, New York, unearthed 35 unique pipe stems. Each one, dating to the mid-seventeenth century, had been carved with finger holes so that they could be used as flutes or whistles. Colonial Fort Orange was once a strategically situated trading post built by the globally powerful Dutch West India Company on the west bank of the Hudson River (Huey 1974). It must have been a lonely enough posting to require the soothing effects of music, if even of a rudimentary kind.

The variety of pipes being excavated throughout eastern North America encouraged some archaeologists to pick up Oswald's trail and to explore clay pipes in new ways. One of the enduring areas of study attracting attention was whether clay pipes could be used for dating archaeological deposits.

After examining a substantial number of specimens from Williamsburg and the surrounding region, Noël Hume realized that beginning in the late sixteenth century, as tobacco became more plentiful and thus less expensive, pipe makers steadily expanded the size of their pipe bowls and added more decoration. A pipe made in 1860 is larger and more elaborate than one made 200 years earlier. Nineteenth-century pipes were often decorated in a vast number of ways, including with human faces, evocative symbols, political mottos, the initials of organizations, and countless other things. The only limit on bowl decoration was the mold maker's cleverness.

Noël Hume's observation about the change in pipe bowl size through time remains relevant, but much more surprising was an observation made in the 1950s by J. C. Harrington, the same man who visited with Audrey and Ivor Noël Hume at the Guildhall Museum. His excavations at Jamestown had yielded over 50,000 pieces of clay pipestems. As he pondered the huge pile of them on his laboratory table, Harrington noticed something intriguing. It seemed to him that pipes made earlier had larger holes through their stems than those made later. He decided to test his impression even though it meant individually measuring each of the stem bores. He doggedly began the tedious task of measurement with a standard set of American drill bits. Noël Hume (2003–2004) mockingly called Harrington's effort a "lunatic operation," but Harrington was undeterred. After withstanding the boredom of inserting a drill bit into the end of each and every pipestem, Harrington discovered that his initial impression was correct: the hole in white clay pipe stems did get smaller through time. Using the scale available on the drill bits, he organized the stem measurements on a chart separated into segments of time and hole diameter. In the 1620–1650 era, the holes measured between 7/64 and 9/64 inches in diameter, with over half of them measuring 8/64 inches. In the 1750–1800 era, nearly 80 percent of the holes measured 4/64 inches in diameter, with the others being either 5/64 or 6/64 inches (Harrington 1954; Noël Hume 1972: 297).

Harrington's insight and tireless labor offered an innovative way for archaeologists to assign dates to deposits containing clay pipes stems. Nonetheless, for the next eight years most archaeologists, except perhaps his colleagues at Jamestown, paid little attention. That changed in 1962.

Just when the push toward a more scientific archaeology was gaining steam in the United States, Lewis Binford discovered Harrington's paper about pipestems. Binford was then in the middle of his doctoral research on the historic-era Native American cultures who had lived on the Virginia–North Carolina state line. Although primarily interested in much earlier history, Binford would remain a peripheral figure in historical archaeology throughout his life.

As he attempted to use Harrington's method, Binford (1962) discovered that the segments of time Harrington had used to divide the pipestems made it difficult to provide precise age estimates. The decades-long periods were simply not accurate enough. So Binford decided to accept Harrington's original stem measurements but to convert them into a statistical formula. By plotting the years against the means of the hole measurements in each of Harrington's time segments, Binford calculated a straight-line regression formula. His hope was that archaeologists could use this formula to date large pipestem collections more accurately. Skeptics, and there were many, quickly pointed out that Binford's straight-line formula contained a fatal flaw. In his straight-line model, the holes in pipestems would completely disappear in 1931! The critics argued that the regression line had to be curved because a pipe stem without a hole is merely a fired-clay cylinder (Hanson 1971; Heighton and Deagan 1972).

The arcane debate over the holes in pipestems has receded into history, but a few archaeologists have maintained an interest in devising ways to use clay tobacco pipes to help narrow down the dates that a building was inhabited or used (Mallios 2005; Shott 2012). Determining the occupation and use dates is especially critical in cases where historical documents are vague or nonexistent, a situation that is often true for many places associated with enslaved Africans.

The enthusiasm surrounding the use of white clay smoking pipes for dating historical living and working spaces is important to archaeology as a discipline, but in the end the technical information offers little opportunity to learn about the people who used the pipes. All that is learned is that past men and women smoked pipes of different sizes, shapes, and decorations.

For several years after the Harrington/Binford pipestem studies were published, archaeologists continued to collect clay tobacco pipes without much fanfare. Except for the occasional devotee, excavators routinely dug them up, washed them off, dutifully measured them, and boxed and shelved them without much enthusiasm. The ho-hum approach to pipes began to change in the late 1970s, just as historical archaeology really began to take off as a discipline.

Archaeologists excavating seventeenth-century properties in the Tidewater region of Virginia and Maryland continued to unearth hundreds of white clay smoking pipes throughout the 1970s. They knew that most of them had been made in English or perhaps even Dutch workshops and imported to the region. But included within the excavated collections archaeologists often found unusual pipes. They had been made in the classic long-stem European form but fashioned from local clays. Instead of being white in color, these pipes were earth-toned, generally dark terra cotta or brown. Some of the pipes appeared to have been made by hand rather than pressed in molds. Archaeologists like Harrington were initially puzzled by these pipes but decided that English settlers must have made them when bad weather, economic slumps, or some other factor affected the Mother Country's ability to supply the colonies with commodities like tobacco pipes.

In the late 1970s Susan Henry (1979), an archaeologist with Alexandria Archaeology Research Center in Northern Virginia, decided to investigate the terra cotta pipes by studying a collection unearthed from the remains of a seventeenth-century house and yard in St. Mary's City, Maryland. Harrington (1951) had foreseen the need for just this kind of study over 20 years earlier. During the excavations, archaeologists had found over 11,000 pieces of white clay pipes, and over 1,800 terra cotta pipe fragments.

During her painstaking analysis, Henry noticed two intriguing things about the pipes. Many made in the classic European shape were highly decorated. Some of the stems had flower designs or decorative bands running around them. Some of the bowls were even more elaborately decorated with figures of deer, diamonds, and stars. One bowl even had an ornate decoration composed of hearts with arrows crisscrossing through them, zigzag lines, dots, and stylized plants. Some of the designs had been fashioned by hand with a tool of some sort. The other feature that caught Henry's eye was that a few of the terra cotta pipes were not made in the usual European form. Instead they appeared to mimic styles long used by Native Americans. A typical form was the "elbow pipe," so named because the angle between the stem and the bowl resembles a bent human arm. One pipe in the collection had even been made in the shape of a bird. Native American smokers had used both elbow and effigy pipes for centuries.

Henry concluded that English settlers may indeed have made their own pipes during periods of reduced importation. She was unable to say with absolute certainty that her hunch was correct but only that she had not been able to disprove it. Without question, more study was needed to unravel the true history of these enigmatic pipes.

The idea that English settlers hugging the eastern coast of North America made their own tobacco pipes raised a series of fascinating questions. Further excavations had shown that seventeenth-century pipe makers had established several small workshops across the region bordering Chesapeake Bay. Findings at dwellings and other buildings indicated that locally made pipes did not travel far after manufacture. It seems that the region's terra cotta pipes, fashioned into both Native American and English styles, were intended for local people (Luckenbach and Kiser 2006).

One of the most skillful, visionary pipe makers in the Tidewater region was Emanuel Drue. An English immigrant, Drue had settled in the 1650s along the northern fringe of Chesapeake Bay, a few miles south of today's Baltimore. Drue was something of a polymath. He owned and operated a plantation, he dabbled in science, he was an accomplished potter, and he made tobacco pipes. But referring to him as a "pipe maker" does him a grave injustice because he was a true artist in clay. He not only turned out European-style terra cotta pipes, but he also experimented with different clay mixtures, producing pipes with richly decorated stems and bowls. He even made pipes with red-and-white-striped stems reminiscent of old barber poles. His most remarkable piece was a pipe in the shape of a crumhorn, an early modern wind instrument shaped something like Sherlock Holmes's famous pipe. He crafted this special piece to demonstrate his extraordinary talents and creative flair (Luckenbach 2004).

That Drue and his fellow Chesapeake pipe makers churned out hundreds of elbow-shaped pipes raises an alluring question: just who were their customers? Two conclusions immediately spring to mind: European colonists and Indigenous men and women. Some European settlers may not have cared what kind of pipe they smoked, thinking that the shape was inconsequential. If a pipe of whatever form was available and functional, then it may have been perfectly fine with them. On the other hand, some pipe consumers may have been Native Americans. Colonial pipe makers like Drue, although they made pipes for the local market, probably kept a trained eye on global economic trends as well as on local consumer desires. As artisans in a world becoming increasingly committed to commodity production, they probably tried to make pipes that appealed to consumers. Viewed this way, the local production of multicolored pipes is especially intriguing. In making them, Drue and other pipe makers may have been specifically attempting to lure Native buyers into the enlarging English economy. Red, white, and black had special significance to local American Indian cultures, but equally fascinating is that the same colors were also meaningful to many African peoples, just those who had been kidnapped, enslaved, and transported into the Chesapeake region at a time when the workshops of Drue and the others were up and running (Gaskins 2020: 141; Orser 2018: 382). Could the Chesapeake pipe makers have cast their nets wide enough to include captive African Americans as consumers?

Questions over who used the locally made clay tobacco pipes in the colonial Chesapeake led to a related question: could Native Americans and enslaved Africans also have been making smoking pipes? It took a full 10 years after Leland Ferguson first expressed the idea that African potters may have been involved in the creation of colonoware pottery for an archaeologist to take this question seriously.

In 1988 Matthew Emerson, now a visiting professor at Amherst College, dedicated his doctoral and subsequent research to the question of African involvement in the creation of colonial smoking pipes (Emerson 1988, 1994, 1999). He decided to investigate the issue after examining several undecorated pipes found at Jamestown. He realized that these pipes had probably been made with tavern-goers in mind. But when he studied pipes unearthed from plantation deposits, he noticed that they simply looked different from the tavern pipes. He was intrigued.

To begin his search into the possibility that Africans could have been involved in making pipes in the Chesapeake, Emerson selected 694 pipes from 15 collections excavated from seventeenth- to early-eighteenth-century dwellings in the vicinity of Williamsburg, Virginia. Roughly one-third of the pipes were undecorated, but the rest exhibited designs Susan Henry had also examined.

Emerson recognized that the region's American Indian cultures had made and used tobacco pipes for generations, and he was aware of the history of the English pipe-making industry. His goal was to follow Ferguson's path to see whether he could discern African characteristics in the terra cotta pipes. He knew that archaeologists in West Africa had proven that African artisans had made pipes for decades, including during the era of the transatlantic trade in human cargo. Archaeologists at the Newton Plantation cemetery in Barbados, in addition to finding English-made pipes, had also unearthed clay pipes closely matching those found in West Africa (Brown 2016; Handler 1983; Ozanne 1962). This tangible evidence proved that West Africans either made pipes in the Americas or that some captives had been able to smuggle a few from their homelands. Despite the discovery in Barbados, Emerson knew that colonial Virginia had been a pluralistic, although grossly unequal, society. Historians, anthropologists, and a growing list of archaeologists have written shelfloads of books and articles documenting the many daily associations, for good and bad, that occurred between Indigenous Americans, captive Africans, and immigrant Europeans in colonial Virginia. Emerson fully accepted that uncovering the hidden information possibly preserved on the pipes would present many of the same hurdles Ferguson had faced when he first approached colonoware. It was likely, as Ferguson had discovered, that no one feature of the pipes might openly declare African involvement. The matter was undoubtedly going to be complicated.

Without question, one of the most distinguishing and visibly obvious features of the Chesapeake pipes was the unique decorations they carried on their bowls. Emerson believed that some of these decorative elements may have been Native American in origin. When archaeologists find a pipe with an image of a deer on its bowl, they typically attribute it to Native manufacture and use. But given the multicultural reality of colonial Virginia, Emerson (1999: 55) reasoned that the widespread distribution of these pipes across the region meant that many different groups may have adopted the image, with each attaching their own culturally relevant meaning to it. Otherwise, perhaps the image was simply that of a deer with no deeper meaning. As he confessed, "we may never know its significance to different smokers."

Something else that Emerson noticed was that some of the images etched into the pipe's surfaces had been filled with a white substance, forcing the image to stand out. White inlaying was an artistic technique known to many cultures throughout the world, but it was particularly common in parts of Africa, including in the west. In these places, artisans used white clay, ash, chalk, and other white substances to give their etchings added pop. The use of white infilling was another element that helped point Emerson to African pipe makers (Emerson 1988: 130–132, 1994: 41).

Encouraged, Emerson pushed ahead and identified four seventeenth-century decorative motifs that shared strong similarities with decorations also found in Africa. A design looking something like a roughly drawn apple core with bites taken out of both sides and known in West and Central Africa appears on a pipe discovered at Green Spring Plantation in Virginia. At Jamestown, archaeologists had unearthed a pipe with two concave designs embellished with small circles. The figures appear next to one another like two bananas lying on their sides. The same design appears on Ashanti pottery in Ghana, West Africa. A decoration called the "Kwardata motif," formed by a series of parallel lines that leave a space between them in the shape of a diamond connected by a horizontal band, is found on pottery in Nigeria as well as on pipes in Virginia and Maryland. And a decoration composed of two concave lenses placed back-to-back, with small circles in both concave areas, appears both in Nigeria and on a number of seventeenth-century properties in Virginia (Emerson 1988: 147–155, 1994: 42–43, 1999: 59–60).

The similarity between the four motifs found on colonial smoking pipes in Virginia and designs present in Africa, although intriguing, did not convince everyone. A group of archaeologists with long experience excavating colonial settlements in the Tidewater, including Noël Hume, countered that some historical archaeologists had been too quick to diminish or dismiss the influence of Native Americans on colonial American life (Mouer et al. 1999). They observed that American historical archaeology, being created largely to investigate the European presence in the Americas, has been too restricted in its outlook. In the early years of research, historical archaeologists focused most of their earliest attention on Europeans. Even the discovery of European artifacts at Indigenous villages often drew attention away from the villagers and toward the European interlopers. In seeking to counterbalance Emerson's argument, the group turned it upside down. They contended that the Europeans and Africans in colonial Virginia had simply appropriated artifacts and decorative motifs from local Native Americans. They proposed that what Emerson was seeing in the pipes was American Indian influence, not African retentions. To their way of thinking, indentured European servants and enslaved Africans, both being "culturally displaced" in the English colonies, although under vastly different circumstances, had seized upon elements of Native culture. The skeptical archaeologists rooted their argument in the rapid way the English had adopted tobacco. English intruders had been so committed to tobacco that they had even created a new industry centered on the use of the plant. For these critics, the adoption of Native things orbited around the cultivation and use of tobacco. They claimed that the development of clear African American traditions did not begin in the region until the eighteenth century.

The critics' position about the primary importance of Native American influence on Chesapeake pipes is strengthened by the sixteenth-century watercolor images made by John White, a well-connected gentleman from London. White had a powerful backer in Sir Walter Raleigh, and it was Raleigh who tapped White as the governor of the ill-fated colony of Roanoke. While in the colony in the late 1580s, an era when Englishmen were first learning to make clay pipes for themselves, White sketched several images depicting the region's native plants and animals. He also painted several images of the area's Indigenous people. In one finely crafted image entitled "A Young Woman of Aquascogoc," White (1585) shows an Indigenous woman standing alone on barren ground. Her right leg is crossed behind her left and her arms are bent upward covering her bare chest. Around her middle she wears a dark-tan-colored fringed wrap that reaches to the middle of her thighs. Her face is covered with tattoos, but most intriguing are the tattooed bands running around both her upper arms and her calves. In style and design, these bands bear an uncanny resemblance to those wrapped around the stems of some Chesapeake smoking pipes.

Despite, or perhaps because of, the controversy swirling around Emerson's identification of African elements on colonial-era pipes, researchers in the Tidewater region continued to be intrigued by them. Most found it hard to imagine that the decorative motifs were merely artistic. Surely they must have deeper meanings, but do those meanings have anything to do with captive Africans? How one perceives art is inherently subjective, so archaeologists who have examined the same pipes have not necessarily reached the same conclusions. And so the meaning or meanings behind the decorative motifs identified by Emerson remain controversial, just as they do for Ferguson's cross-in-circle decoration on colonoware bowls. One especially puzzling motif found on many pipes is a many-pointed star.

The stars present on many of the pipe bowls unearthed in the colonial Tidewater share the same general features. All are made with dotted lines as if they were impressed on the bowls with a toothed comb or perhaps something like a dressmaker's tracing wheel. The number of points on the stars range from 4 to 13, with a common number being 8. All points radiate outward from a dot or circle in the star's center and taper to a point. Some pipes are decorated with 2 stars, 1 facing outward and 1 facing the smoker, whereas others have a single star facing the smoker and a panel decorated with initials, symbols, or even an image facing outward. Many of the world's cultures employ stars as symbols, so pinning down those on the pipes to a specific culture or even a particular place of origin is difficult if not impossible.

In an insightful study, Kathryn Sikes (2008), an archaeologist at Middle Tennessee State University, has documented that the star as a decorative motif was well known to the cultures interacting in the colonial Chesapeake. Stars are less meaningful to many of us today because they are obscured by the effects of light and other forms of pollution. But in colonial times, when people were making and using star-decorated pipes, stars were part of the celestial landscape. Ringed in darkness after dusk, men, women, and children of every heritage gazed upward and beheld a brilliant night sky bristling with stars. What each person or cultural group observed was framed by their own understanding and experience. Europeans had a rich and well-developed iconography of the heavens extending at least into the Middle Ages and arguably all the way back to the Greeks and Romans. European mapmakers originally placed Jerusalem at the center of the world, but through exploration and colonization they increasingly represented the world much as we know it today. Because maps represent an effort to control geography—to make land understandable and thus attainable—they were integral to the European project of exploration. Thus, a tantalizing connection may exist between the eight-pointed stars found on some clay pipes and the eight-pointed compass roses present on many colonial-era maps and early handheld compasses. The plausibility of a link between eight-pointed stars and exploration is increased by the discovery of a pipe at Flowerdew Hundred, a late-seventeenth-century plantation in Virginia. This pipe has an eight-pointed star facing the smoker but a rectangular panel facing outward. Inscribed on the panel is the profile of a square-masted ship (Emerson 1986; Mouer 1993: 146; Sikes 2008: 88).

Whereas the English inscribed many of their thoughts about the night sky in books and on maps of the heavens, the oral cultures of Native North America and the western coast of Africa retained their knowledge in remembered traditions. The personal transmission of oral information complicates our ability to comprehend its many subtle nuances, but it is perfectly reasonable to assume that when individual Africans, American Indians, and English women and men gazed into the darkened sky, they each perceived something different. When the Rappahannocks, who encountered the English soon after the founding of Jamestown, looked upward at what Europeans had dubbed "Orion," they may not have seen a single constellation. Members of the nearby Powhatan Confederacy located just north of the Rappahannocks believed that good men rose into the sky after death. Equally notable, captive African women in Virginia, recalling what they knew from home, used various constellations as guides to the planting season (Sikes 2008: 92–93).

Sikes's most striking conclusion is that rather than seeking to determine the cultural identity of the pipes' makers and users, archaeologists would be better served by trying to tease out the pipes' multiple meanings. English colonists, captive African laborers, and Indigenous Americans all viewed the stars and undoubtedly all the other symbols and marks placed on the pipes through their own cultural and personal lenses. Despite their differences, every colonial person shared the night sky as a common space. The commonality of the celestial experience did not mean that the English colonial world was free of inequalities, humiliations, and unspeakable violence. But what Sikes learned in her analysis of the pipes' stars is that archaeologists' efforts to untangle the cultural threads of African American life may remain largely unrealized. Like our world, the colonial world was far too complicated for simple interpretations.

The many questions surrounding the Chesapeake pipes continued to rumble through the archaeological world for years after Henry, Emerson, and Sikes had offered their innovative interpretations. Emerson's study had perhaps come closest to connecting captive Africans with some Chesapeake pipes, but definitive answers remained elusive. Sikes's (2008: 76–77) reasoning that "the ethnicity of their makers is far less important than the multiple meanings the pipes bore within the diverse communities in which they were used" was increasingly gaining strength among archaeologists.

The idea that archaeologists may have been looking in the wrong direction or at least had adopted the wrong perspective was picked up and scrutinized in detail by Anna Agbe-Davies, an archaeologist at the University of North Carolina. Her interest began in a curious way.

Standing at the museum display, Anna, alongside a fellow archaeologist named David, gazed through the glass at a tiny object (Agbe-Davies 2015: 11–13). The specimen, a fragment of a brown clay pipe delicately seated on a little pedestal, had been excavated from a mid-seventeenth-century fort in Maryland. It was the type of pipe that had intrigued Emerson, Sikes, and so many others. As Anna and David examined the object, each recognized that staring back at them was a face. Their realization was not remarkable by itself. Being able to recognize the human face is part and parcel of what it means to be human. Research shows that newborns, even those only one to three days old, can recognize faces. But innate intuition was not required in the case of this pipe because its facial features were obvious. It had two circles perfectly spaced for eyes with a triangular nose positioned in between. Radiating outward from the nose were six perforated lines just like those that had been used to form the stars that had grabbed Sikes's attention. Two parallel lines extended from the bridge of the nose up across the forehead, and one line each extended outward from the nose across each cheek. Two more lines extended at angles downward from the mouth across each side of the chin. The face itself was unmistakable; its meaning was far less clear. As David studied the pipe, the Native Virginians drawn by John White immediately flashed through his mind. The lines on the pipe's face were obviously meant to represent tattoos, just like those in White's watercolors. But Anna, pondering the same face, imagined peoples a world away in Nigeria and Chad. For her the lines on the pipe were the indelible marks of scarification. Where she saw Africa, David saw Native America. This simple experience with the tiny pipe charted the course for Anna's professional life for the next few years. She had to know more about the pipes and their diverse meanings. But to start down this path, she had to fully understand how archaeologists devise their interpretations.

As a graduate student working toward her doctorate, Anna had become inspired by the debates then swirling around Ferguson's interpretation of colonoware and Emerson's provocative studies of Chesapeake pipes. She realized that arguments about the same specimens, like the one that had occurred between her and David, were irreconcilable (Agbe-Davies 2018a: 182). The argument that either "the pipes and pottery are Native American" or "the pipes and pottery are African" had solidified into such hard positions that further discussion seemed impossible. Archaeologists should ideally work together as a loose collective of colleagues discussing and debating key questions with the goal of working out the best possible interpretations for the puzzles of the past. Interpretation is, after all, at the core of archaeological research, and reasoned disputes are bound to arise. But when it came to the controversy over the African presence in colonial artifacts, the positions seemed firmly fixed. Anna found this circumstance infinitely interesting but frustrating. How could she and David, two well-trained archaeologists, examine the same object and reach completely different conclusions? She had to know more.

To explore the question and its many implications, Anna decided to focus her attention on the Chesapeake's clay smoking pipes. She was not entirely sure why she settled on pipes because she was not particularly interested in them. Perhaps the pipes' many, often mysterious decorations drew her in, or maybe it was colonial history itself. Having originally entered college to study international relations, perhaps it was the colonial era's cultural mix that pulled her in. In any case, she knew that the Chesapeake region had a "vibrant archaeological community" and was "an important center in the development of historical archaeology" (Agbe-Davies 2018a: 182). It was the perfect place to continue exploring the debate with many of the same pipes that had been the subject of past study and dispute.

After immersing herself in the analyses of other archaeologists, Anna began to think that maybe archaeologists had been asking the wrong question about the pipes. Rather than worrying so much about who made them, perhaps archaeologists should also concern themselves with wondering why they, as modern-day scholars, cared so much about who had made the pipes. And rather than thinking about the makers and users of the pipes as members of racial or ethnic groups, perhaps a more fruitful approach would be to concentrate on the social relationships the pipe makers maintained with others in the colony. Instead of focusing strictly on the pipes, maybe archaeologists should also investigate what the pipes reveal about the realities of everyday life in colonial Virginia. When thinking this way, clay pipes offered a lens through which to examine three things at once: the seventeenth-century pipes as objects, the social relations that had been attached to the pipes, and the practice of contemporary archaeology itself. This approach would require coming to terms with how archaeologists carry out their analyses. Only by understanding the analytical process would it be possible for Anna to delve deeper into the history of the pipes, both as items from the past and as tools archaeologists use in the present to interpret the past. To provide the entryway to the answers she sought, Anna turned to a philosophical tradition called pragmatism.

Pragmatism was a late-nineteenth-century American invention ultimately rooted, like so much else in Western thought, in ancient Greece. Like all bodies of philosophical thought, pragmatism includes a rich and complex set of terms and concepts, ideas that have been modified as various thinkers have tinkered with its primary tenets. A central idea of pragmatism is that understanding the world cannot be separated from living in the world and that "truths will emerge within the process of looking for them" (McDavid 2007: 69). The first generation of pragmatists were led by Charles S. Peirce and William James. Their works have spawned a small library's worth of books and articles, and today pragmatism is a lively realm of thought. Anna relied heavily on Peirce (Agbe-Davies 2015: 29–32, 2016, 2017, 2018a, 2018b).

Pragmatists argue that archaeological research can never be divorced from the present. Archaeologists spend their entire professional lives engrossed in studying the past even though they excavate, classify, and interpret in the present. The questions they ask in their research—about race, class, gender, cultural traditions, and many other things—often arise because these issues have profound significance today. It was no accident that Charles Fairbanks decided to excavate at Kingsley's plantation after the rise of the civil rights movement, or that during the Jim Crow era archaeological excavation managers ignored the work of their African American colleagues. Pragmatism pushes critical reflection to the forefront of archaeologists' minds, forcing them to think about the past, the present, the myriad connections between past and present, and how archaeological research is forever embedded within its own time.

Anna's deep dive into pragmatism convinced her that it holds a unique relevance to the archaeology of the African Diaspora because it allows for a broadening of thought. Its perspectives offer a way for archaeologists to develop new insights about stubborn controversies such as the one that had occurred between Herskovits and Frazier. Many African American scholars, including Du Bois and Cornel West, have also found pragmatism to be an appealing philosophy. It allows for a better understanding of the world as African Americans encounter it, and in the process of encountering it, learning to recognize the forces that shape it (Agbe-Davies 2018b: 136; West 1989).

One of the first things about archaeology that pragmatism lays bare concerns how analysts sort objects into exclusive categories. When archaeologists are confronted with a pile of inanimate artifacts, how do they know how to arrange them into meaningful categories? Archaeologists have spent a great deal of time and thought on this question because they know that how they group things together can affect how they understand and interpret them. Anna demonstrated this with an assortment of clay tobacco pipes collected in Virginia. To sort the collection into discrete piles, the original analyst started with the collection as a whole and sorted it into five groups of pipes: English-made and imported, English-made with variations and imported, locally made in molds, locally made by hand, and Native American-made. The archaeologist's second most important feature was bowl shape (Pawson 1969), meaning that they chose to use a combination of pipe-maker heritage (English, Native), location (England, Virginia), and bowl shape as the foremost factors in deciding how to sort the pipes into neat piles. But what if some other attribute had been more important to the potter? Anna decided to create a series of different groups, one using the color of the clay as the most important characteristic. Thus, her plan began with the following categories: agatized (mixed colors), buff-gray, pinkish, and pinkish gray (Agbe-Davies 2015: 43–45). Which system is correct? The answer is both and neither. Each classification system is constructed to address the questions the analyst seeks to explore. The central point is that every system of putting things into piles involves assumptions. A central precept of pragmatism is that analysts must be aware of the assumptions they make because those assumptions will structure their thinking. Furthermore, they must acknowledge that many assumptions can be unconsciously made. Artifact analysts might use an old system of classification because it seems comfortable or because others have used it before. This was essentially the problem when archaeologists unconscientiously adopted Noël Hume's term "Colono-Indian Ware." Systems of classification must be structured to address specific research questions.

Anna examined over 3,000 clay pipe fragments from Jamestown and several other colonial properties in Virginia. One facet of the region that fascinated her was the tight social connections maintained by plantation owners. As is true today, privileged members of society tend to stick together, even when personal conflicts between them arise. Despite the many ties between slaveholding plantation owners and colonial administrators, Anna discovered that these advantaged, White elites were unable to control the distribution of clay pipes. When she divided the upper class into three categories based on their social and geographical relations—distant friends, close enemies, and close friends—and studied the pipes found on their individual estates, she noticed something curious. Two plantations owned by close friends had pipes made in similar ways, whereas at two other properties of close friends, the similarity rested in the pipes' decorations, not their forms. Interestingly, the pipes found at the plantations owned by antagonists shared almost as many features as those of close friends. Also, the pipes found on properties located geographically near to one another, regardless of whether their owners were friends or enemies, tended to share characteristics. This finding reinforced the idea that pipes were made and distributed locally without the estate owners' input, thus highlighting the importance of the pipe makers over the plantation owners. Thus, where pipes are concerned, archaeologists should look closely to the artisans as a class of workers rather than to the privileged owners and their social and economic advantages, as had been the convention for so many years.

Anna's research reveals that questions about who made Chesapeake pipes may not be the only important question to ask by laying bare the multifaceted and confusing nature of social life, both for those living now and for those in the past. One of archaeology's strengths is that it puts things made and used in the past at the core of its efforts. But by putting objects in the center, archaeologists must remind themselves not to let the cherished frameworks of analysis structure their studies or points of view. Focusing strictly on who made and used clay pipes may detract from more intricate questions about the pipes' present and past worlds. Humans, like artifacts, can be put into neat categorical boxes, but should they be?

Such research on the clay tobacco pipes helps to further illustrate that archaeologists face significant obstacles when attempting to discover irrefutable Africanisms. Asking uncomplicated questions about complex artifacts oversimplifies culture and history. Anna's research advises archaeologists to consider asking more searching questions of the objects they collect and to look at their amassed information from fresh angles, never forgetting their own attitudes, biases, and place in today's social fabric. Given the complexities of present-day social life, why should anyone think that society in the past should have been any less complicated than today?

One of archaeology's hallmarks is that surprises are always possible. Some of the most exciting revelations have come from applying the newest, most cutting-edge technologies to old things. This is what happened when four clay pipe stems excavated in Maryland were submitted to DNA analysis.

In 2014 archaeologists with the Maryland Department of Transportation began to search for the exact spot where, during the last gasps of the American Revolution, a French general named the Comte de Rochambeau had camped for one night in September 1781 (Schablitsky 2016). The Comte and the over 4,000 men under his command were on their way to Yorktown to risk their lives in the war's last horrific battle. The general area of the Comte's campsite was known but it had never been professionally pinpointed. Discovering its location was vital because a private school had acquired the land, and what was left of the campsite could be destroyed if the school's administrators ever decided to build on top of it.

The Comte had encamped his soldiers at Belvoir, a huge plantation established in the mid-1730s. Encompassing 700 acres and holding captive Africans as laborers, the army's past visit was deemed important enough to demand a historical marker. The marker memorializes the brief presence of the army but says nothing about the African Americans who lived and toiled there long before the army arrived and long after they left. In fact, enslaved women and men continued to live on the estate until 1864. The historical marker erected there proclaims that the estate was also called Scott's Plantation because Francis Scott Key, the lyricist of the "The Star Spangled Banner," often visited the place during his wealthy relatives' ownership of it.

Julie Schablitsky, the transportation department's head archaeologist, figured that the camp had been large enough to be easily discoverable, even though the army's stay had been only overnight. But what they found when the team began their limited excavations was not what they expected. It was not the Comte's campsite. It was something that completely rewrote the estate's history.

At first, Schablitsky's team found much of what would be expected on an eighteenth-century campsite: pieces of British-made plates and teacups, fragments of German-made stoneware jugs, brass buttons, and scattered food remains in the form of animal bones, fish scales, and seeds. The artifacts were typical, but their location was not because the archaeologists had found them inside the foundation of an unusual 32-foot-square stone building. Stone architecture was extremely rare in the region, and the arrangement of the rooms was unique. Plantation buildings intended for enslaved laborers were often designed as duplexes, with two doors leading to individual living rooms with a common wall in between. But the unearthed duplex at the campsite had a single room in front, probably used as a kitchen, and two living rooms behind it. Although highly unusual, such a house was not unknown, or at least unimagined in colonial Virginia. Thomas Jefferson, while tinkering with ideas about innovative housing for his enslaved captives, had drawn a sketch depicting this exact floor plan. The duplex design suggested that the house had been home to enslaved domestic workers. The few available documents from the plantation revealed that one of the individuals forced into involuntary servitude at the estate was a woman who had been renamed Cinderella by an unknown enslaver or past owner.

Included in the objects the archaeologists excavated from the remains of the stone building were four white clay pipe stems dating to the early nineteenth century. Three of the stems were unremarkable, but the fourth stood out. It carried the unmistakable grooves made by someone's clenched teeth. Despite the pipe's otherwise ordinary appearance, Schablitsky had a brilliant idea. She was aware of the many advances in DNA technology, and she knew that several archaeologists had had astonishing success retrieving DNA from artifacts and other excavated materials. She also knew that white clay pipes, being porous and in daily contact with human saliva, were potentially excellent candidates to undergo DNA testing. She optimistically had her team collect the four pipestems with latex gloves and sterilized tweezers. They then turned the specimens over to DNA specialists.

The scientists were able to extract mitochondrial DNA from two of the specimens, indicating that women had used both pipes. Unfortunately, only the stem with the teeth marks had sufficient DNA for further analysis. Rigorous testing indicated that the pipe smoker was African and most closely related genetically to the Mende people living in what is today Sierra Leone in West Africa. Historians have documented that around 69 percent of the enslaved women and men in the Chesapeake had come from the Sierra Leone region (Schablitsky et al. 2019).

The DNA analysis is provocative, but it cannot tell us anything more about the pipe-smoking woman. We cannot know what she thought of her condition or of the world around her. We cannot even know her name. It is tempting to imagine that Cinderella had once clamped the pipe in her teeth, but that knowledge is unobtainable.

The study of clay pipes followed much the same trajectory as the analysis of colonoware. As is true of the pottery, the easy attribution of specimens to Africans is clouded by the cultural complexity of colonial history. Being a place that experienced several cultural heritages in close, daily contact means that the story of colonial-era artifacts is pluralistic. Some pipes are probably African-made whereas others were the product of English and Native American artisans. New research on Chesapeake pipes always holds out the possibility that much can still be learned, perhaps things that archaeologists have not yet even imagined. But while some archaeologists were focusing their attention on pots and pipes, others were looking directly into the earth.

They were gazing into holes in the ground.

7

Pits

Cellars and Storerooms

Why do people dig holes in the ground and then put things inside them? The answer to this question is as wide-ranging as the individuals involved, but one thing is clear: humans have dug pits for a very long time. All cultures, wherever and whenever they existed, have dug pits and put things inside them.

A pit seems so elementary that no explanation is required. A pit is merely a hole that someone has dug into the ground for some purpose. But it is the "for some purpose" that is tantalizing because pits seem so deceptively simple. Scratch the surface, however, and pits become infinitely complex. So complex, in fact, that archaeologists have included them as examples of "negative constructions." This grand term seems self-contradictory. "Construction" indicates that pits are products of conscious human thought and action, whereas "negative" suggests absence. The term "negative construction" refers to a void or nothingness, but deciding to dig downward rather than building upward requires an equal amount of forethought and action (Schiffer 1987: 218). In some instances the gulf between building upward and digging downward may be the cultural equivalent of the difference between Mount Everest and the Mariana Trench.

At their most profound, purposefully dug pits may contain a society's deepest secrets. A small village with centrally located storage pits may reveal that the village's residents have equal access to the pits' contents. Another village having pits only inside private homes may expose the importance the villagers place on private property or perhaps they may simply demonstrate the people's unwillingness to share with their neighbors. Viewed in this way, the physical location of storage pits may project a society's morality, disclosing its most closely guarded needs, desires, and fears (Hendon 2000).

That the concept of "negative construction" also includes burials, canals, and ditches implies that immense variation is possible, especially when considering the entire sweep of human history. The possible diversity in pits is so vast that even a single culture may have constructed a wide array of styles and forms. In New Zealand, archaeologists exploring ancient Māori villages encounter a range of pit styles, all of which were dug for storage purposes. The most rudimentary pits were mere holes in the ground. These pits' most elaborate feature was a simple lid. On the opposite end of the spectrum were carefully dug rectangular pits. Archaeologists have discovered some as large as 20 feet long, 12 feet wide, and 6 feet deep. The largest such pits may even have had A-frame roofs raised up over them, supported by up to three or more rows of stout posts anchored in the earth (Fox 1974).

Cultures native to the United States also dug pits. People living on the northern Great Plains built some of the most remarkable storage pits on the continent. Living in a region with long, frigid winters frequently raked over by razor-sharp arctic blasts, the Mandans, Arikaras, and Hidatsas constructed their houses using the hearty prairie sod, what Sergeant Ordway of the Lewis and Clark Expedition aptly called "a thick coat of Earth" (Quaife 1916: 149). From a distance these "earth lodges" looked like the conical burial mounds that dotted the valleys east of the Mississippi. For added protection from the weather, the three cultures dug the floors of their houses several inches into the tough ground and oriented their long entranceways away from the biting gusts. When archaeologists excavate these circular homes, they usually discover one or two large storage pits inside each one. Technically termed "undercut cache pits," these pits were true marvels of ingenuity and engineering. Sometimes as deep as eight feet, anyone attempting to reach the bottom would need a sturdy ladder. A two- to three-foot-wide shaft led down to a steadily widening chamber. At its flat base, a large pit might measure several feet in diameter. The earth lodge residents packed these earthen, bell-shaped spaces with corn and squash, and to protect their hard-won produce, they blocked the pits' openings with intermittent layers of grass, earth, and skins (Lehmer 1971: 140–141; Lowie 1954: 22). English botanist John Bradbury, visiting the northern plains in the nineteenth century, reported that part of the reason for the carefully made pits was protection against hunger: "The nations of the Missouri, always liable to be surprised and plundered by the Teton villains [enemy Dakotas], annually conceal a quantity of corn, beans, &c, after harvest, in holes in the ground, which are artfully covered up" (Bradbury 1817: 118n).

Other Native American cultures dug pits as places of storage designed as one element of a survival strategy. Faced with the threat of enemy attack, storage pits were a potent means of endurance. Eighteenth-century Jesuit priest Pierre Charlevoix observed that some Natives in the Great Lakes region "when they apprehend some irruption of the enemy, they make great concealments underground" (DeBoer 1988: 14). Such pits were a hedge against the future. As the world swirled around them, hiding objects in the ground, whether foodstuffs or precious objects, provided a way for villagers to own their surroundings and to prepare for a future they could not foresee.

Not all pits used for storage were as complicated as those dug by the Māoris or the Plains' earth lodge dwellers, but as a rule, pits are as ubiquitous as potsherds at past human settlements. The homes of once-enslaved African Americans are no exception. As archaeologists intensified their excavations of the houses of the enslaved, they began to encounter pits, sometimes lots of them, dug into the floor of a single house. First appearing in the soil as dark stains, excavation could reveal previously unthought-of discoveries.

Archaeologists were at first mystified about the reasons for the pits' presence at African American sites, so they usually opted for the most obvious conclusion. Resting on practicality, they figured that enslaved Africans used the pits for storage. In 1970, when archaeologists were still learning about Fairbanks's findings at Kingsley's plantation, William Kelso, the future excavator of James Fort at Jamestown, began a preliminary study of Carter's Grove Plantation, a huge eighteenth-century enslaved-labor estate on Virginia's storied James River. The estate's grand mansion, sitting today on the 500 acres remaining from the original 1,400, was one of the first places that Ivor and Audrey Noël Hume visited in 1956 (Noël Hume 2010: 216–217). For 15 months, Kelso probed the earth for remnants of the plantation's eighteenth-century houses and outbuildings. He and his team eventually made several significant discoveries, including a dwelling likely built in the late eighteenth century, a garden, several old fence lines, and a network of sandy pathways. Each of these discoveries was relatively easy to interpret, but in one part of the property they found a series of 13 differently sized rectangular pits. These were much more difficult to explain.

Eleven of the pits averaged about 3 feet square and 4 feet deep, but two of them were considerably larger. Whoever dug the two large pits, measuring about 9 × 6 feet in dimension, had placed them somewhat away from the others. Their builders had also lined them with wooden planks and strengthened their sides with wall studs held together with hand-wrought iron nails. Kelso estimated that when the pits were first dug, they were probably about 4.5 feet deep. Inside one of the large pits his team found lenses of lime and oyster shells. In the other large pit, they found traces of lime but no shells. Two of the smaller pits, with scorch marks on their clay floors, raised the question: why build a fire inside a storage pit?

Puzzled by these findings, Kelso and his team started to piece together what the physical evidence told them. They reasoned that the pits, being together in one place, must have been associated and thus meant for some specific purpose. This implied that the pits had to have been open at the same time, meaning that they were likely not dug separately over a long period of time. Kelso's excavation also revealed round soil stains left by posts erected near the pits, meaning that the pits must have had a structure or framework over them. The soils and the artifacts indicated that someone on the plantation, probably its captive laborers, had filled in the pits sometime after 1785 using normal household refuse. Compiling the evidence led Kelso to conclude that the pits had probably been used to tan leather. This interpretation was plausible because eighteenth-century accounts specified that leather tanning required soaking animal hides in vats of lime. This process transformed the rough hides into soft, supple pelts virtually immune to decomposition. Cooking them over low, steady heat was a key part of the tanning process. This interpretation neatly explained the discovery of lime in the large pits and the evidence of burning in the two smaller pits (Kelso 1971: 33–40). Case closed.

By the 1980s the number of excavations at the dwellings of Virginia's enslaved Africans had grown to the point that archaeologists could start thinking about drawing more general pictures of the past lives of the enslaved. As this occurred, archaeologists increasingly interpreted subfloor pits as root cellars dug inside houses. They reached the same conclusion after reopening the cold case of the pits Kelso had discovered at Carter's Grove (Samford 1988). The reasoning behind this new thinking was based on comparisons between different excavated house remains.

The eighteenth-century living spaces plantation owners afforded to captive Africans were typically small and architecturally simple. Always with one eye on their estates' bottom lines, owners of slaveholding plantations sought to minimize their building and upkeep costs as much as possible. And because most of them held racists views about the captives whose labor provided the plantation's wealth, estate owners were able to justify the austere living conditions of their confined laborers.

The range in styles of housing for the enslaved was vast because the materials, designs, and methods of construction depended upon the time, the place, the enslaved occupant's job on the plantation, the estate owner's wealth, and a host of other factors (Carson et al. 1981, 2008). The construction of mud-walled houses was usually a temporary form of housing, and by the middle of the seventeenth century most plantation housing for the enslaved were small post-in-the-ground, or earthfast, timber buildings covered with rough clapboards. In 1710 Thomas Nairne, a self-described "Swiss gentleman," advised, "If any one designs to make a Plantation in this Province, out of the Woods, the first thing to be done is, after having cutt down a few Trees, to split Palissades, or Clapboards, and therewith make small Houses or Huts, to shelter the Slaves" (Nairne 1710: 49). Over time, if the estate owner wished to show off his wealth or attempt to project ethical behavior toward the property's captive laborers, the houses of the enslaved could be refurbished to be reasonably habitable. If the owner was slovenly, the buildings of the estate might reflect it.

The house remains left for archaeologists to uncover often consist of the merest of physical clues: one or two pits, a chimney base, and the dark stains left by vertical wall posts. Upon discovering such unadorned evidence, archaeologists have usually concluded that such simple buildings must have once housed enslaved Africans. But how could they be sure? When the only visible clues are mute, how can anyone know what sort of person lived in the house while it was still standing? Since the remains of small colonial-era houses all look pretty much the same despite who once lived there, archaeologists began to think that a telltale mark of enslaved African occupation might be the pits themselves. If this supposition was correct, then the pits might hold the key to African identity (Kelso 1984: 105). This insight was a breakthrough as potentially revealing as was Ferguson's flash of insight about colonoware.

For the interpretation that subfloor pits suggest African presence to make sense, there must have been good reasons for enslaved Africans to have dug pits into their house floors. The most obvious reason was for storage. In the days before refrigeration, storing something in the ground for the sake of preservation was just about the only option available. Rot and mold could arrive quickly and without warning, so anything that might fend them off, if only briefly, was a definite plus. The coolness of the earth would be a welcome home for precious foodstuffs. Colonial residents also had to defend against armies of ants and swarms of flies, termites, and other insects, and a hole in the earth offered a ready solution (Linebaugh 1994: 7).

The use of simple pits for storage in eighteenth-century Virginia has historical support. Writing in 1705, Robert Beverley, the genteel historian of early Virginia, noted that the region's Native Americans, whom he patronizingly called "our Natives," raised "Spanish Potatoes," what we would call sweet potatoes. These potatoes were monsters, "about as long as a Boy's Leg, and sometimes as long and as big as both the Leg and Thigh of a young Child, and very much resembling it in Shape." Despite their prodigious size, Beverley added that the potatoes were "so tender" that the Natives found them difficult to preserve once the weather turned cold. Because the "least Frost" would destroy them, the villagers chose to "bury 'em under Ground, near the Fire-Hearth." The potatoes would stay there throughout the winter, being eaten as needed (Beverley 1705: 30).

So certain were archaeologists that pits inside the footprints of long-buried house remains had been used for storage that by the early 1990s the term "root cellars" had become solidified in the lingo of American historical archaeology. Beverley had observed them in action among Virginia's American Indians, and numerous excavations at eighteenth-century house sites proved that English settlers had used them too (Linebaugh 1994: 11–12; Orser 2018: 285–316). After all, for those who could afford the expense, cellars were all the rage in colonial-era England.

Cellars in English homes were commonplace by the early sixteenth century. At the time dictionary writers defined cellars simply as places to store things, but only a century later the English had come to recognize the common cellar as having at least two related functions. The first was practical and obvious: cellars were storage spaces. As pioneering lexicographer Thomas Eliot (1538) wrote, a cellar is a place "wherin any thying is kepte." At the time, though, cellars were not like today's garages, spaces where a random collection of things might be put to get them out of the way. Instead, colonial-era Englishmen and women often built cellars to hold a special class of consumables. The most admired cellars were those filled with multiple casks of wine and spirits. Linked to the cellar's liquid contents was the idea that cellars should be meeting places for the well-born, concealed hideaways where upper class "hail fellows well met" could tap exotic casks and enjoy a good time away from prying eyes. As one advice columnist pronounced in 1682, "be sure to store your Cellar well because . . . besides the great number of friends that will come . . . to give you a visit, and with all respect wish you much joy" (Marsh 1682: 114). For Englishmen and women with large enough purses, the overflowing cellar bestowed bragging rights. In 1689 playwright Thomas Shadwell (1689: 33) had a character named Lord Bellamy, upon making his grand entrance, introduce himself by cataloging his copious personal possessions. After listing his flocks of sheep, breeds of horses, and the future venison then grazing in his deer park, Bellamy ends with "my Cellar well furnish'd with all variety of excellent Drinks, and all my own." So ingrained was the cellar in the English mind that speakers sometimes used the metaphor "he has no Wine in the Cellar" to refer to those without economic means and to disparage individuals lacking common sense and intelligence.

English religious commentators also employed the cellar metaphorically to represent the acceptance of Christianity. In the late sixteenth century, just when English adventurers were imagining the spoils they might acquire through exploration, colonization, and perhaps even a bit of piracy, Christian authors often meant the holy books of Christianity when they said "wine," and "Christ" when mentioning the cellar owner and wine master. The central idea was that God "has constituted a good and holy Church which is as a Wine Cellar to supply all our Wants" (De Laune 1681: 19). Being welcomed into the bosom of the Church was akin to being invited into a richly stocked cellar, where bountiful things awaited.

Cellars in England during the colonial era also had two additional uses, one specialized and one sinister. Early physicians, men who combined emerging ideas about science with a healthy dollop of the occult, advocated using the cool darkness of cellars for mixing and aging medicines. In the mid-seventeenth century, Thomas Brugis, who stubbornly believed in the truth of the horoscope and who looked to the phases of the moon for guidance, prescribed "Oyle of Swallows" to his patients suffering with severe aches and pains. To concoct the oil, Brugis first had to capture ten swallows. Once he had them in hand, he had to pulverize their frail bodies in a mortar along with lavender, cotton, walnut leaves, rosemary tops, cloves, and several other leaves and berries. When he had these ingredients fully ground together, he poured the mixture into "an earthen pot" and tightly sealed it with *lute sapientiae,* a mysterious substance used by alchemists. He then stored the pot in a cellar for nine days. When he had concluded that the concoction was fully cured, he removed it from the pot, heated it, and administered it to the unsuspecting patient (Brugis 1648: 32). We are left to surmise the tonic's efficacy.

Lurking within the alchemy of early medicine was a darkness, one that colonial-era English clergymen, many of whom were Puritans, were loath to leave alone. Some of the most steadfast evangelists used the blackness of the cellar as a warning to the unrighteous. Human souls might indeed be like cellars "dark and low," but the lessons of Christian goodness could "go down into the dark cellar of their hearts and make discoveries." Many fire-and-brimstone preachers ranted that "the Devill is in the Cellar" and told terrifying stories of the unwary souls who had been lost to evil in the bleak, dark world of the cellar (Anonymous 1648; Burroughs 1652; Mather 1684; Vines 1656). Such ideas, having crossed the Atlantic, reappeared in colonial America.

Most of the English colonists who landed on the shores of colonial Virginia would have been aware of the cellar's many meanings, even if only vaguely. Archaeologists have discovered that during the earliest years of seventeenth-century settlement, some English colonists were reduced to living partly underground in rudimentary houses made of bark, leaves, and branches. One of the living spaces English men and women called home during the earliest years of settlement was the "cellar house," a dwelling whose floor was dug into the earth like a Northern Plains earth lodge. One colonial Dutch official, living in today's New York and keeping a wary eye on the English colony to the east, observed that new arrivals in both colonies, having "no means to build farm-houses" were reduced to digging "a square pit in the ground, cellar fashion, six or seven feet deep, as long and as broad as they think proper." Once dug, he reported that the inhabitants would encase the pit's walls and floor in timber and cover the roof with "bark or green sods" (O'Callaghan 1856: 368).

The early seventeenth-century cellar house Noël Hume excavated at Virginia's Martin's Hundred had been dug into the earth to a depth of about 4 feet and measured about 296 square feet in floorspace. Its builders had cut a series of steps into the clay down to the floor and had erected an A-frame roof over it. The roof's eaves probably reached to the ground, thus closing the rough house to the elements (Noël Hume 1983: 57–59).

The typical English colonialist in Virginia probably did not have the cellar house in mind when he or she envisioned their homes in their new world and, given the cellar's dark associations pressed upon them by fire-breathing preachers, most were probably happy to crawl out of the cellar house for the last time. As soon as they could abandon them for something better, English colonists did so and quickly. By the end of the colonial era, the English houses raised in Virginia ranged from the grandest brick manor houses with brick-floored cellars to the simplest one-room, earthfast homes pockmarked with irregular subfloor pits.

The well-documented range in colonial housing styles in Virginia is what led archaeologists to conclude that simple structures with roughly dug pits were likely the homes of captive Africans. The plantation owners' racist mindset allowed them to believe that large, well-built homes were intended for slave owners, and that little, poorly built homes were right for the enslaved. Accordingly, big houses had well-built cellars, and small houses had simple holes in the ground. The equation seemed straightforward, but had archaeologists ever actually tested it, or was it something that everyone "just knew"?

Intrigued in the mid-1990s by the seemingly obvious connection between cellar style and enslaved or free legal status, three archaeologists set out on a journey to discover the truth about subfloor pits. Maria Franklin, Garrett Fesler, and Patricia Samford were on the same path of discovery even though each worked independently. They frequently bounced ideas off one another and were inspired by and built upon an idea or finding made by one of the others.

Maria Franklin (1997), now a professor at the University of Texas, Austin, decided to use her doctoral research to study and evaluate the connection between cellar style and legal/racial status using the archaeological evidence then available in Virginia. Her goal was to distill the state's growing mass of excavated information into an easily understood set of characteristics that would create a more thoughtful link between cellar style and past identity.

Franklin's careful survey of the evidence showed that differences did indeed appear in the storage pits of enslaved African Americans and those of free Europeans. She found that, as a rule, compared to the simple root cellars of enslaved captives, the cellars of English families in colonial Virginia were larger and more rectangular. The pits dug by English homeowners were also more often lined with either wood or brick, and when they used simple pits, they were typically found in fewer number than those dug beneath the houses of the enslaved. This generality made abundant sense, but what accounted for the difference? After all, English, Native American, and African American men and women had all used simple pit cellars. Searching for good reasons to account for the distinction between Europeans and Africans living in Virginia, Franklin settled on two possible factors: economics and household makeup.

Franklin's economic interpretation rested on an idea known to every adult living in an advanced, capitalist society: that a close relationship exists between wealth and storage space. For those who can afford it, cellars can be spacious and waterproof, and they can even extend under the entire footprint of the house above. Grand houses have grand cellars. The same relationship between disposable income and material possessions operated in colonial Virginia. Franklin's thinking was that multiple, simple pits were a metaphor for the dispossession of enslaved African captives. The pits were mirrors of the lives of the enslaved themselves: both were fragile yet resilient. The basic pit, being merely a hole, would degrade quickly, and a new pit would have to be dug to replace it. The trick was that the new pit would have to be dug within the same floorspace as all the other disused, refilled pits.

Franklin knew that enslaved captives, often born in widely distant African villages, were frequently thrown together into the same plantation community. Among strangers, individual men and women, unwilling to concede their personhood, may have sought to eke out some degree of privacy, even if it meant burying some of their possessions. Creating a personal space for storage was perhaps one way to retain a sense of individuality within a setting wherein one's life was not necessarily their own and where personal freedom was an ideal rather than a tangible reality (Franklin 1997: 87–90).

Franklin believed that the simple cellars in the dirt floors of captives' houses were thoughtfully arranged and used, rather than dug haphazardly. In her view, residents dug their first pits closest to the hearths so that the heat from the fire would keep their produce from freezing during the winter, a practice also used, as Beverley witnessed, among local Native Virginians. But Franklin realized something else because this was not the only strategy captive Africans employed. Given that their houses were small and cramped, African plantation laborers were mindful to dig their root cellars in spots with low foot traffic. Even when covered with a wooden plank, constant walking over a simple pit might cause its sides to eventually crumble. Since root cellars held such importance to their nutrition, the enslaved were careful to maintain their cellars and to improve them when possible.

Franklin's meticulous examination of root cellars raised a key question in her mind: why do archaeologists find it so challenging to draw concrete conclusions about the pits found in the house floors of captive Africans? The answer to this question hinges on a combination of human and natural processes. As a purely practical matter, no hole in the ground stays open for long. If left alone long enough, any hole dug into the ground will be gradually reclaimed by nature. As Noël Hume learned when excavating the cellar house at Martin's Hundred, rain causes the sides of hole to slump, soil slowly filters in, and the hole is naturally refilled. A carpet of grass will begin to overlay the top surface of any pit, open or filled, even after a few weeks. This means that archaeologists excavating a pit find thin layers of soil that tend to be thicker on the bottom than on the sides. Humans add another element to the puzzle. In the days before curbside trash pickup, an open hole was a yawning beacon for unwanted bottles, empty jugs, broken dishes, windblown paper, and other pieces of unwanted whatnot. As a result, the artifacts archaeologists encounter in pits may have been made and used long after the pit was originally used. The trash inside a pit may have absolutely nothing whatsoever to do with the pit's intended function, period of use, or original users.

When Franklin excavated the remains of two houses that formed a duplex occupied by enslaved Africans at an eighteenth-century slaveholding estate in Williamsburg, Virginia, called Rich Neck Plantation, all that was left was the base of a central brick chimney and 15 subsurface pits. Next to the hearth in one house she uncovered two subfloor pits, clearly dug to protect food from infestation and cold. Although the pits were safe from insects and frost, they were still not entirely secure. At some point rodents had nosed their way into both pits, thus forcing the residents to plug the creatures' points of entry with bricks. The residents must have realized that they were fighting a losing battle because they eventually admitted defeat. As an act of surrender they filled in the two pits and spread a layer of yellowish-brown clay over both, in effect creating a resurfaced floor. Still needing a root cellar, the residents decided to try again, so they built a larger, deeper, and more rectangular cellar directly next to the old pits. Once again nature had its say in the residents' lives because they soon discovered that their neighborhood was prone to flooding. Cellars dug too deeply into the ground may simply fill with water, ruining everything inside. As a defense, the house's residents decided to build up the floor of the cellar with a layer of sandy clay. As an added hedge against the future, they also lined the pit with wood for stability (Franklin 1997: 106–107, 2004: 54–64).

Archaeologists' discoveries of the prevalence of subfloor pits in the houses of the enslaved in Virginia led to an intriguing question: what if the number of pits could reveal something about the people living inside the houses? Put differently, is there more that might be learned about pits beyond their design, methods of manufacture, and practicality? These were the questions Franklin had begun to investigate by attempting to link the history of deposits with the household members' activities and lifecycles.

Regardless of house size and design, an inescapable fact is that the houses' interiors were the domains of the enslaved. Even in the closing years of African American enslavement, when nosy journalists and curious travelers roamed throughout the slaveholding South writing about what they witnessed, remarkably little was written about house interiors. Subfloor pits, even in houses with wooden floors, were domestic features the enslaved could build and use for themselves. Pits formed an integral part of the captive's "homespace," the domestic enclosure allowing residents to practice love and companionship, plan survival strategies, and ponder day-to-day tactics of resistance (Battle-Baptiste 2011: 94–95; hooks 1990: 42–43). The available archaeological evidence proved that enslaved captives in Virginia made the most of their opportunities to exploit the chinks in the system of unfreedom in which they were entrapped.

While excavating at Utopia Plantation on the James River only about four miles from Franklin's excavation, Garrett Fesler (2004), now an archaeologist with Alexandria Archaeology in Northern Virginia, made further discoveries that deepened the archaeological understanding of the subfloor pits' significance. Enslaved captives lived in the Utopia Quarter from about 1675 to around 1775. Their long-term occupation gave Fesler a rare opportunity to examine how enslaved laborers had used their subfloor pits over time.

Fesler discovered that the quarter had contained nine eighteenth-century houses. He was able to divide the lifespan of the quarter into three eras. During the first era, from 1700 to about 1730, when James Bray II was the estate's primary owner, the enslaved laborers lived in three dwellings. During the second era, from about 1730 to about 1750, when Thomas Bray II and James Bray III were owners, the enslaved inhabited two buildings; and in the final period, from about 1750 to about 1775, when Lewis Burwell IV owned the property, the enslaved lived in three buildings, one of which was a duplex. All six of the houses dating from 1700 to 1750 had been made with dirt floors, whereas the later three houses all had plank floors.

When he examined the pits from each era, Fesler discovered that from about 1700 to 1750, the residents had situated about half of their pits near the hearth and half elsewhere on the floor. During the five decades, the quarter's residents had also dug vastly different numbers of pits in their homes. A house inhabited in the 1700–1730 era had about 563 square feet of living space and 12 pits, but another house from the same era, measuring about 336 square feet of living space, had only 1 pit. In the 1750–1775 era, one side of the duplex had 10 pits while the other side had 12 pits. The other 2 houses from the same era had only 1 pit each. Something had caused the variation, but what was it, and was it something that would have left archaeological traces behind?

Fesler realized that one important line of inquiry might be to ponder how pits had appeared in the first place. Could pits have been happy accidents? Houses built for captive Africans were simple structures because enslavers did not wish to spend money on housing materials for people whom they brutalized yet relied upon. Given the houses' modest post-in-ground design, was it possible that the pits were holes left over from the construction process (Kimmel 1993: 105–107)? Builders of dwellings with stick-built chimneys used clay to glue the sticks together and to plug gaps between logs and rough timbers. The most obvious place to get stiff building clay was right under foot. Once the walls of the house had gone up and the occupants moved in, a ready-made hole in the clay floor could be repurposed for storage. This intriguing idea is substantiated in at least one nineteenth-century account. In an article in the *Southern Cultivator* published in November 1850, a man signing his name "Tatler" wrote in "Management of Negroes" that "many persons, in building negro houses, in order to get clay convenient for filling the hearth, and for mortar, dig a hole under the floor." Tatler argued that "such excavations uniformly become a common receptacle for filth, which generates disease" and stressed that such pits should "by no means be allowed" (Tatler 1850: 62). Although an interesting idea, Fesler rejected this idea out of hand. In the first place, there was absolutely no way to prove it. But even if he could prove it, other reasons made the proposition extremely unlikely. For one thing, archaeologists find barrow pits in yard areas, meaning that carpenters saw no reason to dig up a perfectly good house floor when an entire yard was available if earth was needed. Equally importantly, no reason existed to dig barrow pits in houses that are framed with wood, covered with clapboards, and have brick chimneys, like those Fesler was investigating (Fesler 2004: 295).

Fesler decided that the pits probably had three main uses: for food storage, for cold storage, and for personal storage. The successful use of pits for food storage would have required the constant monitoring of temperature and humidity. Enslaved African Americans must have learned these skills because, after all, food storage pits were an important element of their overall survival strategy. Experience undoubtedly taught them to control the pits' environments as much as was feasible given the climatic conditions.

As Fesler noted, evidence for such knowledge was all around them. The archaeology clearly showed that house residents had placed some pits near hearths and others away from hearths. The growing evidence proved that the placement of pits was not haphazard or whimsical.

Despite Fesler's conclusion that most subfloor pits had been used for storage, that was not the end of the story. Another, more startling interpretation was to be made. This idea would come from Patricia Samford, the third archaeologist pondering the past uses of the puzzling subfloor pits. Her innovative idea was that some subfloor pits may have been designed as religious shrines (Samford 1999).

By the time Samford began to analyze subfloor pits, archaeologists in Virginia had discovered and excavated hundreds of them. Her first interest in the pits developed when she became the person who opened the cold case of the 13 subfloor pits William Kelso had excavated at Carter's Grove Plantation. She determined that those pits had been used to store precious foodstuffs. Her curiosity further led her to wonder whether there was more to the story. Was the most commonsense conclusion about the pits where it ended?

Samford understood that determining whether pits contained secrets would require meticulous research and a large mass of data, enough proof to allow her to formulate convincing arguments. She had learned some of the hidden pitfalls by reading Franklin's and Fesler's thoughtful studies. If she could not come up with something startlingly new, perhaps she could at least settle the pits' functions once and for all. To get answers, Samford dove into the mass of existing archaeological information and selected 154 pits from 13 houses occupied by enslaved Africans from about 1680 to 1830. Included in her collection were pits excavated by Franklin and Fesler.

The first topic Samford tackled was the question of whether captive Africans really had used some subfloor pits as root cellars. This interpretation has remained in the forefront of archaeologists' minds because so many excavations have demonstrated that enslaved laborers were often compelled by necessity to spend their "free time" immersed in hunting, fishing, and foraging to supplement the meager diets afforded them by cost-conscious plantation owners. Analysts picking through bags of excavated soil have identified minuscule seeds, shells, and grains to prove that enslaved Africans spent considerable amounts of time and effort raising gardens and foraging in woods and streams. Excavations have added weight to the idea that these efforts were widespread. Excavations at Thomas Jefferson's Monticello proved that his force of captive Africans ate wild species like deer, opossum, birds, and turtles as well as domesticated pig, cattle, and sheep (Crader 1990). A study of food remains found at Rich Neck Plantation revealed that the enslaved laborers there relied on a wide variety of plants, including both wild and cultivated species. Alongside the remains of beans, corn, peanuts, and melon were numerous plant seeds, including those of blackberry and cherry (Mrozowski et al. 2008).

Samford's research added further support to the idea that subfloor pits were used for storage. An eighteenth-century subfloor pit at Utopia Plantation contained pollen proving that the residents of the house had lined the pit with grass and then, as excavated grains of starch revealed, had filled it with either sweet potatoes or corn. Another pit on the same plantation also contained grass pollen (Samford 2007: 134–136). The analysis of pollen, seeds, and other microscopic materials confirms that archaeologists' suppositions about subfloor pits were correct: some enslaved captives did use subfloor pits for food storage.

The second idea Samford reviewed focused on the use of subfloor pits for the safe keeping of personal possessions. At Kingsmill Plantation, she learned that archaeologists had excavated a pit containing a mineral water bottle and 19 wine bottles, 13 whole and 6 partially broken. When the archaeologists uncovered this strange collection, many of the whole bottles were lying on their sides. More intriguing, the partial bottles appeared to have been broken in the pit itself. At the nearby Carter's Grove Plantation, both of the houses in the duplex had rectangular pits lined with what appeared to be prefabricated wooden boxes. In one box, archaeologists found an iron padlock, a key, a scythe blade, the handle from an iron grate, an iron piece from a saddle, and a broken wine bottle. In the box on the other side of the duplex, archaeologists uncovered an iron hoe and nine large iron spikes. Samford (2007: 143–147) concluded that enslaved laborers must have used these pits to store valuables or to hide useful objects they wished to keep out of sight until needed.

Samford's conclusions were significant. Using the growing body of excavated information to concretely determine that enslaved men and women had used subfloor pits to store foodstuffs and valuable objects seemed to put an end to one mystery. Skillfully placing and using the pits within the tiny confines of their floorspaces, captive Africans were able to circumvent some of the restrictions placed upon them by their bondage. To paraphrase Du Bois (1903: vii), root cellars and storage pits help to demonstrate that "herein lie buried many things which if [seen] with patience may show the strange meaning of being [enslaved in the eighteenth century]." The presence of the pits fly in the face of the daily oppression and humiliation meted out on plantations and provide mute testimonies about the determination of the enslaved to survive with dignity in spite of it all. The pits, so silent today, express morality in an immoral place, a homespace beyond the slaver's avaricious grasp. The pits archaeologists find in the house floors of Virginia's captive Africans proclaim a collective righteousness even though, as Samford (2007: 148) concedes, each pit was "as individual as the persons creating them."

Once Samford had substantiated the practical nature of some subfloor pits, her research turned in an unexpected direction. As she closely examined her collection of pits, she noticed something remarkable: some of them seem to have been neither root cellars nor hiding places. Four of the pits discovered at the Utopia Plantation appeared to have had more otherworldly connections, features that extended far beyond the practical needs of storage and food preservation.

In the southwestern corner of an early eighteenth-century captive's house, excavators discovered a pit containing an iron hoe, the body of a wine bottle with its neck and shoulders broken off, a paving brick, a waterworn black stone, a piece of a white clay smoking pipe, and the lower jawbone of a raccoon. Sifting through the soil inside the pit, archaeologists also found pieces of bone and eggshell. The dates of the items in the pit were consistent with those found elsewhere on the site, so excavators knew that the artifacts must be more than a disconnected jumble of things thrown together haphazardly. So why were they together in the pit?

In a pit in another house in the Utopia Quarter, occupied during the middle of the eighteenth century, archaeologists found a second strange assortment of things. The residents of the house had dug a rectangular pit, but on its clay floor they had raised an earthen mound, about five inches high. Carefully resting on the top of the mound were seven whole scallop shells, a pelvis and two leg bones from cows, two white clay smoking pipe bowls, and a piece of a pipestem. Animal bone specialists said that the bones had come from two different cows, and that two of them carried the telltale marks of butchering; one had been cut and the other chopped.

Archaeologists found another curious pit at the Utopia Quarter. This one was placed in the center of the house and the objects inside it were arranged into four quadrants. In the northeastern quarter of the pit were two scythe blades, an adze, and a wagon hitch. In the northwestern quarter were a bone-handled knife, a clay marble, an iron hook, and an iron file. In the southwestern quarter were a brass candlestick and cuff links, and in the southeastern quarter lay an iron padlock and key (Samford 2000: 207–211, 2007: 157–162).

In another pit, dating to the mid-eighteenth century, archaeologists discovered a copper frying pan about 12 inches in diameter. Inside the pan and lying on its side was a whole wine bottle dating to the early 1760s. Also in the pan were pieces of animal bone, fragments of wood, and pieces of three white clay tobacco pipes. The pan also held one more item: one of only two cowrie shells found during the entire excavation (Samford 2000: 214; 2007: 164–165).

Samford was especially intrigued by the cowrie shells, and for good reason. When archaeologists first imagined that they could find Africanisms in and around the houses of enslaved Africans in the United States, they hailed the cowrie as a possible signifier of African culture. This was surprising because cowries were not native to Africa; they were most abundant in the Indian Ocean. But cowries had figured into so much African art that their connection to Africa seemed obvious. In 1986 William Kelso, while excavating a row of houses inhabited by enslaved Africans on Jefferson's Monticello Plantation, unearthed what he called an "African cowrie shell" and concluded that it helped prove that "African tradition was very much alive with the Monticello slave community" (Kelso 1986: 30). He was not alone in this kind of optimistic thinking. As was true of colonoware pottery and etched white clay smoking pipes, the idea that a single object could be evidence for the continuation of African culture in the Americas was alive and well. But as was true once again, the story was much more complicated than anyone initially imagined.

The use of cowrie shells was not unique to the United States or even to the Americas. The small, folded white shells were already well known to Africans long before the first European slave trader ever touched the shore. A few cowries had probably trickled into West Africa prior to the 1400s, carried by the caravans of the Saharan trade (Heath 2016; Ogundiran 2014: 70). The Portuguese, who had established a series of richly rewarding trading bases in and around the Indian Ocean, had transported sack loads of cowrie shells to West Africa in the sixteenth century (Ogundiran 2002: 438–439). By the time the English had arrived, the shells were already embedded into several West African societies. As the English interest in the transatlantic slave trade grew, ships flying the banner of the Royal African Company were in the practice of scooping up the shells by the thousands in the Indian Ocean and unloading them onto West African docks ready for sale or barter. Along with the shells, English merchants sold

African customers iron, cloth, powder and muskets, knives, swords, and countless other goods. In return the company extracted "Gold, Elephants Teeth, Hides, Malagueta or Guinea Pepper, Red Wood... with several other good Commodities." Another major commodity were "numbers of Negroes for supplying the American Plantations, to their great Advantage" (R. B. 1708: 8). Between 1662 and 1703, cowries made up about 44 percent of all European imports into Africa (Ogundiran 2014: 71), and in 1719 alone the *Heathcote,* owned by the East India Company, made 421 bags of cowrie shells available for purchase (East India Company 1719: 45–47). The cowries most desired were the species *Monetaria moneta* and *Monetaria annulus,* shells that became widely used as currency throughout much of the colonial world, including within West Africa. Eurocentric English aristocrats perceived the cultural significance of cowrie in terms of the then-popular theory of cultural evolution, so that "Nations [like those in Africa], in emerging from barbarism, improved their currency from cowrie shells to gold" (Miles 1842: 3). In 1738, 65 shells had the equivalent value of about a halfpenny sterling (Chambers 1738: 389).

Africans also used cowrie shells for decoration. Excavators unearthing the seventeenth- and eighteenth-century cemetery at Barbados's slaveholding Newton Plantation found an elaborate necklace in the grave of a man about 50 years old at the time of death. His remarkable jewelry included 21 drilled dog canines, 14 glass beads, 5 drilled fish vertebrae, a large red-orange, cylindrical carnelian pendant, and 7 cowrie shells (Handler 1997; Handler and Lange 1978: 125–130). At the eighteenth-century African Burial Ground in New York City, archaeologists discovered the remains of a woman aged between 39 and 64 who when buried was wearing around her waist a strand of 112 circular glass beads and 9 cowrie shells (Perry et al. 2009: 460–462).

The curious contents of the pits at the Utopia Quarter, combined with the information from the burials, led Samford (2007: 155) to pose a momentous question: might the odd collections of artifacts found in pits express something spiritual? Perhaps the lone cowrie shell was pointing archaeologists in this new direction, imploring them to consider the profound importance of spirituality to African peoples. As a well-trained and experienced historical archaeologist, Samford knew that the answer might be found in the history of England's tragic experience with colonial-era human trafficking.

By the year 1700, English slavers had developed an intense interest in the entire west coast of Africa, but they had become especially enthralled with the region they revealingly dubbed the "Slave Coast." This region, now part of present-day Ghana and Nigeria, was home to the Igbo culture. English slave traders had extracted thousands of Africans from this region during the seventeenth and eighteenth centuries, sending them to toil as unpaid cooks, maids, field hands, and skilled artisans throughout the English colonial world. Of the approximately 84,000 captive Africans taken to Virginia by the end of the seventeenth century, most of them had been born in the "Slave Coast" region (Newby-Alexander 2019: 195; Orser 2018: 135–138).

Unlike many of the cultures surrounding them who had arranged themselves into class-type societies, the Igbos were content with small-scale, family-based groupings that survived by growing crops and collecting natural foods. Their social organization began with the extended family and expanded from there. If a male member of a family was a successful husband, father, and provider, he could absorb less successful relatives and create a minor lineage or "compound." As the leader of a compound, he served as the group's provider, disciplinarian, and mediator. If his compound decided to adsorb more people, the minor lineage would become a major lineage or "village." An assemblage of villages could be formed into a clan, a collective identity held together by the members' united belief in their descent from a common ancestor (Cookey 2011: 337; Isichei 1997: 353).

Anthropologists have written a small library's worth of books and articles about the cultures of West Africa, often documenting their patterns of life in minute detail. By far, however, some of the most compelling information about the eighteenth-century Igbo comes from the remarkable autobiography of Olaudah Equiano (1837) first published in 1789.

Born in Igboland around 1745, Equiano was kidnapped at the age of 11 and forced to tramp to the coast along the trail of enslavement. As he trekked through villages whose residents increasingly used European objects, he saw "iron pots, and . . . European cutlasses and cross bows," all things unattainable to his friends and family deep in the interior. After eventually reaching the shoreline and gazing up at the massive *African Snow* bobbing at anchor in the harbor, Equiano realized for the first time that he would never see his homeland again. He would be stowed on board the floating castle as cargo and shipped off to a strange place like a barrel of African pepper. His initial astonishment "was soon converted into terror" (Equiano 1837: 41–43). The unworldly Equiano wondered whether the "white men with horrible looks, red faces, and long hair" lived in that "hollow place" and whether they planned to eat him. Africans on shore assured him that the ship's crew did not live on the ship except when it was under sail and that they were not going to eat him. They told him that the crew were just men who came from a far-distant land.

With Equiano stowed below deck, the ship slowly slipped away from the African coast, and after sailing for what seemed to him like an endless chain of days, the *African Snow* slid into a harbor at Barbados. The busy island was then the undisputed jewel of the English sugar empire. Having now reached a colonial society completely propped up by African enslavement, Equiano was even more a commodity, and he was quickly sold and soon on his way to Virginia. The process of resale entailed another humiliation. His new master changed his original slave name, Michael, to Jacob. An officer in the Royal Navy purchased him in Virginia and renamed him yet again. He was now Gustavus Vassa, in honor of a sixteenth-century Swedish king. After many adventures, including serving as his master's valet during the Seven Years' War, Equiano was sent to England to receive a respectable Anglican education. While there he converted to Christianity, was again sold and this time transported to Montserrat, where he was resold, now to an American Quaker from Philadelphia. After several difficult trials, including a trip to the North Pole, Equiano settled in London as an outspoken critic of African enslavement. He died in 1797.

Having had such a momentous life with so much to tell, Equiano left behind surprisingly little about Igbo spirituality. He did note, though, that the Igbo believed in a supreme deity, the Creator God or the Greatest of the Gods, who created everything.

The Igbos believed in three dimensions of spiritual space, and it was the uppermost dimension, the sky, where the Creator God lived, as did the gods of rain, lightning, and thunder as well as several other major deities. The middle dimension, including humans, was home to an earth goddess named Ala and numerous minor deities and spirits. The lowermost dimension was the world of the ancestors, an individual's personal god, and demons. Igbos believed that deceased friends and relatives were transformed into ancestor spirits who "always attend them, and guard them from the bad spirits or foes." Individual Igbos, free to worship all the gods they believed in, erected shrines for lesser gods but never for the Creator God (Egboh 1971: 269–270; Oriji 1989: 115).

One realm of the earth deity, Ala, was morality. If a man was charged with adultery, a priest would plead with Ala and the man's ancestors to contain their anger and not punish the people for the man's breach of morality. Murder, kidnapping, poisoning, stealing, giving birth to twins or unhealthy children were all crimes against Ala. Equiano added that adultery was punishable by slavery or death. Whatever the infraction, rites had to be performed to purge the village of the evil caused by bad actions. Equiano (1837: 10, 23) said that "priests and magicians, or wise men" performed the purifying rites. In addition, no village would be complete without a shrine to Ala because she was one of the strongest spiritual forces holding Igbo society together (Meek 1943: 113).

When he visited the Igbo in 1900, English missionary G. T. Basden discovered that individual villagers maintained close connections with their personal and family gods. He observed that people erected shrines to these deities and venerated objects they believed were inhabited by spirits. Basden also learned that the Igbos were careful to protect their shrines, many of which could be quite old, from outsiders. One of the shrines he was able to visit was entrusted to a village whose residents dutifully watched over it to ensure that no trespassers might gain access to it. To find it, he had to follow a narrow, twisting path that ended at a clearing. Devotees of the shrine's deity who served as its custodians occupied small dwellings erected in the clearing. On the far side of the clearing was another narrow trackway that disappeared through a curtain of dark, overhanging trees. Following this path, Basden eventually came to a wall with a narrow opening. Beyond it was the shrine (Basden 1921: 246–247).

Basden was not an impartial eyewitness, and much of his language is overtly racist. But as a Christian missionary, he would, we may well suppose, present what he thought was an accurate picture of Igbo shrines because the spiritual world was one facet of life that would have captured his undivided attention. Only by attempting to understand Igbo beliefs could he hope to offer arguments against them as he tried to pull the people toward his brand of Christianity. Igbo culture obviously experienced many changes between Virginia's eighteenth century and Nigeria's early twentieth century, but a striking similarity exists between the shrines archaeologists have discovered in colonial Virginia and those observed by Basden. His account of the twisted path he had to negotiate to reach the shrine proves that one feature of Igbo shrines was inaccessibility. Individuals with no good reason to see them would have trouble finding them. Eighteenth-century Igbos enslaved on Virginia's plantations lacked the freedom to clear, maintain, and monitor paths through the woods, so they did the next best thing: they buried their shrines in the ground. The Igbo viewed the ground itself as sacred, and by cutting shires into the earth, they solidified the connection between themselves, their ancestors, and Ala (Samford 2007: 181). So concealed, the shrines retained their power, but only for the cabin dwellers living above them. As was true in Nigeria in 1900, eighteenth-century Igbo shrines were intended only for the initiated.

Neither Equiano nor Basden ever mentioned cowries, but the little shells were important in Igbo spiritual life, at least in the twentieth century. In the 1950s Igbo diviners built houses over their shrines and decorated their exterior mud walls with cowrie shells, mirrors, coins, dinner plates, and other reflective objects. They also painted the house walls in bold colors and patterns to attract attention. The sparkling outer walls of the shrine houses were designed to advertise the diviner's skills (Cole and Aniakor 1984: 72).

The attention Igbo diviners sought in mid-twentieth-century West Africa was not something that would have been easily practiced in slaveholding Virginia, even if cowrie shells had been widely available. Slave owners looking to set their captives on the righteous path of Protestant Christianity or who sought to destroy all vestiges of African culture may have been horrified to discover some walls on their estates plastered with cowrie shell decorations. Shrines hidden in subfloor pits were a clever way for enslaved men and women to circumvent some of the restrictions imposed upon them. Captives also may have believed that their captors were unworthy of setting their eyes on their sacred shrines, so they installed them in pits, far out of sight. The secrecy embodied in the shrines found at Utopia Plantation was a practice that captive Igbos had adapted within the vicious surroundings they encountered in slaveholding America.

At the time Samford's discovery that some pits at Utopia Plantation were Igbo shrines seemed as monumental as Fairbanks's decision to excavate the houses of captive Black laborers and Ferguson's idea that colonoware had a profoundly intriguing backstory. Samford's research promised to open further avenues of inquiry into West African religious practices and their transference to the eastern coast of the United States. The apparent Africanisms she identified were not composed of a single, telltale object but an assemblage of things buried in the ground. Many archaeologists readily accepted her findings because it confirmed what the clay pipes and potsherds also seemed to be signaling: that Africanisms were identifiable in the deposits of houses once inhabited by enslaved African laborers. But was this the end of the story? Careful archaeologists are reluctant to ever think that the past has been completely understood because every archaeological excavation has the potential to reveal something new or to overturn an accepted interpretation. This may also prove to be the case with subfloor pits.

New research by James Davidson (2021), a professor of archaeology in

Fairbanks's former anthropology department at the University of Florida, indicates that archaeologists may have been too hasty in accepting the African origin of subfloor pits. Davidson has extensive experience in the archaeology of the African Diaspora and had excavated at Kingsley's plantation, the same place originally explored by Fairbanks. Davidson, being as intrigued by the pits as Samford and others, combined his experience at Kingsley's plantation with information he collected from the Bulow Plantation located about 100 miles to the south. He also studied nineteenth-century, English-language reports mentioning West African cultural practices and considered them in relation to the archaeological information from the two plantations.

The distinctions between the Kingsley and Bulow plantations fascinated Davidson because, as readers will remember from Chapter 1, many people in the nineteenth century considered Kingsley to be an odd character, someone out of step with the conventional practices of White elites in the antebellum South. He did not practice Christianity, so he did not attempt to convert the captives he held on his estate; he allowed a practitioner of traditional African rituals to keep his paraphernalia; and he did not force Africans to change their names. And he had an African wife—Anta Madgigine Jai, mentioned in Chapter 1—whom he wed in an African ceremony. The owners of the Bulow Plantation, on the other hand, had no interest in African cultures and were extremely cruel to the Black captives they detained as unwilling laborers (Davidson 2021).

The differences between the plantation owners were mirrored by the archaeological findings at the homes of the enslaved. Davidson's excavations at Kingsley's plantation did not expose any subfloor pits, whereas he did find them at Bulow's estate. Added to this finding is that ethnographic information indicated that the Igbo and other West African cultures, just those peoples known to have been present on both plantations, did not bury their agricultural produce in the ground. They typically suspended their stored crops from the ground in baskets or on racks. Davidson also discovered that West African ancestor shrines were built above ground, not buried in pits. He did concede, though, that in conditions of bondage in the United States, White surveillance may have caused practitioners of African traditions to use hidden, underground shrines.

The evidence Davidson amassed caused him to reframe the questions swirling around subfloor pits. If they were not a West African retention brought into the United States within the minds of kidnapped, captive Africans, then the pits must have been an African American invention. If this interpretation is correct, then what function did the pits serve? In agreement with the views of archaeologists at the time the pits were first encountered, Davidson concludes that the pits must have been used to store agricultural produce and other mundane things. To drive home this interpretation, he returns to the term "root cellars" to describe them.

Davidson's conclusion is especially fascinating in the light of the two plantation owners' personalities. Both estate owners found it perfectly acceptable to keep Africans on their property and force them to work without remuneration, but Kingsley was not as overtly cruel as the enslavers at Bulow Plantation. Viewed from this vantage point, perhaps the storage pits at the Bulow estate were created out of necessity. Given the brutality meted out at the Bulow Plantation, perhaps the enslaved captives believed they had to hide their produce and other objects from being confiscated. Perhaps subfloor pits were a measure of African ingenuity and resilience in the face of the harsh reality they endured. As Fairbanks student Theresa Singleton, a historical archaeologist at Syracuse University, wrote in 1995, "The use of storage pits in slave quarters may have related to the conditions of slavery . . . and several archaeologists have proposed that they reflect a form of day-to-day slave resistance to planters' control and domination" (Singleton 1995: 124).

Despite the likelihood that Samford may have been too eager to accept the religious nature of some subfloor pits, one of her most important contributions is that she followed Du Bois's advice and accepted the profound significance of spiritual beliefs to African Americans and their captive ancestors. Her interpretations about West African shrines in America, although perhaps ultimately invalid, caused archaeologists to pause and consider that what they may have initially perceived as mundane may in fact have had deep cultural meanings. Her findings, coupled with those of a growing number of archaeologists, spurred others to acknowledge that enslaved men and woman may have devised subtle ways to express their spirituality. Nowhere did this become more apparent than in slaveholding Maryland.

8

Bundles

Hoodoo, Fear, Protection

By the beginning of the 1990s it was becoming increasingly obvious that identifying clear-cut Africanisms in one or two artifacts from African-associated houses, yards, and workshops was, if not a lost cause, at least one requiring extraordinary amounts of patience. Africans, Europeans, and Native Americans, each with their own distinctive traditions and points of view, met, interacted, and exchanged ideas and objects throughout the colonial era and beyond. Recognizing one telltale artifact as African-inspired from within the dense cultural mix of America often felt like trying to identify a single drop of water in a whirlpool.

Studies on pipes and pots revealed that some decorations might have been more than merely ornamental. The cross-in-circle, the Kwardata motif, and the multipointed star may have been originally impressed into pots and pipes for specific reasons, but what they were assumed to represent might depend upon the mind of the viewer. It seemed that Africa was indeed represented in these objects, but despite the compelling cases made by Ferguson, Emerson, and others, serious questions remained. Subfloor pits appeared to offer a more profound element to the story because it appeared that some buried objects may have had spiritual or even magical properties.

Once the door was unlocked to the possibility that everyday artifacts like bottles and seashells could have supernatural implications, the archaeology of the African Diaspora tore off in a new and exciting direction. It was in this realm that archaeologists would make their most insightful inroads into appreciating African American life. Here they would also make some of their most astounding discoveries.

At the heart of the matter are magic and religion. The discussion of what separates the two can quickly spin off into an unsolvable theological debate. One person's religion might be another's magic and vice versa. Attempts to distinguish between religion and magic are as old as anthropology itself, extending to E. B. Tylor's (1871: 101–102) unfortunate view that magic was for the "lower level of civilization," whereas religion was practiced by more enlightened peoples—oddly, just like those found in Victorian England. Luckily, scholars have now freed us from espousing earlier, less enlightened thoughts about the similarities and differences between religion and magic.

At their most basic, both religion and magic seek to introduce supernatural intervention into human life: to use certain rituals and incantations to make life better on earth. In this respect the two are identical. What sets them apart is how the specialists in each realm seek to accomplish their goals. In religion a priest may lead a prayer or incantation seeking relief with the understanding that their plea may or may not be answered. Success depends upon the intercession of the deity to whom the appeal is directed, and the outcome is uncertain. Conversely, a magician's spell, if properly performed, is guaranteed to work. A prayer is an appeal to a god figure, whereas a spell is an effort to manipulate a supernatural power. Another significant difference involves the person conducting the rituals. In highly organized religions, the assumption is that priests work on behalf of the spiritual health of their flock. In the Western world, most celebrants of formal worship services have attended schools to learn the rites, liturgy, and appropriate behaviors. Practitioners of magic, often called "witches" or "cunning folk," can perform rituals with good or bad designs. Workers of magic tend to be born with special insights or gifts, but if they happen to have learned their craft, they will usually have done so at the foot of a master rather than in a formal setting (Hutton 2017: xi–x; Thomas 1991: 46).

Despite the definitions separating magic from religion, the distinction between them remains fuzzy and controversial (Hammon 1970; Thomas 1975; Wallace 2015). To thwart discord, many scholars adopt the term "magico-religious" to avoid having to make potentially regrettable value judgments about spiritual belief.

The first person to devote serious attention to magic as it might be observed by historical archaeologists was Englishman Ralph Merrifield. Like Noël Hume, Merrifield had spent time as a curator at London's Guildhall Museum. While Noël Hume left town for the humidity of Williamsburg, Merrifield stayed in rainy London and accepted the job of deputy director of the city's Museum of London. Principally an expert on Roman London, he authored a series of books on the subject. Several of them remain standard reference works. But Merrifield was not so focused on the Roman conquest and colonization of his homeland that he ignored everything else.

He also kept a keen eye focused on British folklife, a subject that fascinated him throughout his life. Merrifield would often ramble through the English countryside jotting down information about the peculiar practices and unusual objects he observed. These notes became the raw material for articles he submitted to folklore journals (Merrifield 1967; Merrifield and Smith 1956). One especially noteworthy project of his came about accidentally after a gentleman appeared at the door of the museum clutching an object in his hands.

It seems that one day the man, Charles Johnson, had decided to enlist in the army of mudlarks trooping along the banks of the Thames. Sloshing along in the mud wearing an assortment of wellies and other boots, the amateur legion was searching for ancient coins, clay pipe stems, and anything else that struck their fancy and was worth the effort of stooping over to retrieve. After some time spent ambling slowly over the soggy ground with his head bent down and his determined eyes fixed on the sticky mud, Johnson saw something that immediately grabbed his attention. Just poking out of the wet earth was the unmistakable belly portion of a jug made of thick, heavy ceramic. The vessel was missing its curved handle, but the rest of it was in remarkably good shape. Only one small crack marred its otherwise pristine condition. Carefully picking it up, Johnson discovered that the jug was still stoppered with a stiff, clay-like material. Once he got the jug safely home, he peeled the substance from its mouth and began running water into the container's interior. Tipping the jug over to release the water, Johnson was astonished to find a few brass pins and iron nails tumbling out along with it. Shaking the jug, he could hear that something was still stuck inside, so grabbing a pair of surgical forceps, he was able to carefully extract a dark brown piece of felt cut in the shape of a heart. Whoever had jammed it and the other objects into the jug's mouth had first pierced the heart with five brass pins.

Merrifield's wide-ranging knowledge of British folklife immediately told him that the jug was a Bellarmine. Bellarmine jugs, also called "beardedman," "Bartmann," and "greybeard" jugs, have a long and fascinating history. With roots buried in the Middle Ages, the jugs are distinguishable by their globular bodies and the unmistakable face of a bearded man on their necks. The man's flowing beard usually reaches to where the neck meets the body. Sometimes the vessels bear a circular or rectangular medallion beneath the bearded man. Generally made in Germany, these jugs were immensely popular throughout Western Europe in the late sixteenth and seventeenth centuries. The exact details are in debate, but the name "Bellarmine" is generally believed to refer to the Roman Catholic Cardinal Robert Bellarmine (or Roberto Bellarmino). Bellarmine was an outspoken cleric universally despised by early modern English Protestants because of his steadfast support of Catholicism. Diehard English Protestants meant their name for the jug as a satirical taunt (Orser 2018: 361–371, 2019). In truth, the earliest Bellarmine jug is dated to 1550, a year when the cardinal was only eight years old (Noël Hume 1972: 55).

The most surprising thing about Bellarmine jugs is that they often became objects of magic. Popularly known as "witch bottles," Merrifield's research revealed that in addition to the objects Johnson found inside his mudlarked jug, witch bottles could also contain urine, fingernail clippings, human hair, thorns, and other items (Merrifield 1954, 1955). At last count, over 200 examples have been found in England, although many more undoubtedly remain undiscovered (Hoggard 2004, 2016). Believers in the bottles' power to ward off a witch's evil spells generally buried or otherwise concealed them (Augé 2022: 18).

Archaeologists have found Bellarmine jugs, whole and in pieces, throughout the colonial United States, and several "witch bottles" have been found along the Eastern Seaboard (Augé 2013: 263–264). During an excavation on an island in the Delaware River archaeologists unearthed a dark olive-green glass bottle containing six straight pins. The bottle had been tightly sealed with a whittled wooden stopper. Someone around 1748 had buried the bottle upside down and had placed a long, thin bird bone under one of the bottle's shoulders and stuck the rim of a black-glazed, red-bodied bowl under the other shoulder (Becker 1980). The discovery of these bottles—in both ceramic and glass—demonstrates that the practice of casting spells in stoppered jugs and bottles had been brought to the colonies from the Old World, and that belief in the charm's power lasted well into the eighteenth century. (Today the mystically inclined need not contact a cunning person to obtain a "witch bottle." They can order one online.)

Archaeologists barely noticed it when Merrifield published his study on witch bottles. They showed greater interest with the appearance of his book on the archaeology of ritual and magic, first published in Great Britain in 1987 and then in the United States the following year (Merrifield 1988). In the book Merrifield begins with Neolithic stone axes, runs through the Roman era, and ends with the early eighteenth century. His pioneering effort to connect archaeology and folklore is widely appreciated today, but at the time few historical archaeologists professed much interest in ritual and magic. It took the development and growth of archaeologists' commitment to exploring the African Diaspora to dramatically change the situation. As the study of African American ritual and magic was pushed to the forefront of historical archaeology, its importance could no longer be denied. It was here that archaeologists may have discovered the Africanisms they had so long sought.

Like everything else in archaeology, the game changer in thinking is always just one excavation away. This is what happened on an otherwise typical enslaved-labor plantation in east Texas.

Starting in 1986 and continuing for several years, Kenneth Brown, a professor at the University of Houston, gathered a team of archaeology students and traveled about 60 miles south of Houston to the Levi Jordan (pronounced "Jerdan") Plantation in Brazoria County. Early in his career Brown had trained his intellectual sights on the cultures of ancient Mesoamerica, principally concentrating on Guatemala. Over time he had become increasingly intrigued with history that was not only more recent in time but also more locally accessible. His gravitation to historical archaeology is what led him to Jordan's plantation.

In the 1840s Georgia-born Levi Jordan migrated to southeast Texas, forcing 12 enslaved laborers along with him. He decided to settle on a 2,000-acre piece of lush bottomland, a spot guaranteed to generate wealth. Before he was finished expanding his economic empire, Jordan had purchased over 140 captive Africans. Like thousands of others across the United States, Jordan's captive Africans toiled to raise a steady stream of hugely profitable sugar and cotton from the fertile earth. Seeking to squeeze even greater returns from his estate, Jordan commissioned the construction of a sugar mill, a facility designed to vacuum up all the sugar cane grown by the captive Black laborers of his neighbors. With the end of the Civil War and emancipation, Jordan was forced to diversify even further, so he added cattle to his property. Around 102 emancipated African Americans opted to stay on the estate after 1865 (Brown 1994; Brown and Cooper 1990).

Jordan's African workforce had been on the estate starting in 1848, living in a series of 8 barracks-type buildings grouped in twos. Jordan's main house had been built of wood, but the barracks, placed about 400 yards away, were brick. The 8 long buildings were subdivided into 26 small living spaces, each one allowing just 32 square feet of interior room. Freed African Americans continued to live in these dwellings as impoverished sharecroppers until 1892.

When Brown and his students arrived at the property for the first time, archaeologists elsewhere were deeply engaged in the spirited debate about

Africanisms. Given the prominence of the topic, Brown turned his interest to the workers' housing, with one goal being to determine whether he could identify African "holdovers" at the property. That the workers had lived in the houses as both enslaved and freed men and women gave Brown a rare opportunity. It also made the investigation immensely exciting. At the time neither Brown nor anyone else could have guessed just how important his findings would be.

Each individual housing unit in the Jordan barracks had been constructed with a narrow gap, no more than six inches deep, between the ground and the wooden floor above. It was in these otherwise ordinary "crawl spaces" that Brown and his students changed history.

Many of the things the team pulled from the soil under the floorboards were the usual assortment of objects common at nineteenth-century dwellings: ceramic fragments, buttons, pieces of glass and porcelain, and the ever-present white clay smoking pipes. If this was all the team had found, the excavation would have been just another interesting case study. Their findings would have added more evidence to the growing catalog of information being assembled from enslaved-labor estates. But the collection of items pulled from the small housing units revealed so much more.

Under one housing space Brown's students discovered that someone had carved into a brick something that looked exactly like a football-shaped cross-in-circle. In the earth under another cabin once occupied by a person Brown identified as a "shell/bone carver," the excavators found numerous species of shell, several knives and files, a punch, two small drills, and a small saw blade. The resident of the house had apparently used these tools to make shell buttons. Close inspection revealed that someone had etched a six-pointed, Star of David–type star onto one of the store-bought buttons also unearthed at the dwelling. Curiously, the star was found on the back of the button. Facing inward, the star could not have been purely decorative because no one would have been able to see it when worn. Only the wearer would have known of its concealed presence.

The carved brick and the six-pointed-star button were intriguing enough, but they were just the beginning. Equally fascinating was the handle of an elaborately carved-bone fly whisk and 12 pieces of carved bone, 4 of which may have served as oracle bones. Elaborately carved fly whisks, known throughout Africa, are typically associated with royalty. In addition to shooing away pesky flies, whisks can also be used to ward off evil spirits (Gott 2003). The use of special bones to divine the future are also known in many parts of the world, most famously in ancient China, but they are also

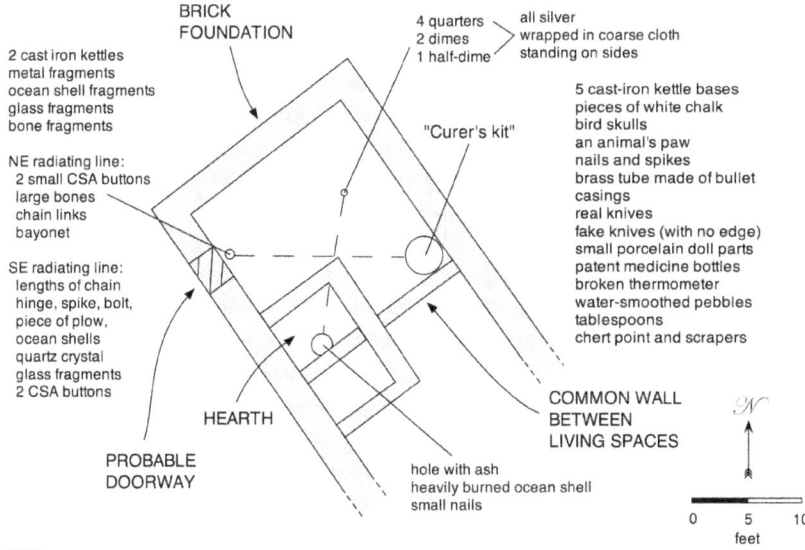

Figure 8. House excavated by Kenneth Brown at Jordan Plantation. Drawing by author.

known in parts of Africa (Campbell 1968). Brown reasoned that one of the community's leaders must have owned and used the whisk and the bones.

These tantalizing artifacts, just by themselves, would have set the archaeological world abuzz with excitement, but even they were just the tip of what remained to be exposed. Far more surprising was what Brown and his team discovered beneath the cabin of a person they labeled a "magician/curer" or "conjurer" (Figure 8).

The curer's cabin, located on the northern end of one of the barracks, was a treasure trove. Brown and his students discovered four individual clusters of artifacts that had been placed in such a way that lines drawn between them would create a cross, just like those found in the cross-in-circle. The cluster on the north contained seven silver coins—four quarters, two dimes, and a half-dime. The excavators thought that the coins had once been placed inside coarse cotton cloth and that the coins had been placed so that they sat on edge in a roll. Excavation under the dwelling's hearth on the south side revealed a hole that someone had dug under it after removing some of its bricks. The person had lined the hole's bottom with a thin layer of clay and then covered it with ash, broken and heavily burned ocean shells, and a few small nails. The person then refilled the hole with soil and replaced the bricks, thus completely hiding the hole.

The two clusters of artifacts had obviously been planned and situated in a specific pattern. These diverse objects could not have ended up together by chance. Their placement across from one another at the cardinal points was far too deliberate.

The western side of the cross held even more objects. Two whole cast-iron kettles made up the central feature of this group of items. Someone, presumably the house's resident, had placed the kettles, one inside the other, under the floorboards directly inside the dwelling's doorway. The uppermost kettle contained a few small fragments of metal, shell, glass, and animal bones along with about three inches of ash. Another small cast-iron kettle had been broken apart and placed over the top of the other two. Two lines of items radiated outward from the kettles. Northeast of the iron pots the excavators found two small Confederate uniform buttons, several large animal bones, links from an iron chain, and a bayonet. In the southeast were more chain links, numerous shells, a quartz crystal, pieces of glass, and two more Confederate buttons. The cluster also included a fragment of a plow and an iron bolt, a spike, and a hinge.

The western cache of artifacts was deeply interesting, but the collection discovered on the eastern side of the cross was truly extraordinary. It contained the bases of five cast-iron kettles, several pieces of white chalk, pieces of a small balance scale, bird skulls, the paw of an animal, a brass tube made of joined bullet castings, patent medicine bottles, ocean shells, small doll parts, iron nails and spikes, several tablespoons, knives, thick knives lacking a cutting edge, and a pre-Columbian chert point and two scrapers (Brown 2004, 2011).

Brown's discovery was inspiring. Prior to this find, one or two archaeologists had made brief reference to the possibility of locating objects related to African American spiritual beliefs and ritual behavior, and at other sites some had even excavated Christian medals and other religious objects from African American dwellings and graves at other sites (Klingelhofer 1987; Orser 1994; Patten 1992). But no one had ever guessed that a find of the magnitude of Brown's discovery would ever come to light. It left no room for skepticism. No reasonable person could cling to the idea that the objects in the four groups had been pushed together by accident, that somehow they just happened to come together without conscious human intention. There was no doubt that the plantation's caches were intentional clusters gathered for some special purpose. The cross-in-circle on colonoware and the decorations on clay pipes might be open to interpretation, but it required little imagination to appreciate the profound nature of what Brown and his team had unearthed.

Other objects thought to have African connections were so tightly intermingled with possible Native American traditions that interpretation was necessarily fraught with hesitation and uncertainty. As was the case with colonoware and clay pipes, teasing out and separating the African from the Native North American was extremely challenging. Interpretations would always be controversial and open to debate. But what Brown and his students uncovered at Jordan's plantation could not be confused with the practices of Native Americans or Europeans.

Native Americans have lived in east Texas since time immemorial, but the US Army had begun its full-throated effort to disrupt, displace, and destroy the Indigenous inhabitants the same year that Jordan moved into the newly created state. The US government continued its harassment almost exactly the length of time his plantation was in operation (Smith 1996). Various Native Americans are known to have buried objects in holes, some possibly for ritual reasons, and the use of sacred bundles was a long-held tradition of many Indian cultures (Amick 2004; Bamforth 2013; Zedeño 2008). Nothing, however, suggests that Indigenous traditions had played any role in the four clusters found at Jordan's estate.

By the same token, burying everyday objects in clusters is not a practice typically associated with the recognized religions of England or Europe. For centuries those who believed that supernatural forces might do them harm often hid protective objects in walls, under floorboards, and in other hidden places. In old house walls, renovators in the United Kingdom often find shoes, mummified cats, horse skulls, garments, and pieces of parchment with mysterious symbols and strange words. And, like Bellarmine witch bottles, worried individuals could also bury protective items. These intriguing concealments appear to have nothing in common with the bundles Brown and his students had found in Texas (Hutton 2016).

Based on the objects themselves, including their careful arrangement under the floorboards, Brown reasoned that the clusters represented a *minkisi*, a ritualized collection of powerful objects. As noted earlier, peoples throughout western Africa, including by the Charter Generation BaKongo, had used such items for generations. *Minkisi* generally consisted of a container of some sort, perhaps a cloth bag, a wooden cup, or clay jug. Believers accepted that the container was infused with a spirit that could be invoked for numerous reasons, including the treatment of illness and for protection, both personal and communitywide (Fennell 2007: 55–67; Janzen and Janzen 1988; Thompson 1983: 121–123).

Brown supposed that the objects his team had discovered were indeed *minkisi* but that their containers, possibly cloth bags, had deteriorated or had been removed. The disappearance of the containers, regardless of the reason, did not diminish the significance of the find. The discovery raised a tantalizing question in the minds of many archaeologists. Was Brown's discovery a purely African expression or was it the creation of a transformation adapted for life in a new land (Fennell 2007: 68–95)?

Shortly after Brown had made his dramatic discovery, other archaeologists began to document findings that were similar to the objects used by the enslaved and emancipated at Jordan's plantation. Archaeologists excavating a nineteenth-century estate in south Louisiana found an 1855 British coin with a drilled hole running through it, several flint arrowheads, and a piece of a cowrie shell (Wilkie 1995). At a plantation in northern Kentucky archaeologists excavating the ruins of three dwellings occupied by captive African laborers found a small blue bead, a US two-cent piece, and a Chinese coin. Someone had cut four notches in the American coin so that a string tied between them would create the cross-in-circle design (Young 1996). Each of these artifacts may have served spiritual purposes or had supernatural associations. Findings such as these deepened the mystery about the use of ritual objects by African Americans and forced archaeologists to wonder whether some of the things they had unearthed in the past were really highly charged, powerful *nkisi*.

The undeniable presence of African spiritual beliefs, as told by the objects left behind, produced the first significant fissure in the wall that archaeologists had constructed between African culture and the history of the United States. The crack, begun with studies of colonoware and clay tobacco pipes, was now a noticeable fracture because it was possible that Brown's extraordinary discovery may have been completely unique, a fascinating example, but one of a kind. Despite the cynicism in some quarters, the wall of separation was about to crumble in 1999. From that year forward, the archaeology of the African Diaspora would never be the same. The demolishers of the wall would be two widely respected scholars. They had begun by traveling different lanes on the same road, each unaware of the other's expertise, but their paths would eventually converge and, having done so, would transform the archaeology of African American life. One was a folklorist named Gladys-Marie Fry, and the other was an archaeologist named Mark Leone.

As a scholar dedicated to learning all she could about African American folkways, Fry would become renowned as an expert on Black quilting traditions (Fry 1990; White 2017). She had earlier written a well-received book on the folklore surrounding the dreaded night riders who terrorized Black families in the American South (Fry 1975). She had come to the decision to write about these vigilantes on a dark Halloween night. In her effort to draw stories out of African American informants reluctant to relate oral traditions about enslavement, Fry realized that she had hit a wall of stubborn resistance. As she contemplated how best to pull slavery-era stories from her otherwise amiable interviewees, the comfortable house in which they sat made a loud crack as it settled for the evening. Taking the opportunity offered by the spookiness permeating Halloween, Fry asked "Mrs. Smith" if she knew any ghost stories. This woman, who Fry described as a "short, pinchfaced women who had previously said little," suddenly sprang to life and said with feeling, "Don't you know the white man taught them all of that about ghosts. That was a way of keeping them down—keeping them under control." From this unexpected remark, the woman's animation soon consumed her, and as she exploded in a torrent of words, her grandmother's rich account tumbled from her lips. She told of the time the plantation overseer rode through the community of the enslaved covered in a white sheet with tin cans tied to his horse's tail. She said this display was intended as a not-so-veiled threat to ensure that the enslaved men and women would stay in their tiny houses throughout the night. This remarkable and wholly unexpected tale of intended intimidation led Fry to delve deeper into the night-riding domestic terrorists, the psychological impacts of their threats, and the injurious depredations of the Ku Klux Klan (Fry 1975: vii–viii).

Leone's career had developed along a completely different trajectory but ended up in the same place as Fry's. His archaeological training began in the early 1960s at the University of Arizona, and his first fieldwork focused on an ancient pueblo northeast of Phoenix. As a graduate student taking courses during the first heady days of the New Archaeology's intellectual revolution, Leone became swept up in the excitement. He would soon edit one of the core texts of the movement, a book that archaeologists still regularly consult (Leone 1972). As an academic, he maintained his interest in archaeological theory, eventually developing "critical historical archaeology," a perspective that challenges archaeologists to acknowledge the political implications of their research and to admit that they operate within a capitalist socioeconomic system that includes structural inequalities (Leone 2010; Leone et al. 1987; Mullins 2016). Because they live and work within this environment, Leone stressed that one of the archaeologist's most critical objectives should be to make archaeology relevant to present-day society. After all, most historical archaeologists are immersed in the study of a world that was primarily capitalist or was increasingly impacted by capitalist activities, motivations, and material objects. His interest in understanding the relationship between physical objects and belief systems led him to investigate the history and architecture of the Church of Latter-Day Saints (Leone 1973a, 1973b, 1977).

Leone is also widely admired for having developed "Archaeology in Annapolis" in 1981. Still in operation, this project has helped train some of today's most well-respected historical archaeologists, dedicated scholars who have excavated many iconic properties in the eastern United States. Under Leone's direction the project has cast a wide net over the history of America's one-time capital, with one of its central commitments being to illuminate the city's and the region's African American history. It was in this context that Leone's path intersected with Fry's.

What unexpectedly brought Leone and Fry together was the excavation of the Charles Carroll House in Annapolis. Three generations of Charles Carrolls—Charles Carroll the settler, Charles Carroll of Annapolis, and Charles Carroll of Carrollton—are considered royalty within America's colonial pantheon. The Carrolls were arguably the most prominent Roman Catholic family in early American history, with Charles Carroll of Carrollton putting his name to the Declaration of Independence on behalf of Maryland. He was the only Catholic to sign the document.

The Carrolls' brick mansion, still one of the city's most outstanding architectural marvels, was also home to enslaved Africans who unwillingly labored to make the lavishly wealthy Carrolls' lives ever-more comfortable. During an excavation at the house, archaeologists discovered a series of intriguing clusters of objects like those found by Brown's team in far-distant east Texas. About 18 inches under the earthen floor of the east wing were 14 crystals, several white bone discs measuring over an inch across, a polished black pebble, a coin dated 1790 and another marked 1810, and a few straight pins. Inverted and placed over the top of these objects was the bottom portion of a small ceramic bowl decorated with a large, stylized blue asterisk. Leone and his colleagues contemplated various options to explain the collection. Perhaps it was just a pile of haphazardly thrown-together household refuse discarded in an unusual place? The bowl was broken and useless, and the pebble was just a stone. But on the other hand, there was no reason to throw away perfectly good coins and pins. Not giving much more thought to the curious group of artifacts, and because the discovery occurred before the appearance of Brown's first article about Jordan Plantation, Leone's team treated the artifacts in the usual manner: they were cleaned, recorded, photographed, and carefully stashed away.

After a newspaper article appeared detailing the mysterious discovery at the Carroll House, an expert on West African cultural traditions contacted Leone to tell him that the objects discovered at the Carroll House were not discarded trash. Far from it, the objects were an example of a West African *minkisi* (Logan et al. 1992: 137). Leone was stunned by the weight of the Carroll discovery and wished to know more.

By happy coincidence, Fry, who had heard of Leone's find, was interested in speaking with him, so one day she simply stopped by his office at the University of Maryland and introduced herself. She told Leone that she had been trained as a folklorist and had spent years scanning the narratives collected during the 1930s from once-enslaved men and women living in 17 US states. Fry declared that she had read the over 10,000 typed pages three times. She had also read the few other collections that folklorists and others had collected. Remarkably, she read all this before any of the collections were digitized and electronically searchable.

Fry had also recognized the significance of the Carroll House cache. Unlike many scholars who stubbornly refuse to leave the comfortable boundaries of their own scholarly silo, she appreciated the insights that archaeology could offer. She had developed a fondness for the field while holding a postdoctoral fellowship at the Smithsonian Institution under the mentorship of Theresa Singleton, a widely regarded expert on the archaeology of African enslavement and plantation life. Fry had also examined the artifacts Brown had collected from Jordan's plantation. For Leone, meeting Fry was a godsend.

Fry and Leone, along with Timothy Ruppel, whom Fry had trained, decided to submit a grant proposal to catalog all the artifacts that academic and cultural-resource archaeologists had found along the East Coast but had failed to recognize as possibly sacred African bundles. They also planned to search for white powder, chalk, ash, and other substances that archaeologists might not usually think of as "artifacts" per se.

Being successful in their grant application, the three set about by diving into the pile of archaeological reports from the region. They soon realized that bundles or caches had a long history in the United States, first appearing around 1700 and continuing into and beyond the 1920s (Brown 1990).

The folklore accounts revealed that African Americans referred to spiritually powerful objects and caches as "hands," "mojos," or "tobys" (Leone 2005: 200–204; Leone and Fry 1999, 2001; Ruppel et al. 2003).

The system of belief incorporating these practices and their associated caches is broadly called hoodoo but is also known as conjure, conjuration, or root work. As the practice of enchantment, divination, and spiritualism, hoodoo is a fusion of concepts from the religious traditions of west-central and western Africa as well as elements adapted from Islam and Christianity (Cochran 1999: 26–27). Hoodoo is, in Leone's (2005: 214) words, "part of what is left of Africa in America."

The goals of hoodoo, as it stretched from Texas to at least Delaware, was to request protection, curing, and healing. By creating and installing bundles, conjurers hoped to anticipate floggings, keep families together, end lifetimes of drudgery, and generally protect community members from harm. Turning a mojo, bag, or bundle against someone who intended to harm another person was a way to put the world back in balance. Each bundle was made for personal use, meaning that each one is distinct from every other one even though they exist within a unified realm of thought. The personal element accounts for the variety of objects inside them. One feature that makes hoodoo unique is that the bundles are presumed to contain a living spirit (Chireau 1997).

African American informants told folklorists that in hoodoo, individual objects can be used for certain kinds of protection. A man might carry a black cat's bone in his pocket to avoid being whipped, and a woman might pin a piece of red flannel at her neck to protect her from a devious, ill-tempered conjurer. Another person might use the red flannel and the black cat bone to cause harm, in a practice known as "fixing" (Leone and Fry 2001). The meaning of these "personal charms" (Davidson and McIlvoy 2012) could change and shift at any time because the beliefs that underpinned them had been passed from mouth to mouth and from generation to generation. They were not to be found in any book of spells.

Leone and Fry disagreed about whether hoodoo had a true theology, a guiding set of principles that gave it consistency. Fry could not find a common thread because hoodoo had no named deities and, although it required practitioners, anyone could assemble a bundle if they wished. Leone, deciding to dig deeper, discovered that hoodoo contained an African-based worldview that developed during America's Great Awakening, the era of Protestant religious excitement in the 1730s and 1740s. His research further suggested that hoodoo became much more important during the second

Great Awakening, an era beginning in the 1780s and extending into the 1830s (Leone 2020).

As is true of crossroads, the bundle, or mojo, has remained prominent in the blues. "Got My Mojo Working," written in the 1950s and made famous by Muddy Waters (McKinley Morganfield), was, like the crossroad motif, appropriated by British blues musicians (Allen 2007; Clar 1960).

One person who explained hoodoo to a broad American audience outside of the blues world was Zora Neale Hurston. Born in Alabama, probably in 1891, Hurston spent her formative years in what she termed "a pure Negro town" just north of Orlando, Florida. When she decided to leave Florida and head north, she slid easily into life in New York City and, taking a special joy in Harlem, she became a celebrated member of the already star-studded Harlem Renaissance (King 2019: 189–192). A gifted and evocative novelist, she sought to lay bare the realities of African American life in the South by employing muted power and quiet sensitivity.

One of the realms of Hurston's focus was American racism, and it was toward this subject that she vented her anger with sarcastic rage. Writing a piece in *Negro Digest* titled "Crazy for This Democracy," she directly confronted the inequalities of American democracy as they stood in 1945. Starting with the courageous sentence, "They tell me this democracy is a wonderful thing. It has freedom, equality, justice, in short, everything!," she outlined how Americans have patted themselves on the back since 1937, an era when "nobody has talked about anything else." She decided, based on "all this talk and praise-giving," that she wanted to "try some of the stuff . . . to get hold of a sample of the thing." Citing Franklin Roosevelt's claim that the United States was the "arse-and-all" of democracy (she claimed that his accent made "arsenal" sound this way), she converted it into the "Ass-and-All of Democracy." Taking aim at the efforts of the Indo-Chinese to eject the colonial French from their land, she artfully observed that American soldiers were "fighting along with the French, Dutch, and English to rivet chains back on their former slaves." Hurston believed that the involvement of the United States in the campaign of colonization was linked to segregation and Jim Crow, with her proof being the relationship between dark skin color and second-class citizenship. She protested that Jim Crow laws were designed as psychological tools of oppression that gained expression in the "back seats in trains, back-doors of houses, exclusion from certain places and activities." The fact is, she said, that "talent, capabilities, nothing has anything to do with the case." Exasperated, she resolved that she would like to believe in "this democracy thing," but while discriminatory laws keep people like her on the outside, she would continue to find it difficult to accept democracy's promise. Only with the repeal of Jim Crow laws would she and thousands of others have the chance to experience true democracy in their own country. She believed the only reasonable solution was to end Jim Crow, "not in some future generation, but repeal *now* and forever!!" (Hurston 1945).

In addition to her gifts as a novelist and sharp social critic, Hurston was also an insightful ethnographer and folklorist. She supplemented her inborn talents with academic training by some of the giants of twentieth-century American anthropology, including Boas and Herskovits. In the mold of Boas, Hurston was a tireless collector of tales, stories that propelled her deeper into African American historical life. She added to her southern experience with fieldwork expeditions to Haiti, Jamaica, and the Bahamas, working mostly under Herskovits's direction (King 2019: 275–278).

Hurston's many treks into the dense backwoods of Florida are legendary. In one of her rambles in the 1920s, when she was employed by the Association for the Study of Negro Life and History, she unearthed information that would eventually be used by archaeologists (Hurston and Lynch 1927). Documents about Fort Mose, the free settlement of Africans established outside Spanish St. Augustine, would only be noticed by archaeologists several decades later when they first explored the settlement (MacMahon and Deagan 1996).

In the backwaters of the Sunshine State, Hurston slogged from cabin to cabin patiently recording tall tales, herbal cures, and menacing curses. In the evenings, she diligently typed up her notes, and when she had gathered them into book form, she shipped them off for comment to Boas, whom she referred to as "King." Like most of Boas's students, she had been trained to view ethnography as an act of salvage, part of a larger, heroic effort to record oral traditions before they were lost forever (King 2019: 201). At the time of her hoodoo research, Hurston was under the direction of Herskovits, so she accepted that the "shreds of Hoodoo beliefs and practices" would exist across Black America but in different degrees, being more pronounced in some places, and less in others (Hurston 1931: 318). Her diligence had convinced her that hoodoo was more prevalent among people of African heritage living in the Caribbean than it was in the American South. She said that the greatest incidence of hoodoo in the American South occurred along the Gulf Coast, especially in New Orleans and its environs. The reason for the presence of hoodoo along the Gulf, she thought, rested in the violent ouster of the French from Haiti in the early nineteenth century (James 1989). As

Black revolutionaries took control of the island, thousands of families of African heritage went to the American continent, many as enslaved laborers, taking hoodoo along with them (Hurston 1931: 318). In her mind, individuals of African descent in the United States had fewer African retentions than in the islands because steel-hearted American enslavers had traded men and women willy-nilly without regard to family ties, personal skills, or much else. To such cruel traders, dark-skinned humans were mere commodities whose value was rooted solely in their ability to work.

As Hurston trekked through New Orleans in her search to understand conjuring, she learned that a person could become a "hoodoo doctor" by heredity, by serving as an apprentice to a recognized practitioner, or by receiving the "call." Informants explained to her that the most influential hoodoo doctors are born to it. One of the most celebrated doctors in New Orleans was Marie Leveau (or Leveaux), a woman still revered as the city's "Voodoo Queen." People said her gifts were so profound that even the queen of England and the emperor of China were among her many clients (Fandrich 2005).

Hurston, who studied under a hoodoo doctor in New Orleans for five months (Hurston 1990: 202), stressed that the practices and beliefs of hoodoo were affected and modified by their cultural contexts. In Louisiana's Crescent City, hoodoo became intermixed with elements of the Catholic Church, where holy water, incense, and blessed oils stood side by side with herbal remedies and tales of devious spirits. Hoodoo practitioners, many of whom were Catholic, could obtain holy water by setting a receptacle on the ground to catch rain. Thunder and the sun would defile the water, so it could only be used if the rain had fallen in the absence of thunder, and if sunlight had never touched it. If these stipulations were met, the practitioner had to put their hand in the water and say the Lord's Prayer nine times. Only then could the water be bottled and given out to believers.

Hurston (1990: 183) declared that hoodoo's significance to African Americans could not be underestimated because its deeds "keep alive the powers of Africa" in those places that received cargoes of captive African women and men. Leone and Fry's research, including the material collected by Hurston and other fieldworkers, substantiated that hoodoo was a nineteenth-century phenomenon that had developed in the last decades of the eighteenth century.

Once archaeologists began to appreciate the evidence from folklore—that fieldworkers like Hurston had gathered and that Fry and Leone had compiled—and to accept the significance of artifacts found in tight groups, excavators began recognizing ritual caches elsewhere. The contents of each cache were completely unique, but when viewed at a distance, they clearly formed part of a unified tradition.

At the Brice House in Annapolis, built in the eighteenth century, archaeologists discovered an intact perfume bottle filled with soil and a single seed placed on a bed of yellow sand. Surrounding the bottle were seashells, two buttons, half of a wooden disk, a piece of glass, a matchstick, and a few animal bones. Nearby were a brass military button from an American Civil War uniform, an ornament from a cartridge case embossed with an eagle, several glass buttons and beads, a piece of red-cotton fabric, numerous straight pins, two polished black stones, three late-nineteenth-century coins, and a small brass pendant inscribed with an M (Cochran 1999: 28–30).

Excavations at the Slayton House, a late eighteenth-century row house also in Annapolis, uncovered seven individual bundles. One bundle included porcelain doll parts, a peanut shell with a pin, a brass button, white shell buttons, and a gold ring. The second collection included shell buttons, white glass buttons, and a straight pin; and the third cache contained two buttons and the pieces of a soup bowl, a basin, and a butter crock. The fourth Slayton House bundle included three buttons (one each of bone, shell, and metal) and sherds from a white soup plate and wash basin. The fifth cache contained a black bead, a gray glass button, straight pins, and a piece of a crab claw. The sixth bundle included a glass tumbler and a bottle, glass fragments from a lamp chimney, and pieces of a white-and-pink lamp globe. The seventh cache contained a Chinese coin, a brass bell, and straight pins (Leone 2005: 207–210).

At another house in Maryland, one first occupied during the early decades of the nineteenth century, archaeologists discovered a layered series of four bundles placed within the courses of a stone chimney. The first cache contained a metal button, white ceramic sherds, pieces of glass, lead shot, mica, iron cut nails, pokeberry and grape seeds, eggshells, teeth from a rabbit and a squirrel, and the bones of mice, a large mammal, birds, and fish. In the second bundle archaeologists found lead shot, iron cut nails, straight pins, glass fragments, a round metal lid, iron jewelry, iron mesh, a fence staple, a piece of a copper alloy wire, a shoe grommet, pieces of white dinnerware and heavy, gray crockery, mica, black beads, a white clay tobacco pipe stem, pencil lead, buttons made of various materials, a white glass shirt stud with a bull's-eye pattern, pokeberry seeds, pig teeth, and bones from several species of small mammals as well as fish and snakes.

The third cache included iron-wire mesh; iron cut nails; a brass percussion cap; clear glass fragments; three beads (white, black, and gray); a copper alloy rivet; iron lids; pokeberry and grape seeds; eggshells; teeth from rabbits, pigs, squirrels, and opossums; and the bones of turkeys, snakes, birds, fish, and small mammals. The fourth and smallest bundle contained a bead, pokeberry seeds, a squirrel tooth, and bones from fish, birds, turtles, and small mammals (Schablitsky 2011: 54–55).

Yet another site in Maryland, dating from about 1680 to 1720, contained two bundles. Both had been placed where archaeologists had found them, in a pit in the southwestern corner of the house. The first consisted of a door staple resting on a large section of a pewter plate. Underneath the plate archaeologists found a broken stone tool made of chipped quartz, a small circular disk, two hand-wrought nails, and several rocks. Close to these objects was an iron spike driven into the side of the pit. Lying directly under it was the bowl of a white clay smoking pipe (Lucas 2014: 114–119).

In northern Virginia archaeologists found a bundle containing a pre-Columbian American Indian projectile point and six crystals in the remains of a small dwelling dating to the mid to late nineteenth century (Galke 2000: 21–22). And in the South Carolina Lowcountry, a plantation occupied (like Jordan's plantation) both before and after emancipation, archaeologists discovered 21 separate ritual deposits, over half of which contained pieces of white ceramics tightly bound together with two nails (Moses 2018: 146).

Archaeologists intrigued by the bundles have noted the presence of iron and other metal objects in practically every example. Cultures around the globe have imparted special properties to metal and objects made from them. Many West African cultures considered iron, brass, bronze, and copper to have unique characteristics. For many peoples in West Africa, iron signified strength and resiliency, whereas brass, bronze, and copper were thought to have protective properties, which, in addition to being present in bundles, also explains why archaeologists have found nonferrous metal bracelets and other jewelry in African American burials (Davidson and McIlvoy 2012: 137–138; Fennell 2007: 61–62; Handler and Lange 1978: 125–127; Moses 2018: 145).

Iron objects are among the most deceptive items found in caches because when unearthed, they are usually unimpressive lumps of rust-colored corrosion. Many are so unidentifiable that X-rays must be used to determine what lies hidden within the misshapen mass (Leone et al. 2014: 207–208). When someone first buried the nails, the lengths of wire, and the other metal items in the soil, the objects still had their original shape and shiny appearance. They no longer looked the same when excavated, leading one to wonder whether the rusty, flaky lumps may have encouraged archaeologists to decide that the items were insignificant.

Archaeologists have discovered that African Americans also used ancient Native American artifacts as likely "house charms," in addition to putting them in bundles. Such amulets were designed to protect a dwelling's inhabitants (Davidson and McIlvoy 2012: 138–144; Leone et al. 2014: 208–209). A building inhabited by a Black family in Maryland was found to have had a stone ax incorporated into its stone foundation while eight quartz stone tools had been placed around the inside of the foundation (Schablitsky 2011: 58). Archaeologists have found similar stone artifacts at other dwellings associated with African Americans, both enslaved and free, throughout the Eastern Seaboard. Before Leone and Fry's in-depth look into the folklore accounts and archaeological reports, archaeologists excavating African American houses and yards often misidentified pre-Columbian arrowheads, spear points, axes, and other stone tools, thinking that past individuals had probably collected the artifacts as interesting curios (Orser 1985: 52). The power assumed to be locked inside ancient stone artifacts was made abundantly clear to a folklorist traveling through parts of the South a decade before Hurston. An "old conjure-doctor in Mississippi" told the collector that "the Indian arrowheads often found in the locality were not made by man at all, but were fashioned by God out of thunder and lightning" (Puckett 1926: 315).

The possible spiritual connection between some hoodoo beliefs and pre-Columbian Native American stone tools is perhaps further borne out by the practices of some Black Spiritualist churches in New Orleans. The roots of this religious tradition are thought to have begun with Mother Leafy Anderson, a woman who relocated from frigid Chicago to steamy New Orleans in 1918. She espoused a complex religion mixed with features from traditional American Protestantism, Pentecostalism, Roman Catholicism, nineteenth-century Spiritualism, and Caribbean voodoo (Wehmeyer 2007: 18–19). After Anderson established her church, 11 others quickly appeared in the city. Unlike Anderson's church, most of the others openly accepted hoodoo.

Leafy Anderson had several spirit guides, one of whom was Black Hawk, the famed freedom fighter from the Thakiwaki (Sauk/Sac) nation who fought against death and displacement at the hands of US forces in 1832. Some of New Orleans's spiritual churches, venerating Black Hawk for his efforts to protect his people, seek to call forth his spirit by chanting, touching his statue, or lighting candles in his honor (Wehmeyer 2000: 62–63). Altars dedicated to him are adorned with plastic tomahawks, spears, bows, and arrows (Hurston 1931: 320; Jacobs 1989: 54). Mother Anderson was not a hoodoo doctor, but the connection between the plastic artifacts and ancient specimens in buried bundles and house charms is intriguing.

Archaeologists have now discovered so many African American spiritual bundles that summarizing them all is far too tedious. Because the bundle was related to a specific individual, hoodoo practitioners used a wide variety of objects, in combination and alone. Any comprehensive list, no matter how seemingly complete, is likely to become obsolete after only one or two additional excavations.

Perhaps unsurprisingly, the sheer number of artifacts, in addition to their ordinary character (Reeves 2014), inadvertently contributed to the skepticism some archaeologists expressed about African-associated artifacts. This was the same incredulity Ferguson, Emerson, and others had faced over their interpretations. As one archaeologist complained, when it comes to the African presence in artifacts, the amassed evidence "is always prefaced by 'maybe,' 'might be,' and 'could be.'" Cautious hedges such as these encouraged this critic to conclude "So what?' It 'might be' a lot of things. Archaeologists will never know" (Steen 2011: 169). True, archaeologists will never know with perfect certainly. No one alive today will ever be able to work out the indisputable truth about every nuance of African American spiritual belief, or even daily life, expressed since the early seventeenth century. After all, most of what archaeologists have learned derives from largely undocumented sources like a cross-in-circle etched into a clay pot, stars on smoking pipes, irregular holes dug into cabin floors, and the magico-religious use of buttons, straight pins, and ordinary glass bottles. It is this uncertainty that forever challenges archaeologists, urging them to stockpile as much supportive evidence as possible to develop reasonable interpretations. The caveat, of course, is that what seems reasonable to us today may have nothing to do with what was thought reasonable in the past. When it comes to ritual bundles, however, the weight of the evidence most certainly points to African American practices.

The everyday nature of meaningful, ritualized objects associated with free and enslaved African Americans, rather than being a cause for skepticism, should be a reason for celebration. The use of ordinary household objects for ritual purposes makes abundant sense. The cross-in-circle on clay pots, meaningfully marked clay pipes, and objects with spiritual connotations each had special meanings known to the initiated. Considered as a group, the objects represent a united front of resistance, persistence, and belief—tiny expressions of defiance that laughed in the face of their oppressors. Slave owners and their associates were permitted the see the marked pots, decorated pipes, and red-flannel swatches, but they had no idea what they meant. Outsiders would never be able to fully judge or understand their profound significance. Oppression of the body does not necessarily mean the colonization of the mind.

That archaeologists have had a difficult time unraveling the subdued, hidden meanings of these objects is not surprising. Remarkably, even Charles Fairbanks, who specifically went looking for Africanisms, failed to recognize them when he excavated at Couper Plantation, the next stop in his search after Kingsley's (Davidson and McIlvoy 2012: 109). The cleverness of the objects' desperate meanings was never meant to be broadcast to one and all. Leone's initial confusion over the true meaning of the bundle found at the Charles Carroll House characterized archaeologists' views for many years. A stark example comes from the heart of New York City.

Beginning in 1983 and extending through the first frigid days of 1984, a team of archaeologists huddled under the bulky tents they had constructed over the sizable hole they had dug into the unforgiving, cold earth. Most people viewing archaeology from the outside might find the setting unusual. This dig was not taking place in the depths of a primeval jungle or on some windblown desert. No, this excavation was situated smack in the center of Lower Manhattan, one of America's most frenetic pieces of real estate. The New York City Landmarks Preservation Commission had hired archaeologists to scour the earth within the footprint of what would become yet another immense tooth jutting from the city's jagged skyline (Grossman 1985). The Broad Financial Center, at 33 Whitehall Street, was to be a 27-floor megalith of gleaming glass, a modern monument to finance, one that would unabashedly proclaim its right to occupy the spot in New York's gallery of steel leviathans.

Every great city in the world sits atop layer upon layer of earlier cities. Urban excavations for the deeply sunk foundations required to keep highrise apartments and office buildings upright often expose remnants of the past. In Mexico City, building contractors regularly come across evidence of the mighty Aztecs, and in London, construction teams often find traces of the conquering Romans. In Lower Manhattan, builders often unearth evidence of colonial Dutch settlers. Aware of the cultural value of New York's colonial history, the Landmarks Commission sent the archaeological team to the financial center's plot to ensure that no surprises were exposed at the business end of a backhoe.

The Dutch colonial empire first arrived in what is today's New York in 1609 when Henry Hudson, in the employ of the world-grasping Dutch East India Company, coaxed his tiny *Halve Maen* due north up the river that would soon bear his name (Fabend 2012; Shorto 2004). Thinking the waterway might be a shortcut to porcelain-rich Cathay, Europeans' name for China at the time, Hudson found not a sea lane to the East, but a staggeringly fertile land already occupied by Native peoples. By the early 1620s the Dutch had fully moved onto Manhattan Island and raised the wooden buildings of New Amsterdam, a tiny colonial outpost perched on a triangle of land poking into the Atlantic. The Dutch settlers marked the northern boundary of their embryonic settlement with a wooden palisade, or wall, strung across the entire breadth of the island along what is today Wall Street. As recorded at the time, the Dutch quickly established gardens and raised houses "according to each person's means and fancy" (Piwonka 2008: 405). The colonists also brought with them a few enslaved Africans, and by 1629 the newly formed Dutch West India Company had accepted the ugly responsibility of supplying captive African laborers to Dutch planters throughout the colonial world.

Unsurprisingly, because the Dutch always looked toward the sea (at home, they had wrested acres of land from the water's grip), the plots laid out along Manhattan's two rivers and near the docks were prime real estate. Voracious merchants and shippers, jostling with one another for economic supremacy, were willing to shoehorn their warehouses onto the river's edge. One such person was the enigmatic Cornelius van Tienhoven.

Van Tienhoven served as secretary to the Dutch colonial governor. As a powerful official representing New Amsterdam's administration at home and in the colony, Van Tienhoven fully accepted that Africans were innately suited to enslavement and that Africans in the colony could only be freed on condition that their children would remain enslaved (De Jong 1971: 431).

Attitudes about the natural suitability of Africans for enslavement was only one of van Tienhoven's attributes, for he was an especially dodgy character. Van Tienhoven and scandals were frequent companions, and any weekday was likely to find him standing before the court pleading his case. He was even involved in a sex scandal. While in Amsterdam on colony business and engaged in a torrid affair with Elysabeth Croon van Hooghvelt, the daughter of a basket maker, he failed to mention that he had a wife and children back in New Amsterdam. The secret love affair quickly became the subject of gossip, and before long van Tienhoven was arrested and standing before a judge once again. After paying his fine, both he and Elysabeth escaped across the ocean to New Amsterdam. In 1656 van Tienhoven mysteriously disappeared, never to be seen again. His hat and cane were found floating in the Hudson River, so many presumed that he had walked into the water or had simply fled before having to face another trial, this one for embezzlement. Elysabeth's fate is unrecorded, and van Tienhoven's end remains a colonial mystery (O'Callaghan 1856: 514–517).

The archaeologists hired by the Landmarks Commission were aware of van Tienhoven's checkered past, and they had done detailed research on the history of his warehouse's plot. Digging in an urban area, the team expected to find plenty of artifacts, and they were not disappointed. The collection totaled over 43,000 pieces of dishes, bottles, clay pipes, and hundreds of other things.

As the archaeologists smoothed out the soil in and around one of the Dutch-era stone foundations they had discovered, they noticed a perfectly circular dark stain in the soft brown soil. Uncertain about the stain's meaning, they decided to meticulously remove the earth from inside it, thinking its interior might hold the key to explaining the circle's past use. In doing so, they amassed an intriguing collection of artifacts. The largest item they found inside the stain was one half of a blue-and-white colonial Dutch dinner plate decorated in a Chinese pattern. The most numerous objects were 100 iron nails, but also in the circular hole were 6 pieces of other dishes, 17 marbles, 28 straight pins, 26 pieces of glass, and 4 clay pipe fragments. As they continued digging, the archaeologists also found an iron key, 2 pieces of round lead shot, 3 shell wampum beads, bird and fish bones, fish scales, mollusk shells, and flakes of stone and brick. At the bottom of the stain they found an almost intact round, wooden base with holes in it. Everything appeared to date to the late seventeenth century (Cantwell and Wall 2015: 41; Grossman 1985: x69–x70).

The sides of the pit presented the archaeologists with a puzzle. Around the meticulously excavated pit, they could see the telltale impressions of a coiled rope. This meant that the soil stain was what was all that remained of a deteriorated, cord-wrapped wooden barrel. Knowing that it was impossible to take the soil impression back to the lab for further study, the archaeologists created a mold of it. They poured a mixture of vulcanizing rubber into the hole, waited for it to set, and then removed a perfect model of the cord-wrapping that had once existed around the outside of the barrel.

The remarkable rubber duplicate remains today as all that is left to document the resting place of the assortment of artifacts retrieved from the soil stain. The archaeologists struggled to understand the meaning of the soil stain and its rope impression. Interpretations varied. Perhaps the holes in the wooden base and the marbles were from a long-forgotten Dutch game, or maybe the barrel and the holes were components of an ingenious colonial filtration system and the artifacts had simply been sucked into it. At the time of excavation, the realization that Africans in the United States made ritual bundles was still years away, and it would be another decade before archaeologists would begin to accept their magico-religious meaning. The large and growing number of examples from Texas to New York and from van Tienhoven's seventeenth-century warehouse to late-nineteenth-century sharecroppers' cabins became irrefutable. Remarkably, the jumble of artifacts from the cord-wrapped barrel had lain quietly dormant, misidentified for about 25 years.

More recently, archaeologists excavating at Levi Jordan's Texas plantation have called into question Brown's interpretation of the structural foundations found on the property (Ryan et al. 2022). The archaeologists argue that rather than constituting housing units for enslaved and later emancipated tenants, the buildings Brown unearthed were antebellum livestock barns. The new interpretation identifies what Brown and his team called fireplace foundations as the bases for heavy, roof-supporting beams.

This new interpretation, although intriguing, highlights the severe difficulties all archaeologists encounter when they attempt to offer lasting interpretations. New interpretations are always possible. The new understanding of the outbuilding's remains, however, neither negates Brown's interpretation of the artifacts as sacred objects nor damages the impact his findings had on the archaeological community. The discovery of the cache from Dutch New York City demonstrates that sacred bundles may not always have been secreted within living quarters. It now appears possible that some bundles may have been buried at places of work, just those locales where captive laborers have faced brutal work environments and harsh treatment.

In any case, by 2000 the case on Africanisms was seemingly closed. Archaeologists had finally recognized spiritual bundles as ironclad proof of the Africanisms they had sought since Fairbanks first stepped onto Kingsley Plantation. Identifying them was much more difficult than anyone had ever expected. When the archaeology of the African Diaspora was in its infancy, archaeologists generally underestimated the creativity of enslaved Africans and had miscalculated the amount of secrecy that captive Africans had to exercise to keep themselves and their families safe in a harsh and unforgiving world. The bundles document the resilience of the enslaved women and men and their tireless ability to pass spirituality on to future generations, even while living under the ever-watchful eye of their White captors.

Secrecy was a survival tactic that would serve enslaved African Americans well. The account of one nineteenth-century self-emancipated captive, Henry Bibb, offers ample illustration.

9

Secrets

Henry Bibb and the World of Subterfuge

At birth, Walton Bibb was already enslaved because his mother, Milly Jackson, was enslaved (Bibb 1849). The ambiguity of a life spent in bondage meant that Bibb, called Henry, was unsure of his birth year. He thought that it may have been 1815, but either late 1813 or early 1814 would do as well (Coon 2005). Owners of humanity considered captive Africans' birth dates irrelevant. What mattered was whether the enslaved was old enough to work but not too old or too young to be a financial burden.

Milldred Jackson (Henry always spelled her name with two ls) was probably born in Virginia in the late eighteenth century, perhaps in 1795. She gave birth to seven children, with Henry being the oldest. The next two oldest, George and Granville, were both given the surname White, and the next four children were called Jackson. Their surnames suggest their likely parentage because Bibb confessed that being "fathered by slaveholders," he, his mother, and his siblings all had "slaveholding blood flowing" through their veins (Bibb 1849: 14).

Bibb's first home was on a plantation in northern Kentucky owned by a William Butler. Because the estate was directly on the south bank of the Ohio River, the soil of freedom was tantalizingly near, just across the water in Indiana. Butler's was an unhappy place. Bibb asserted that he had been "flogged up" rather than raised and that he "drank deeply of the bitter cup of suffering and woe" from an early age. He knew nothing of his father. When Bibb asked about him, his mother identified James Bibb. Bibb was the maiden name of slave owner John Sibley's wife. But as Henry wearily admitted, "It is almost impossible for slaves to give a correct account of their male parentage" (Bibb 1849: 13–14).

Recoiling at the "utter helplessness in perpetual bondage," Bibb ran away at almost every opportunity. His first escape, in 1835, was from the home of a Mr. Vires, to whom he had been hired out. He was on his own for several days but was soon caught and returned. The whipping awaiting him did not quench his undying thirst for freedom, and when he ran off again, Vires sent him back home for good. While Henry was working for Vires, his new owner, named White, had married a "tyrant" who worked Bibb mercilessly. Bibb described her as "too lazy to scratch her own head" (Bibb 1849: 16). She demanded that he rock her in her rocking chair while he shooed away the flies. She also made him scratch her feet, and fan her while she napped. These daily indignities further imbued Bibb with the spirit of flight.

As he aged, Bibb became an ever-more accomplished escape artist. Sadly, his skill at avoiding capture was not as well honed, and every escape was followed by capture and some form of barbaric punishment. After pondering this cycle, Bibb realized that his problem would be solved if he carried a bridle with him when he fled. Then, when asked what he was doing out on his own, he could simply say that he was searching for the master's escaped livestock. This realization taught him that deception was his best "weapon of self defence" (Bibb 1849: 17).

In 1833 Henry, at 18, met a field hand named Malinda, who lived about four miles away. She was an excellent singer, and Bibb was soon captivated and fell in love. As they became closer, he confessed to her that his goal was to run away to Canada. Confiding that she had the same goal, she and Bibb agreed to marry, but only if they felt the same way toward one another in a year's time. If their strong feelings continued, they "would embrace the earliest opportunity of running away to Canada for our liberty" (Bibb 1849: 38).

Legal marriage for enslaved women and men was nonexistent. In the eyes of the law, they were mere chattel. A Kentucky statute made their legal status abundantly clear: "All negro, mulatto, or Indian slaves, in all courts of judicature and other places within this commonwealth, shall be held, taken and adjudged to be real estate" (Littell and Swigert 1822: 1155). In quiet defiance of this unjust law, Henry and Malinda took vows during the Christmas holiday and from then on considered themselves married. Their unlicensed union came with all the humiliations inherent within slavery: they lived on separate plantations miles apart and Bibb was only permitted to visit her on Saturday nights.

A few months into their marriage, Albert Sibley, the Bibbs' new owner, decided to sell his estate and move west to Missouri. To his good fortune, Sibley sold him to Malinda's owner, meaning that for the first time he and

Malinda could live together. Malinda soon gave birth to a daughter they named Mary Frances.

Chafing under the stress of being an enslaved husband and father, Bibb found it increasingly galling to stand by and watch his wife suffer the many humiliations that accompanied involuntary servitude. His attitude grew even darker when the owner's wife began to physically abuse Mary Frances. Henry's owner may also have raped Malinda because Bibb (1849: 43) alluded to an act "so violently and inhumanly committed upon the person of a female."

By 1837 Bibb had determined, despite his love for Malinda and Mary Frances, that he had to escape to Canada. He began to save what little money he could scrape together, and with a bank roll of less than "two dollars and fifty cents," he set off on Christmas Day. It took "all the moral courage" he could muster to leave his small family behind (Bibb 1849: 46).

Using the ruse that he could find work in a slaughterhouse at high wages just to the north, Bibb was able to reach the Ohio River. His owner allowed him to go knowing that he would seize Bibb's pay when he returned. In open defiance, Bibb avoided the slaughterhouse and instead found "a conveyance" to cross the river to Madison, Indiana. Setting his feet on free soil, Bibb was truly unchained for the first time. He found a hiding place, changed into the clothes he had carried with him, and waited for a steamboat to chug by on its way to Cincinnati. After a while, a steamer passed and slowly sidled up to Madison's dock. With all the courage he could muster, Bibb decided to step on board as if he had every right to do so. Being light skinned, he was able to burrow into the crowd of White men idling on deck and avoid discovery. Although pleased with his deception, Bibb was disgusted that his light skin had aided in his freedom. He acidly remarked that slave owners had "not only robbed me of my labor and liberty, but they have almost entirely robbed me of my dark complexion" (Bibb 1849: 49).

Bibb spent an uneasy night, but in the morning the boat docked in Cincinnati. He was one step closer to Canada; he had acquired the name of a helpful Black man and was soon directed to his house. Being wary of strangers, Bibb was uncertain whether the man was in favor of Black self-emancipation. To be safe, he lied to the man saying that he had arrived in Cincinnati only for Christmas and that he would soon return to Kentucky. The man, named Job Dundy, told Bibb he would never go back if he were Bibb, and advised him to go to Canada instead. It was then that Bibb first learned of the Underground Railroad. Enlightening him, Dundy revealed the existence of abolitionists and abolition societies and of the means one could use to escape to Canada.

Stunned by the information, Bibb assumed that abolitionists must be "a different race of people," a strange culture that accepted human freedom as a right. Dundy led him "to the house of one of these warm-hearted friends of God and the slave" (Bibb 1849: 51).

Invigorated with the knowledge that he was not alone in this quest for freedom, and fed a good meal, Bibb went on his way, using the North Star as his guide. After 48 hours, he reached the house of another abolitionist. With every step forward, he was gripped with intense fear over the likelihood that vicious dogs and venomous slave catchers were closing in on him. Such vile men would happily return him to slavery and cheerfully accept the reward money.

On his second night north of Cincinnati, Bibb was exhausted, cold, and starving. Feeling faint, he approached a farmhouse for help but was shooed away. Continuing northward, he soon found a humble cottage with a table spread for breakfast. Approaching the woman of the house, Bibb agreed to pay her sixpence for a slice of bread and meat. She refused the money but handed him the food anyway. Bibb was on the road again and before long he was near Bowling Green, where he decided to spend the night at a tavern. Realizing he had already spent his meager funds, he informed the tavern's landlady that, being a cook, he could help her feed the large number of travelers who had unexpectedly arrived. The woman was so pleased with Bibb's work that the next day she offered to hire him for the winter. Fearing recapture if he stayed, he refused her offer, lying that he was eager to unite with his brother in Detroit.

Continuing the trek north, Bibb came to Perrysburg on the Maumee River just south of Toledo, where he found a community of once-enslaved African Americans. Welcoming him, they persuaded him to stay through the winter, telling him that in spring he could catch the steamboat north. Bibb took a job chopping firewood, and with his pockets growing heavy for the first time, he was able to buy a suit of clothes and to save $50 (over $1,000 today). Bibb planned to use this money to go back to Kentucky and rescue his wife. His new-found friends urged him not to go back, pleading with him to hire someone to go in his place. Bibb stubbornly believed that only he could accomplish his wife's release, so he determined to retrace his steps back into the land of enslavement.

The condition of American banking in the late 1830s was such that money from one place was not always accepted someplace else, so Bibb took the steamboat to Detroit, where he used his treasured $50 to buy dry goods. Planning to sell them on his way back though Ohio, he reasoned that upon arrival he would have enough hard currency to purchase Malinda and Mary Frances. As a precaution, he bought a pair of false whiskers as a disguise.

Having eventually reached Cincinnati, Bibb went to the home of the friends who had initially helped him escape. Like the residents of Perrysburg, they too advised him not to return to Kentucky. But being who he was, he thought, "it has ever been characteristic of me to persevere in what I undertake" (Bibb 1849: 57). He then booked passage on a steamboat and landed that night near Bedford, Kentucky, where his mother was working as a tavern's cook. Remembering that she slept in the kitchen, Bibb rapped on the window, awakening her. She at first failed to recognize him through the false whiskers, but when he took them off, they embraced in happiness. To his surprise, Malinda and Mary Frances were also there. Malinda had begun her own effort to escape. After moments of intense joy, Bibb and Malinda laid plans for her and her daughter's escape. Agreeing that she and the child should leave on Saturday night, Bibb gave her money for a steamboat ticket from Madison, Indiana, to Cincinnati, Ohio. The plan was for her to go to the river on Saturday night and cross if a boat was there to meet her. If no boatman appeared or no boat was on shore, she was to try again the following Saturday. Until then, she should stay on the plantation and make it appear that nothing unusual was being planned.

Bibb left Malinda on Wednesday night and, winding his way back to the Ohio River, discovered a small boat chained to a tree. Freeing the boat, he quietly paddled across the river and went straight to the home of his abolitionist friends. They asked why his family had not come with him, which in hindsight was an excellent question, but Bibb apprised them of his plan. They encouraged him, once Malinda and Mary Frances met him in Cincinnati, to take the first stagecoach to Lake Erie rather than risk being trapped by slave catchers during the long, exhausting walk north. Since Bibb lacked the money for three stagecoach tickets from one end of Ohio to the other, his friends started a collection. As donors began to arrive at the house, many of them asked Bibb searching questions: did he need their help to escape? how could someone as white as him be a slave? what was the name of his master? Bibb was disturbed by these questions because he knew that hiding among the abolitionists could be "traitors or land pirates," men both White and Black who made their living as slave hunters. True enough, word of Bibb's location was soon on its way south, where the informants received a $300 reward (about $8,000 today). As Bibb wryly observed, "This being the last and only chance for dragging me back into hopeless bondage, time and money was no object when they saw a prospect of my being retaken" (Bibb 1849: 61).

William H. Gatewood, Malinda's owner, fearing she would try to follow Bibb north, lied to her, saying that abolitionists had convinced Bibb to run away and instead of helping him, they had shipped him off in chains to New Orleans. He claimed that instead of crossing the Ohio River, Bibb was really on his way deeper into the diseased heart of enslavement. Malinda accepted the lie and so decided not to follow Bibb's plan.

Knowing Bibb's true location, Gatewood encouraged two of his neighbors to accompany his son to Cincinnati to recapture Bibb. Upon reaching the city, the three-man posse rallied around them a mob of ruffians willing to do the dirty work of the slaveholders. By then Bibb had gotten a job digging a cellar under a woman's house. Unaware of the impending danger, he was hard at work when the slave catchers entered the house and discovered him. Realizing his dire situation, Bibb tried to run past the nearest man, who threatened to shoot him. Before the man could take aim and fire, Bibb had broken free and was attempting to jump a fence when the posse pounced on him. He violently fought back, but his situation was hopeless.

Bibb's captors roughly led him to "a justice office," a place Bibb viewed as "more like an office of injustice" (Bibb 1849: 64). There he was met by the three Kentucky slave owners. Several people, including many African Americans, having seen Bibb pushed through the streets, had crowded into the small room. The show of support for Bibb convinced the enslavers that staying in the city overnight was not a good idea. Knowing that a steamboat was scheduled to depart in two or three hours, they had Bibb locked in the local jail. This was his first experience with imprisonment.

Later that night and under the guard of the three slaveholders and two hired men, Bibb was shoved on board a steamboat heading for Louisville. As the boat slid by the bend in the river near Malinda's home, Bibb (1849: 66) reflected on his condition as "a wretched victim for Slavery without limit." He likened himself to an ox, a being to be used, lashed, and worked to death.

As the steamboat slowly lumbered down the Ohio River, Bibb began to calculate what his escape had cost Gatewood. He arrived at the figure of just over $1,200, or over $33,000 today. The large amount told Bibb that selling him was the only way Gatewood could recoup his money. Keeping Bibb on the plantation with his wife and daughter was not an option because Bibb had proven himself to be an incorrigible escape artist. He determined to flee once more when he realized that he might end up being sold to the death-dealing Deep South or even into the lethal sugar fields of the Caribbean.

In Louisville, Gatewood hired a notorious slave catcher to guard Bibb while he and the others scoured the city for potential buyers. Before long, the men returned with two slaveholders interested in Bibb. Upon seeing him, the two said that he had the look of a runaway. The slave catcher, knowing that runaways were worth less money, swore that Bibb had never run away in his life. But before the sale could be completed, Bibb bolted for the door. By running fast and jumping fences, he was able to elude the pursuing slave catcher, but as he ran, he realized that a Black man running through the streets of a slave city was not a good look. His fear of being shot in the back convinced him not to move during the day, so he found a pile of boards and, crawling under it, found refuge.

When it grew dark, Bibb was ready to move on, but finding himself in a strange city on a dark night, he felt "like a person entering a wilderness among wolves and vipers, blindfolded" (Bibb 1849: 76). Bibb was 40 miles south of Malinda and Mary Francis's home on Gatewood's plantation, but on the upside, the estate was on the way to Canada.

Bibb was able to reach Gatewood's plantation, but by this time Gatewood's son had returned and reported that Bibb had once again escaped. Gatewood was forced to offer another reward.

Word quickly spread through the area that Bibb had escaped from Louisville. Everyone on the estate, Whites and some Blacks, eyed Malinda suspiciously, looking for signs that she had been in contact with him. The intense surveillance convinced Bibb that he must once again leave for Canada by himself, but he found it distressing to desert Malinda and Mary Frances.

That night Bibb climbed on board a steamboat but disembarked before it reached Cincinnati. He knew that armed slave hunters would be guarding the city's docks waiting for him. Walking quickly to his friends' house, Bibb learned that the two men who had betrayed him were also back in the city. Eluding them, he retraced his steps north to Perrysburg, the home of his fellow runaways. He waited in their settlement for nine months, hoping that Malinda would appear. When she failed to arrive, he made the momentous decision to go back to Kentucky for one last attempt to rescue her and Mary Frances.

Bibb followed the same route back to Kentucky, met with his mother again, and told her of his rescue plan. A young enslaved girl overheard their discussion and informed on Bibb, so that when he went to Malinda's house, he discovered several men with dogs walking around the house. Meeting in secret, he and Malinda once again hatched an escape strategy. The danger was great because the area's slave owners offered a reward to any slave who would betray them. Bibb had found a hiding place in a nearby barn, but a mob of slave owners soon appeared and surrounded it, shouting that they would shoot him if he resisted or ran. Once again, "the grim monster slavery with all its horrors" stared directly in his face (Bibb 1849: 87). The men captured him and, rifling through his pockets, stole $14, a silver watch, a pocketknife, and a Bible. His captors dragged him to a blacksmith shop, where they clapped irons on his arms and legs and took him to jail. This was his second imprisonment, and he would remain incarcerated until someone agreed to buy him.

On the third day of his confinement, the jailer removed him, and along with Malinda and Mary Frances, who had also been captured, and sent them to the Louisville slave market. After spending time in jail, Bibb was in rough condition. The sellers at the market put him on one horse and Malinda and Mary Frances on another. Bibb's feet were manacled together under the horse's belly. When the horse reared and Bibb was thrown off, his appearance became even worse, and no one wanted to purchase him or the small family. Unsold, the three were thrown into a jail swarming with bed bugs, fleas, lice, and mosquitoes. After a couple of days Bibb and his family were moved to an impregnable brick workhouse, a prison with high walls and two rows of small cells. Women were housed on the upper floor and men on the lower. Bibb was shocked by the appearance of the heavily shackled men, Black and White, who were busy breaking rocks and sawing stones. For the first time in his life, he was surrounded by society's most desperate gamblers, drunkards, thieves, robbers, murderers, and pickpockets. As he surveyed the conditions around him, Bibb (1849: 94) realized that "no man would give much for a slave who had been kept long in one of these prisons." Nonetheless, a sadistic man named Garrison bought Bibb, Malinda, and Mary Frances with the intention of selling them at the infamous slave market in New Orleans.

The family was duly marched off to the Ohio River and on the way to New Orleans. They stayed in Vicksburg for three weeks while Garrison searched for buyers. It was there that Bibb was first examined by slave inspectors. Treating him like a horse, they peered into his mouth, studied the back of his hands, and examined his bare back for scars, the telltale sign of a habitual absconder. The inspectors' most complicated job was to assess a captive's mental ability, while the enslaved individual's challenge was not to appear too smart because intelligence "lays the foundation for running away, and going to Canada" (Bibb 1849: 102). Inspectors also believed that intelligence led to insurrection, bloodshed, and the eventual death of slavery itself. They were especially determined to discover whether an enslaved man or woman could read or write because they viewed these skills as especially dangerous weapons.

While in Vicksburg, Garrison was intent on selling Bibb and his family but was unable to find a buyer. Bibb soon found himself standing on the docks of steamy New Orleans, with Garrison looking to offload him at any price. Every day precisely at 10 o'clock, Bibb and the other captives would be herded onto the public auction block. They stood in a line as potential buyers measured their every feature and asked probing questions. Captives who did not answer quickly or correctly and went unsold were later beaten with a hickory paddle. Enslavers realized that marks left by the lash would reduce prices, whereas marks from a paddle would be much more difficult to identify during a quick inspection.

The small Bibb family stayed in the New Orleans slave prison for several months without being sold. Fed up with trying to get rid of him, Garrison finally told Bibb to wander through New Orleans and find his own buyer. Garrison advised him to visit hotels, taverns, and boarding houses with the message that he was a good servant, driver, or porter and that his wife was a good cook, washerwoman, or servant. Being sold as a pair was the only way Bibb and Malinda could remain together and keep Mary Francis. So Bibb, dressed in Garrison's cast-off clothes, roamed the streets of New Orleans for several weeks, but without success.

One day Bibb learned that a Baptist deacon and cotton planter from northern Louisiana named Whitfield was in the city looking to buy laborers. Bibb approached the man, who showed interest in him, and when asked whether he could read and write, Bibb said no. Whitfield remained cautious because he thought Bibb was "a little too near white" (Bibb 1849: 109). The man inquired whether Bibb had ever run away, and Bibb, knowing he was not under oath, said yes, but only for one month. He did not mention Ohio or Canada. Whitfield was impressed enough to purchase Bibb and his small family.

Upon reaching Whitfield's estate, Bibb was appalled by the laborers' half-starved and ragged condition. The food allowance was pitiful. Every week each enslaved person received only a peck of corn, one pound of pork, and sometimes a quart of molasses. Anything else they had to steal, hunt, or trap for themselves. The accepted wisdom among "enlightened" slave owners at the time was that each enslaved captive should receive "a peck of meal, four pounds of good meat, with such vegetables, potatoes, peas, etc., as can be provided without any expense" (A Citizen of Mississippi 1847: 420). Whitfield, obviously not "enlightened," was scrimping on meat and vegetables, both required for vitality and general good health. Prosperous slave owners understood the delicate balance they had to strike between the cost of food and the nutrition the enslaved needed to maintain their demanding work schedules. Weak men and women were unable to work as long or as hard as those who were well fed and healthy.

Careless slave owners like Whitfield may have realized that his negligence simply meant that undernourished workers had to be out in the woods at night gathering plants and hunting animals to supplement their poor diets. The discovery of domestic and wild animal bones and seeds at excavated house sites demonstrates that enslaved men and women, often toiling from sunup to sundown for the owner's benefit, would by necessity also have to work throughout much of the night (Crader 1990; Scott 2001). Many owners allowed their captive laborers to keep tiny garden plots, but these required tilling, weeding, and harvesting, all of which had to be done during precious moments of "free time." Even the allotments of food required work. As Bibb observed (Bibb 1849: 117), the "corn they had to grind on a hand mill for bread stuff, or pound it in a mortar." All this extra work meant that many enslaved workers could not fall into their beds until midnight or later, only to be jolted awake before dawn by a bellowing overseer or his clanging bell.

Bibb discovered that Whitfield's captives labored from first light until after dark with only a half-hour break at noon, including on Sundays. The seven-day work week proved to Bibb, along with the many beatings, that his Baptist owner was more devil than deacon. Whitfield's cruelty even required new mothers to take their infants into the fields with them and lay them on the ground during working hours. Some young mothers tied their babies to nearby shade trees, and others left them in clusters of high weeds.

The poor treatment and neglect led to Malinda having a near-fatal illness and the death of their second child. Bibb had to dig the child's grave and bury it without a coffin or even a box.

One Sunday, Bibb asked the deacon for permission to attend a prayer meeting at a nearby plantation. The deacon agreed and Bibb attended the meeting without difficulty. When he returned, he told his fellow captives about the meeting and encouraged them to accompany him to the next one. They agreed and asked Whitfield for the necessary permission slips. He refused, saying that no one could attend. Bibb went anyway.

Upon his return, a tearful Malinda told Bibb that Whitfield was furious that he had defied him and gone to the meeting. The deacon sent his overseer to find Bibb, but the meeting had adjourned when he arrived, and Bibb was already gone. Whitfield ordered the overseer to stake Bibb, when found, to the ground and give him 500 lashes. Seeking to avoid a possibly fatal punishment, Bibb determined to steal a mule and a saddle and escape. After less than 10 miles, he found the mule to be troublesome and possibly dangerous if anyone heard it braying. On his second night away and while camping in a cane break by the Red River, the mule heard nearby horses' hooves on the road and began to bray and struggle to break free. Bibb decided this situation was far too perilous, so he returned the mule that night. When he quietly slipped into Malinda's cabin, she told him that Whitfield was intent on punishing him. Stealing the mule was a capital offense, but Bibb concluded that if he himself was a piece of real estate like the mule, then his taking the animal was the same as if two mules had gone off together (Bibb 1849: 121). He appreciated that this bit of logic would not save him, so he and Malinda decided to take Mary Frances and leave that night.

The small family wandered through the neighborhood swamps and ate whatever they could gather as they sought to find a way across the Red River. Searching up and down the riverbank, they eventually found a way across. Before long, they heard the howls of the bloodhounds and knew that slave catchers were on their trail. Malinda and Bibb, with his daughter in his arms, tried to flee, but it was hopeless, and they were recaptured.

As expected, Whitfield had Bibb staked to the ground and given over 50 lashes and several whacks with a wooden paddle. The overseer then washed Bibb's back with salt brine.

The punishment left Bibb unable to work for several days, but during this time Whitfield had him taken to a blacksmith's shop where they affixed a heavy iron collar around his neck. The collar had prongs extending over his head; each prong had a small, attached bell. Bibb was forced to wear the tinkling instrument of torture for six weeks.

The punishment only deepened Bibb's defiance, and throughout these ordeals he continued to learn to write and dream of escape. Soon after his release from the collar he and another captive, a man named Jack, decided to run away. Traveling by night they headed toward Little Rock, Arkansas. When they reached a large plantation they saw an enslaved female cook walking from the planter's house to the kitchen. Jack decided to see if the woman would give them food.

Bibb knew that revealing themselves was risky because "domestic slaves are often found to be traitors to their own people, for the purpose of gaining favor with their masters" (Bibb 1849: 136). He was aware that owners encouraged them to report every developing plot, whether it concerned stealing, running away, or merely disobedience. Although filled with its own daily horrors and humiliations, on average, domestic work was less physically demanding than fieldwork or industrial labor. Tending a slave owner's fireplace might be demeaning, but it was not as physically demanding as the back-breaking labor of harvesting cotton in the broiling southern sun or stirring a pot of boiling cane syrup. Bibb remembered the humiliation he felt when he was forced to scratch his languid owner's feet. Bibb recognized that the imposed division of labor between the field and the house was one of the main reasons that the enslaved were divided among themselves. He guessed that without the division, the slave regime would not last longer than one year. True to form, Jack was betrayed, and he and Bibb were forced to run for their lives.

Bibb and Jack tried to get food at another plantation. Jack left Bibb behind and returned shortly with a bag of suckling pigs he had strangled and stolen. With this bounty in hand, they continued their trek north, and soon found a white hat sitting in the middle of the road. A short distance beyond it they saw a man lying in the road either drunk or asleep. Jack, having only the remnants of a hat, decided to take the new-found white one. After walking a short distance, they were accosted by five armed men who appeared suddenly from the woods. The men were after the $50 reward for Bibb, payable whether he was dead or alive. Bibb learned that the slave catchers had been alerted by the man who had lost the hat. Upon awakening, the man had seen the old hat and the tracks of two men, whom he guessed were runaways. The slave hunters soon took Bibb and Jack back to Whitfield, who had them hogtied and flogged.

After several more escapes and trials, Bibb eventually made it to Jefferson City, Missouri, where he hoped to either cross the Missouri River or hop on board a steamboat. Boarding a steamboat was ripe with danger because if he claimed he was free, he would have to show papers to prove it. If enslaved, he would be required to present his owner's permission slip. Either way, Bibb needed proof of his legal status to board the boat. No ship captain would dare take a Black man down the river to St. Louis without first inspecting his papers. Bibb's first thought was to have himself boxed up and shipped to St. Louis, but this was impossible because he had no friends in town who could help him. He then decided to pass himself off as a servant for one of the well-to-do passengers he had seen at the town's hotel. When the steamboat blew its shrill whistle announcing its impending departure, Bibb hoisted his newly purchased trunk on his back and followed the wealthy White passengers up the gangplank. His subterfuge worked, and as the boat backed away from the dock and pointed downriver to St. Louis, he heaved a momentary sigh of relief. He knew he was far from safe because the porter would eventually work his way through the ship ringing his bell and requiring passengers to show their tickets (Bibb 1849: 167).

Nineteenth-century steamboat travel reflected the era's class system. Riders who could afford to pay double fare, between $6 and $8 ($172 to $237 today), could enjoy a relaxing and calm journey, spending the days in upper-deck, private cabins. They would dine and drink in rooms as well appointed as those in St. Louis's finest hotels. Passengers who could afford only the minimum fare, about $3 or $4, had a much different experience. Boxes and bales of freight, rather than passengers' fares, made up the bulk of a steamboat owners' profits, so they were more concerned with cargo than with second-class riders. Owners gave steamboat captains explicit orders to allow the first-class passengers to board first. These were the men and women Bibb had stealthily followed up the gangway. After these travelers were safely on board, the crew would then load the cargo and livestock on the bottom deck. Only after each was properly stowed would the deck passengers be allowed on board. These low-fare riders had to find available space to stand among the stacks of barrels, the bales of cotton, and the bodies of skittish cows and horses. The deck passengers' trips were crowded, uncomfortable, and dirty. Soot and ash from the boat's smokestacks floated in the air and the muck from the livestock made the deck slippery (Lieffring 2019).

Bibb deposited his empty trunk outside one of the first-class cabin doors as if it belonged to the occupant, found the stairs, and descended to the deck to stand among the low-fare passengers, many of whom were Irish immigrants. Noticing that they were drinking whiskey, Bibb joined in and started buying rounds. When it appeared that the porter was making his way toward them, Bibb asked one of the Irishmen if he would buy his ticket when the man purchased his. The man, grateful for the free drinks, agreed and Bibb, with his ticket in hand, had an uneventful trip to St. Louis.

The colonial French founders of St. Louis had situated the city on bluffs high above the Mississippi River, away from the danger of the treacherous river's recurring floods. They saw the city not as a western doorway but as the northernmost Caribbean outpost of the French Empire (Berger 2015:

19–15). It was westward-gazing Americans who had designated the city the gateway to the West. In the 1840s, when Bibb arrived, the city still had a palpable Gallic atmosphere. Many houses were built with Acadian features, including truncated hipped roofs, cedar shingles, and verandas wrapping around at least two sides. Where the plaster had peeled off walls, passersby could see the buildings' upright posts and the small stones and pieces of straw that the houses' French builders had embedded in the mortar for added strength and insulation. The occasional house still had its wooden palisade of small posts encircling it. The city was a multicultural amalgam of people and languages: French and American fur traders, Indigenous men and women from many nations, free and enslaved African Americans, and rough-hewn boatmen from almost everywhere (Arenson 2009). Directly across the river was the massive earthen mound at Cahokia, Illinois, constructed over generations by an ancient and long-deceased Native culture.

Upon reaching this bustling city, Bibb determined to catch a steamboat to Cincinnati, from which he would once again begin his journey north to Canada. He found a boat going that day to Pittsburgh, and upon getting on board he discovered a Black steward he had met in Cincinnati in 1838. As the boat slowly chugged into the Ohio River, Bibb was saddened by the sight of enslaved men and women on the Kentucky riverbank "still toiling under their task-masters without pay" (Bibb 1849: 170).

When the captain had maneuvered the boat to the dock at the river town of Portsmouth, Ohio, Bibb once again hoisted his trunk on his back and crossed the gangway to freedom. Having no money in his pockets, he hired himself out to the proprietor of the American Hotel as a porter for $12 a month in wages.

In Portsmouth he met J. W. Smith, a man he had known in Perrysburg. Smith was planning to drive a herd of Kentucky-bred horses back north. Bibb agreed to join him, and they made the over 200-mile drive without incident. After arriving in Perrysburg, Bibb decided to head for Detroit, which he did in January 1842. His long ordeal was finally over. Bibb settled across the Detroit River in Sandwich, now Windsor, Ontario, where he created *The Voice of the Fugitive,* the first Black newspaper in Canada (Stanton 2001).

Bibb was able to rescue his mother from enslavement, but he never saw Malinda again. She had decided to live with another man, undoubtedly for security and to gain some affection in the brutal, unforgiving world around her. In June 1848 Bibb married a Bostonian named Mary E. Miles. In the early 1850s Bibb and his mother were reunited with three of his brothers in Sandwich.

Bibb was convinced that his tale sounded so fantastic that readers would think he invented it. His belief was justified because, being written during the era of American enslavement, advocates of slavery were likely to argue that formerly enslaved authors had created bizarre stories to prove the institution's inherent brutality. To them, it was simple: Bibb, like Frederick Douglass and the other self-emancipated writers, were liars. They countered that Bibb's articulate narrative must have been written by a White person because those once enslaved were not smart enough to write an entire book. And, anyway, enslaved men and women were not legally permitted to read and write. Their case was strengthened by Bibb's acknowledgment that he had gotten only about three weeks of formal education after reaching Detroit. To White supremacists, his much-read book was a simple example of antislavery propaganda.

Anticipating the potential misuse of the book, the Detroit Liberty Association appointed a committee of three men to investigate the truth of Bibb's account. They wrote a series of letters to people Bibb had mentioned in the text, and after receiving their replies, the committee concluded that the book contained no inconsistencies or falsehoods. They determined that readers could hold his account in "public confidence and high esteem" (Bibb 1849: ii–x).

Bibb's remarkable story, although compelling, seems irrelevant to the cross-in-circles, decorated tobacco pipes, subterranean pits, and ritual bundles discovered by archaeologists. On one level, little similarity exists. Nowhere in Bibb's account does he mention any of the objects explored in this book. His account is an extraordinary tale of one man's struggle to escape the cruelty of perpetual enslavement, but on the surface perhaps little else seems relevant.

If we look deeper, however, it becomes apparent that Bibb's series of trials share a strong connection to the objects archaeologists have unearthed and associated with enslaved African Americans. The link comes via the dual concepts of resistance and secrecy. Viewed this way, Bibb's account is dramatically pertinent because his story is brimming with subterfuge, lies, and secrets.

Social psychologists agree that people living in conditions of oppression find numerous ways to deal with the everyday stresses that subjugation entails. Beleaguered men and women caught within the monstrous grasp of enslavement invent, through necessity, hundreds of ways to struggle against their bondage. Some ways are seen and obvious; others are hidden and obscure (Ayanian et al. 2021; Cortland et al. 2017).

The range of resistance for enslaved African Americans extended from simple acts of defiance, like willfully forgetting how to chop wood or being unusually clumsy with the family's expensive porcelain, to open rebellion, the act of seizing control with the goal of self-emancipation. In between, but just short of revolt, was absconding. Running away was a constant threat that not only proved costly to the captive's owner but also undermined the entire foundation of the institution of African enslavement (Orser and Funari 2001; Sayers 2014; Weik 2012). It also belied the idea that Black individuals were naturally submissive, something abundantly clear in Bibb's life story.

Most students of African American enslavement accept the proposition that enslaved women and men found numerous ways to resist their condition (Rodriguez 2006; Walters 2015), but resistance was not always accepted, even among professional historians. There was a time when reputable American historians completely rejected the idea that enslaved Africans were capable of defiance or any kind of collective resistance. In the late nineteenth century, James Schouler (1882) wrote an authoritative seven-volume history of the United States. A Harvard-educated lawyer, Schouler had taught at two of the country's most prestigious private universities, Johns Hopkins and Boston University. Law students and those already in the profession respected Schouler's many books on American jurisprudence. In addition to his prominence as a legal scholar, Schouler was also a respected historian, having served in 1897 as the president of the American Historical Association, the oldest professional organization of historians.

In his history, Schouler depicted African Americans using terms that were then generally accepted by many White scholars but were extremely negative and racist. In keeping with much of the dominant society's thinking about human diversity, he described enslaved African Americans as characterized by "innate patience, docility, and childlike simplicity." The enslaved, he wrote, exhibited an "almost canine" attachment to a kind master or mistress, such that the compassionate treatment they received would be enough "to make a dog's life happy." He assured readers that enslaved men and women were "musical, imaginative, dramatic" and wished to excel "in oratory" (Schouler 1882: 236). Schouler's bigoted picture of African Americans tried to make it clear that sustained rebellion or resistance would have been impossible for such "childlike" people.

Diatribes like Schouler's were as much political as they were scholarly. He used his prejudiced reading of history to affirm the racist policies of his time.

The failure of large-scale insurrections does not mean that enslaved men and women did not rebel (Aptheker 1943). The truth is far more interesting because, as archaeological research clearly demonstrates, quiet mutinies were an everyday occurrence.

The easiest kind of resistance to recognize is overt expression. Overt resistance occurs when an individual or group behaves in a manner that is perceived as rebellious by both the targets of the action and those observing it (Hollander and Einwohner 2004: 545). Revolts by the enslaved involving firearms, taking possession of a slaveholding estate or a slaving ship, or seizing hostages are obvious acts of overt resistance. The targets, the holder or transporter of captive Africans, recognize the threat, just as do the observers, journalists, and other writers eventually recounting the particulars of the event. These were the mass uprisings that inspired legislatures throughout the United States to enact harsh laws severely restricting the rights of men and women of African heritage. As Du Bois (1896: 80–81) cogently observed about one rebellion in particular, "The wild revolt of despised slaves, the rise of a noble black leader, and the birth of a new nation of Negro freemen frightened the pro-slavery advocates and armed the anti-slavery agitation." Open rebellions suggested that thousands of enslaved Africans and African Americans could find or create ways to free themselves from bondage.

Covert resistance is much trickier to identify (Bauer and Bauer 1942: 389). This kind of resistance is intentional on the part of resistors, but it goes unnoticed or misunderstood by its targets and as a result often goes unpunished. Observers also tend not to notice the disobedience (Hollander and Einwohner 2004: 545). The lack of written documentation proves that plantation owners, other enslavers, visitors, and journalists failed to notice colonoware, the cross-in-circle, decorated pipes, subfloor pits, and ritual bundles. An additional group of observers are archaeologists, and it took years for these "delayed observers" to recognize what they were seeing.

Henry Bibb's extraordinary life in enslavement reveals that he engaged in both overt and covert resistance. As an open resistor, he ran away whenever the opportunity presented itself, crossed the Ohio River, fled from his captors in Louisville, and attended a banned prayer meeting. He also wore a fake beard and frequently lied to his oppressors. But Bibb was also skilled at covert resistance. He realized that the simple act of carrying a bridle could free him from suspicion. He could even get secretly married and learn to read and write.

In at least two cases Bibb was forced to use a mixture of overt and covert resistance. His many escapes, which were out in the open, caused William Gatewood to spend several thousand dollars on his recapture. And when Bibb wanted to board the steamboat at Jefferson City, Missouri, he hoisted a trunk and lugged it up the gangway on behalf of his supposed White owners. The act of shouldering the trunk was an overt act, but the reasons behind it were strictly covert because he was exploiting the racist White American assumption that being a beast of burden was the proper role for a healthy Black man.

Every action Bibb took during his many escapes involved various degrees of secrecy. His activities are in sync with meanings behind colonoware, decorated pipes, subfloor pits, and concealed bundles. Marked colonoware and pipes, subterranean holes dug in the floors of cabins, and carefully assembled and concealed clusters of unlikely objects were secret storehouses of resistance. Tobacco pipes and colonoware pots were in plain sight, but White slaveholders, plantation visitors, and journalists must either have viewed them as insignificant or failed to notice them at all. Their racist ideology, embedded in restrictive laws and upheld by distorted histories, assured them that Africans and African Americans were too simple minded to inscribe meaningful symbols on artifacts or that their symbols and actions could have profound substance. The subfloor pits and bundles were covert elements of resistance, but each required secrecy because they were dangerous to the dominant society's status quo. Secrecy might also be required to protect against those enslaved individuals who, as Bibb recognized, had decided that their best chance for survival rested in their having agreed to serve as informers.

Secrecy is as old as humanity, so anthropologists have been obsessed with secrets from the beginning. Field ethnographers, starting in the mid-nineteenth century with Lewis Henry Morgan, have been asking people around the world about their secret societies, their rituals, and the mysterious nuances of their kinship systems (Jones 2014: 60–62). Archaeologists have been less concerned with secrets per se, with the caveat that much of what they find has remained secret until discovered.

Social scientists are interested in secrets because having a secret is a social act requiring at least two people: the secret-keeper and the person or persons kept from knowing the secret. The process seems straightforward, but social psychologists say that keeping secrets is not as simple as it may appear. Secret-keeping is hard work. It requires acute mental awareness and serious deliberation. Success comes in the form of a performance, the deliberate act of concealing the truth without appearing to do so. Mental gymnastics are required to ensure that verbal and nonverbal behaviors do not unconsciously reveal the secret. As Sigmund Freud (1963: 96) famously remarked, "He that has eyes to see and ears to hear may convince himself that no mortal can keep a secret. If his lips are silent, he chatters with his finger-tips; betrayal oozes out of him at every pore." Studies show that lying while smiling carries significant risks because the feigned mask of happiness might slip and expose the truth (Ekman et al. 1988: 414–420).

In many cases a person keeping a secret is worried about the repercussions that may occur if the secret is revealed (Lane and Wegner 1995: 237). Keeping secrets for enslaved Africans was especially important because the consequences of discovery could be dire, even fatal. Henry Bibb (1849: 26) knew that he would be flogged if, after running away, he decided to return or was caught. Suppressing one's thoughts and restricting one's actions to ensure that a secret stays hidden is a source of stress.

The mind-wandering that accompanies keeping a secret is especially stressful. Psychologists say that thinking about a secret when not actively engaged with behaviors associated with the secret may have a negative impact on the secret-keeper's mood and general well-being. The mental fatigue of secret-keeping can cause a person to perform tasks less efficiently. One of the greatest threats comes from the persistent fear of discovery (Davis et al. 2021; Slepian et al. 2016, 2017, 2019). In the case of enslaved African Americans, distracted thinking about a secret could be catastrophic. A wandering mind while washing expensive porcelain teacups, tending the fireplace, or overseeing sugar boiling could result in costly accidents, incidents that might entail severe punishment including flogging, confinement, sale to an even-harsher owner, and even death. Mental anguish increases in situations where a secret-keeper cannot trust everyone in the community. This is precisely what Bibb encountered in Cincinnati, when he feared that Black men looking for White favor or reward money might divulge his location.

Despite the significant hardships that accompany secret-keeping, secrets can have a beneficial side. Secrecy can create group solidarity.

Enslavers and their allies accepted that bondage could create convivial associations between individuals, so they sought to minimize the possibility of group cohesion by enacting laws against it. As early as June 1680 the Virginia legislature passed "An act for preventing Negroes Insurrections."

It began with the words, "Whereas the frequent meeting of considerable numbers of negroe slaves under pretence of feasts and burialls is judged of dangerous consequence." The law made it a crime for enslaved Africans to carry "any club, staffe, gunn, sword or any other weapon of defence or offense" and required written passes for enslaved individuals traveling outside the places of their bondage (Hening 1823 [1680]: 481). Enslavers in Virginia were so concerned that they reaffirmed their fears in October 1792 with a law stating that enslaved individuals were not permitted to "consult, advise, or conspire to rebel, or make insurrection" (Shepherd 1835 [1792]: 125). Of course, consulting, advising, and conspiring all require collective action, and this is what troubled owners of captive Africans.

Researchers investigating the social aspects of secrecy have learned through a complicated series of experiments that tightly held secrets can create solidarity. The point of contention revolves around the conflict between an individual's interest and those of the group. An unhappy individual within the group can decide to go against the group's needs and cause it harm by revealing the secret (Bonacich 1976: 202–203).

The tension between an individual's interests and those of the wider group is lessened in cases where the entire group experiences repression. Events of resistance caused by repression can be short term, such as the storming of the Bastille, or of medium duration, such as one or two riots during a six-week election campaign. A dynamic process of repression and resistance occurs in places with sustained environments of repression, such as a city occupied by a foreign army or a working plantation relying on the labor of captive laborers.

Experts say that all conflicts involving repression and resistance involve power struggles over space (O'Hearn 2009). The spaces on a typical American enslaved-labor plantation were usually determined by the wishes and whims of the owner or owners, with specific places designated as either living or working spaces. Enslaved Africans were largely unable to renegotiate these spaces. The tobacco barn was the place for tobacco; the "quarters" were for the enslaved.

But the oppressed could negotiate other spaces, albeit clandestinely. Subfloor pits represent an obvious effort to recapture space. Other spaces that could be claimed by enslaved men and women were the inside bases of colonoware pots and the sides of clay smoking pipes. The cross-in-circle, stars, and other symbols on clay pipes thus function as forms of resistance like the V-sign in territories occupied by German forces during the Second World War (Carr 2010). The symbols are out in the open for all to see, but their true meanings are obscured. Is a star simply a star, or is it meant to represent the North Star, the direction-finder for escapees like Bibb, something to lead them north toward freedom?

Ritual bundles were the greatest form of covert resistance in the enslaved African American's arsenal. As Du Bois (1903: 96) observed, the "Priest or Medicine-man" was a holdover from Africa, someone who was "the healer of the sick, the interpreter of the Unknown, the comforter of the sorrowing, the supernatural avenger of the world." As "bard, physician, judge, and priest," the healer channeled "the longing, disappointment, and resentment of a stolen and oppressed people." In an important sense, conjurers were a "revolutionary vanguard," leaders who inspired day-to-day resistance (Rucker 2001). And rather than being the exception, they were the rule. Self-emancipated Charles Ball observed that the enslaved living on cotton plantations "uniformly believe in witchcraft, conjuration, and the agency of evil spirits in the affairs of human life." He disparaged these beliefs as "superstition" and wrote that the believers are "either natives of Africa, or the descendants of those who have always, from generation to generation, lived in the South, since their ancestors were landed on this continent" (Ball 1837: 165).

Bibb agreed with Ball that conjuration, which he also called "tricking, and witchcraft," was superstition. But he was not so dismissive of conjuration that he would not try it. Once, when he expected to receive a severe lashing for one of his many escapes, he visited a conjurer seeking a protective powder. After paying the man a small sum, he received a powder and a bitter root. The lack of a whipping convinced him to have "great faith in conjuration and witchcraft." But his belief in the powder led him to overconfidence. After leaving the estate without permission and "talking saucy" to his owner upon his return, he was brutally beaten. Discouraged, Bibb visited a second conjurer. This man assured him that the first conjurer was a fraud. He claimed that for a fee, he could prevent Bibb from being struck in the future. He instructed Bibb to go into the cow pen at night, collect fresh cow manure, and mix it with red pepper and White people's hair. He was to put this concoction in a pot over a fire and scorch it until the mixture could be ground into a fine powder. When the compound was ready, Bibb was to sprinkle it about the slaveholder's bedroom and into the man's hat and boots. Every chance Bibb had, he would dust the bedroom with the powder, finally seeding so much of the stuff that at bedtime his estate owner began to cough and sneeze. Expecting the worst, Bibb decided to run away before he could be interrogated (Bibb 1849: 26–28).

Secrecy played a huge role in the daily lives of enslaved Africans and African Americans. Much of what archaeologists have learned about the lives of the unfortunate captives has lain hidden in the earth for generations, only to be exposed within the last several years. Exciting discoveries continue to be made and new ideas revealed. Through it all, one thing remains true: enslaved Africans had several tools in their arsenal of resistance, rebellion, and resilience. The most revealing were those that remained secrets within the communities of the enslaved.

10

Kingsley and Beyond

The Transformative Future

When Charles Fairbanks stepped upon the Kingsley Plantation soil for the first time, one of the goals firmly in his mind was the discovery of African retentions or survivals, the things more academically known as Africanisms. That he did not know precisely how to identify them was not a major deterrent. Herskovits and others had made it plain that elements of African culture and heritage should be present in the earth as tangible artifacts, so Fairbanks accepted that he and his students would be able to recognize them in and around the small tabby houses inhabited by Kingsley's enslaved laborers. As his excavation ended and the shovels, trowels, rulers, data sheets, and innumerable other tools were stowed away, Fairbanks left Kingsley's one-time fiefdom perplexed but not defeated. Determined, he knew he would go to another nearby plantation and try his luck again. That he again missed the signs of past African heritage was not entirely his fault (Davidson and McIlvoy 2012). He had no way of knowing exactly what to expect because no one had searched before him. He had no roadmap to follow, no guide to lead his way, and he could not consult the notes of earlier archaeologists because no such notes existed. He was even unsure when he would know for certain that his quest for Africanisms would end, and if so, how.

Fairbanks's lack of knowledge was not his alone. American archaeologists had ignored the African Diaspora, one of the largest and most-protracted enforced movements of people in world history. Before the late 1960s archaeologists collectively treated the Diaspora as if it had no relevance to their world. To them the transshipment of millions of bound human beings from one continent to another was a subject for historians. African American history and culture swirled around the archaeological world, but for most White academics it flew by like an unnoticed apparition. Plenty of works by Black authors, including those of Henry Bibb, Zora Neale Hurston, and W.E.B. Du Bois, sat quietly on library shelves, but these, too, went largely unopened by archaeologists. At the time few archaeologists thought to read folklore, and if they did, they seldom imagined how it could be relevant to their research. Shifts in thinking about American society—generally set in motion by groups protesting racism, social inequality, and war—changed American archaeology for the better. Much of the impetus for a more enlightened archaeology came from pressures exerted by African Americans (LaRoche and Blakey 1997) and Native Americans (Buffalohead 1992; Echo-Hawk and Zimmerman 2006; Hammil 1987). In demanding that their voices be heard, their actions forever transformed archaeological practice.

Fairbanks's willingness to undertake the first serious investigation into the lived realities of the African Diaspora was a clear expression of how things had changed. Despite Fairbanks's ultimate failure to find an African smoking gun, his investigation at Kingsley changed American archaeology forever. After 1968 it was no longer possible for archaeologists, and historical archaeologists specifically, to blithely ignore what was all around them and literally right under their feet. Fairbanks's excavations revealed that the realities of daily life under conditions of enslavement could be dug out of a deserted ruin or revealed as dark stains in the soil.

When Fairbanks first approached Kingsley's plantation, some archaeologists were just beginning to ponder the connections between the past and the present. By the 1990s the idea that archaeology was solely about the past had begun to fade. Part of the impetus for the new perspective came from an archaeological excavation in New York City.

In the 1980s the US federal government sought to construct a towering new office building in Lower Manhattan. Initial archaeological testing suggested that the "Negros Burial Ground" shown on eighteenth-century maps had long since been destroyed. When archaeologists began to excavate the site, it was obvious that the original testing had been wrong, because 419 burials of African Americans were still present at the site. Archaeologists excavated the remains, but during their analysis at Lehman College, bioarchaeologists from Howard University, led by Michael Blakey, questioned the analysts' methods (Nelson 2013: 528–529). Pressure by local activists from the city's descendant community demanded that the remains be accorded the cultural sensitivity they deserved, so the collection was transferred to Howard University (Paterson 1993). Blakey and his team examined the skeletal remains for 10 years, and in 2004 the remains were respectfully reburied in a ceremony attended by thousands (Blakey 2004). The Howard University effort was profoundly significant because it was "the first major project in which blacks have been able to direct the anthropological study of their early ancestors and to tell the story using bioarchaeological methods" (Blakey 1995; also see Watkins 2020). Today the site of the cemetery, now known as the African Burial Ground, is a national monument (Purnell 2010).

Today's archaeologists widely accept that an unbreakable link exists between their research and the present. Historical archaeologists understand this as well as anyone because the distance in time between their present and the past they study can sometimes be as small as a couple of decades or even less.

The transformation of archaeological thinking has meant that excavators now no longer view the people of the past and their living descendants as unrelated. Once, an archaeologist might have sought out a descendant or local resident to learn a few details about a property or family in the same way that a folklorist would collect legends and memories. More often, though, many archaeologists simply ignored living communities. The past was the past, and that was that. Most archaeologists now find the avoidance of descendant communities and concerned citizens as not only unfortunate but terribly wrong. The dominant approach today requires archaeologists to contact descendant communities and stakeholders at the beginning of a research project and to engage with them as full collaborators. In addition to acquiring fresh views of the past, archaeologists now accept that their discipline can be used as an effective tool for civil engagement, social activism, and antiracist research (Barton 2021; Blakey 2020; Flewellen et al. 2021; Franklin et al. 2020; Little and Shackel 2007).

Archaeologists who investigated the histories and meanings of clay pots and smoking pipes, subfloor pits, and bundled collections of otherwise ordinary artifacts knew that their interpretations were always open to reinterpretation. Innovative perspectives and new understandings emerge as younger scholars cast new eyes on old subjects. Even the history of Kingsley's plantation is being reevaluated and reimagined, highlighting once ignored parts of the estate's past (Flewellen 2017).

One study including Kingsley Plantation conducted by anthropologist Antoinette T. Jackson (2004) focuses on the resilience of African American communities in the American Southeast. Like many other captive-holding estates, Kingsley's rapacious behavior gave birth to a tightly knit community of people, individuals who built rich lives as his and Anta Madgigine Jai's descendants. To learn more about the community, Jackson interviewed the plantation's descendants and combined what she learned with the available historical information. She discovered that every generation and each descendant has had to work out their own relationship with the Kingsley legacy, especially as it pertains to their lives as descendants of a couple who once owned human beings.

A prominent aspect of the Kingsley legacy revolves around the complex figure of Anna Kingsley. Jackson's interview with Johnnetta Betsch Cole—noted anthropologist, director of the Smithsonian's National Museum of African Art, and seventh-generation descendant of Anna and Zephaniah—revealed that Cole had a conflicted view of the Kingsley legacy as a "profoundly moving story" but one with "extraordinary complexity and contradictions" (Jackson 2004: 146). Cole accepted that Anna was a remarkably gifted African woman but was disturbed by her having been a holder of enslaved Africans. Cole lamented that the personal histories of countless other African women, all of whom may have been as talented as Anna, are unknown today and perhaps even unknowable.

The descendants of the Black community that rose from Kingsley's plantation became prominent within Jacksonville, Florida, and the surrounding region. One family member was Abraham Lincoln (A. L.) Lewis, who, with his wife, Mary Sammis Lewis, were among some of the wealthiest and most respected individuals in the state's African American community. During the 1920s Lewis helped create the Afro-American Life Insurance Company to assist African Americans denied coverage by prejudiced, White-owned insurance companies. He also bought several parcels of land and had a hand in many profitable businesses, including the Lincoln Golf and Country Club, begun in 1929. Mary Lewis was equally active in many civic organizations and church activities. Zora Neale Hurston became part of the Afro-American Life Insurance family in 1939 with her brief marriage to the grandson of one of the company's founders (Jackson 2004: 160).

Jackson's research into the family history of Kingsley Plantation demonstrates that the relatively short history of the plantation, as a working estate operated by enslaved laborers, is dwarfed in importance by the continuing history and experiences of the Kingsley descendants. As Jackson (2004: 155) cogently observes, the history of the Kingsley Plantation community is "more than a distant memory." The history is alive and celebrated by the descendants who collectively lived through and survived segregation, discriminatory laws, lynching, and everyday racist behavior.

One of the features of community life that the descendants Jackson interviewed makes clear is the importance of the African American family. Du Bois (1908), Frazier (1928, 1932, 1939), and others (Gutman 1976) have also made this abundantly clear. Bibb's repeated efforts to keep his small family intact provides another example. The significance of the Black family has led several historical archaeologists to situate their studies within the context of the community (Barton 2022; González-Tennant 2018; Shackel 2011). Such studies provide testimony to how far the archaeology of the African Diaspora has come since 1968.

Perhaps Fairbanks's greatest mistake was to assume that Africanisms would be obvious to a middle-class White academic. Theoretically, it seemed to make sense. Because the cultures of western and west-central Africa were distinct from all European and Native American cultures, material objects reflecting African heritage should appear different too. But Fairbanks did not appreciate that his most formidable obstacle was the cultural cauldron that was colonial America. He also failed to account for the life-and-death need for enslaved African secrecy. A glaring reminder of the African homeland could have signaled danger to captive-owning planters, complicit government officials, and proslavery hangers-on, individuals who were wholeheartedly dedicated to maintaining White supremacy and the status quo of human bondage. Obvious expressions of Africa would have proven that the oppressors, who saw themselves as all-powerful and omnipresent, had failed in their task to cow enslaved Africans and African Americans. Overt expressions of Africa would have been especially hazardous in the mid-nineteenth century as the enslavers' hold on the American South was becoming increasingly tenuous. Subtlety and secrecy were far better than open expression. Clay pipes and pots, holes dug into the floor, and ritual bundles proved that Africa had not died in the hearts of thousands of forcibly transplanted women and men, even in generations far removed in time from the Charter Generation.

Without question, African Americans, whether enslaved or emancipated, did not spend all their time contemplating the cosmos or scratching symbols into pipes and pots, digging holes beneath their house floors, or creating and secreting powerful bundles. Every Black person undoubtedly had entire days of simply trying to make it through each day, acting in practical and symbolic ways when they were able or when the opportunity arose. Likewise, not all archaeologists committed to the study of African American history and culture have exclusively investigated clay pots and smoking pipes, holes in the ground, and ritual bundles.

In this short book we have focused on clay pots, smoking pipes, subfloor pits, and bundles as one way to tell the story of how archaeologists awakened to one huge part of American history, an entire panorama of events that had escaped them for far too long. The story indeed began with Fairbanks's search for African retentions at Kingsley's plantation in north Florida, but since then archaeologists have fanned out across the territory of the African Diaspora asking questions about every facet of past Black life in the Americas. The areas of inquiry are too vast to detail here, but one topic will further demonstrate the linkage between past and present.

Archaeologists of the African Diaspora have long known that enslaved men and women, when they were not forced to labor for their captors, spent a good deal of their time out of doors in the yards surrounding their houses (McKee and Thomas 1998). It makes abundant sense that individuals relegated to small, cramped houses in warm and semitropical environments would do things outside. As a result, much of the cultural expressions of daily life might be found outside rather than inside the close confines of tiny dwellings (Heath and Bennett 2000). When interviewed, emancipated African Americans often mentioned their yards and gardens, where they often cooked, washed clothes, made objects, butchered animals, told stories, worked on quilts, watched small children play, and did countless other things, including acts of conjure (Leone et al. 2018; Perdue 1976). For many African Americans, the simple act of sweeping the yards around their houses had important connotations, including creating shared racial, gender, and class identities and serving as spaces of socialization (Barton 2022: 62–63; Gall et al. 2020). The use of yards provides continuity between Africa and the Americas and between the past and the present (Gundaker and McWillie 2005; Westmacott 1992). Yards, like dwellings, are important places for archaeologists to investigate.

Many archaeological ideas and interpretations may be as controversial as were those that swirled around and, in some cases, continue to swirl around colonoware, clay pipes, subfloor pits, and ritual bundles. Constantly rethinking and redesigning one's interpretations are as ingrained in archaeology as is the thrill of discovery. What began at Kingsley Plantation in the late 1960s is an ongoing story, one whose entire history may never be told in full because the next excavation might reveal its own unimagined secrets. Despite the incomplete story, history changed when one archaeologist stepped onto an old plantation. That the secrets of the past will continue to be revealed is a testament to the ingenuity and creative abilities expressed by the millions of Africans stolen from their homes and repeatedly reflected in the resilience of their countless descendants.

References

A Citizen of Mississippi
1847   The Negro. *De Bow's Commercial Review* 3(5): 419–422.

Adair, James
1775   *The History of the American Indians, Particularly Those Nations Adjoining to the Mississippi, East and West Florida, Georgia, South and North Carolina, and Virginia.* Edward and Charles Dilly, London.

Agar, Ben
1643   *King James, His Apopthegmes or Table-Talke.* B. W., London.

Agbe-Davies, Anna S.
2015   *Tobacco, Pipes, and Race in Colonial Virginia: Little Tubes of Mighty Power.* Left Coast Press, Walnut Creek, California.
2016   How to Do Things with Things, or, Are Blue Beads Good to Think? *Semiotic Review* 4; https://semioticreview.com/ojs/index.php/sr/article/view/12.
2017   Where Tradition and Pragmatism Meet: African Diaspora Archaeology at the Crossroads. *Historical Archaeology* 51: 9–27.
2018a   Dr. Stage-Love, or: How I Learned to Stop Worrying and Love My Dissertation on Race, Pipes, and Classification in the Chesapeake. In *Engaging Archaeology: 25 Case Studies in Research Practice,* edited by Stephen W. Silliman, pp. 181–188. John Wiley and Sons, Hoboken, New Jersey.
2018b   Laboring Under an Illusion: Aligning Method and Theory in the Archaeology of Plantation Slavery. *Historical Archaeology* 52: 125–139.

Alexander, J.
2001   Islam, Archaeology, and Slavery in Africa. *World Archaeology* 33: 44–60.

Allen, Dave
2007   Feelin' Bad This Morning: Why the British Blues? *Popular Music* 26: 141–156.

Amick, Daniel S.
2004   A Possible Ritual Cache of Great Basin Stemmed Bifaces from the Terminal Pleistocene–Early Holocene Occupation of NW Nevada, USA. *Lithic Technology* 29: 119–145.

Anderson, David
1997   As I Remember Jimmy: On the Value of Museums and Collections. *Midcontinental Journal of Archaeology* 22: 129–130.

Anonymous
1648   *The Devill Seen at St. Albons, Being a True Relation How the Devill Was Seen There in a Cellar in the Likeness of a Ram.* N.p.
1675   *The Women's Complaint against Tobacco.* N.p., London.
1700   *Nicotianae Encomium: Or, the Golden Leaf, Tobacco Display'd in Its Soveraignty and Singular Vertues.* N.p.
1773   A Remedy Universally Practiced in Holland, and Known to Some in England, for the Recovery of Persons Seemingly Dead from Drowning or Succession. *Manchester Mercury and Harrop's Genrral [sic] Advertiser*, 1150, August 17; www-18thcjournals-amdigital-co-uk.proxy1.lib.uwo.ca/Documents/Images/CHE_Harrops_Manchester_mercury_1773/132?searchId=9f935a68-f778-48c6-a136-3d01a77f377e; accessed November 2020.

Aptheker, Herbert
1943   *American Negro Slave Revolts.* Columbia University Press, New York.

Arenson, Adam
2009   The Double Life of St. Louis: Narratives of Origins and Maturity in Wade's *Urban Frontier. Indiana Magazine of History* 105: 246–261.

Atalay, Sonya
2006   Indigenous Archaeology as Decolonizing Practice. *American Indian Quarterly* 30: 280–310.

Atwater, Caleb
1820   *Description of the Antiquities Discovered in the State of Ohio and Other Western States, Communicated to the President of the American Antiquarian Society.* American Antiquarian Society, Worcester, Massachusetts.

Augé, C. Riley
2013   Silent Sentinels, Archaeology, Magic, and the Gendered Control of Domestic Boundaries in New England, 1620–1725. PhD dissertation, Department of Anthropology, University of Montana, Missoula.
2022   *Field Manual for the Archaeology of Ritual, Religion, and Magic.* Berghahn, New York.

Ayanian, Arin H., Nicole Tausch, Yasemin Gülsüm Acar, Maria Chayinska, Wing-Yee Cheung, and Yulia Lukyanova
2021   Resistance in Repressive Contexts. *Journal of Personality and Social Psychology* 120: 912–939.

Ayto, Eric G.
1990   *Clay Tobacco Pipes.* Shire, Aylesbury.

Baker, Lee D.
1998   *From Savage to Negro: Anthropology and the Construction of Race, 1896–1954.* University of California Press, Berkeley.

Baker, Steven G.
1972   Colono-Indian Pottery from Cambridge, South Carolina with Comments on the Historic Catawba Pottery Trade. *South Carolina Institute of Archaeology and Anthropology Notebook* 4(1): 3–30.

Baker, Vernon G.
1978   *Historical Archaeology at Black Lucy's Garden, Andover, Massachusetts: Ceramics from the Site of a Nineteenth Century Afro-American.* Robert S. Peabody Foundation for Archaeology, Phillips Academy, Andover, Massachusetts.

Balandier, Georges
1968   *Daily Life in the Kingdom of Kongo from the Sixteenth to the Eighteenth Century.* Pantheon, New York.

Ball, Charles
1837   *Slavery in the United States: A Narrative of the Life and Adventures of Charles Ball, A Black Man.* John S. Turner, New York.

Bamforth, Douglas B.
2013   Paleoindian Perambulations and the Harman Cache. *Plains Anthropologist* 58: 65–82.

Baptist, Edward E.
2016   *The Half Has Never Been Told: Slavery and the Making of American Capitalism.* Basic, New York.

Bardolph, Dana N.
2014   A Critical Evaluation of Recent Gendered Publishing Trends in American Archaeology. *American Antiquity* 79: 522–540.

Barnhart, Terry A.
1989   Of Mounds and Men: The Early Anthropological Career of Ephraim George Squier. PhD dissertation, Department of History, Miami University, Oxford, Ohio.
2005   *Ephraim George Squier and the Development of American Anthropology.* University of Nebraska Press, Lincoln.
2015   *American Antiquities: Revisiting the Origins of American Archaeology.* University of Nebraska Press, Lincoln.

Barrow, John
1759   *A New Geographical Dictionary, Containing a Full and Accurate Account of the Several Parts of the Known World.* J. Coote, London.

Barton, Christopher P.
2022   *The Archaeology of Race and Class at Timbuctoo: A Black Community in New Jersey.* University Press of Florida, Gainesville.

Barton, Christopher P. (editor)
2021   *Trowels in the Trenches: Archaeology as Social Action.* University Press of Florida, Gainesville.

Basden, G. T.
1921   *Among the Ibos of Nigeria.* Seeley, Service, London.

Battle-Baptiste, Whitney
2011   *Black Feminist Archaeology.* Left Coast Press, Walnut Creek, California.

Bauer, Raymond A., and Alice H. Bauer
1942   Day to Day Resistance to Slavery. *Journal of Negro History* 27: 388–419.

Becker, M. J.
1980   An American Witch Bottle. *Archaeology* 33(2): 18–23.

Berger, Henry W.
2015   *St. Louis and Empire: 250 Years of Imperial Quest and Urban Crisis.* Southern Illinois University Press, Carbondale.

Berlin, Ira
1996   From Creole to African: Atlantic Creoles and the Origins of African-American Society in Mainland North America. *William and Mary Quarterly* 53: 251–288.
1998   *Many Thousands Gone: The First Two Centuries of Slavery in North America.* Harvard University Press, Cambridge, Massachusetts.

Beverley, Robert
1705   *The History and Present State of Virginia in Four Parts, Book II.* R. Parker, London.

Bibb, Henry
1849   *Narrative of the Life and Adventures of Henry Bibb, An American Slave.* Henry Bibb, New York.

Bieder, Robert E.
1986   *Science Encounters the Indian, 1820–1880: The Early Years of American Ethnology.* University of Oklahoma Press, Norman.

Binford, Lewis R.
1962   A New Method of Calculating Dates from Kaolin Pipe Stem Samples. *Southeastern Archaeological Conference Newsletter* 9(1): 19–21.

Blakey, Michael L.
1995   What Makes Burial Ground Project a Milestone. *New York Times,* May 30, A16.
2004   Field Note. *Archaeology* 57(1): 74.
2020   Archaeology under the Blinding Light of Race. *Current Anthropology* 61: S184–S197.

Blassingame, John W.
1979   *The Slave Community: Plantation Life in the Antebellum South.* Rev. ed. Oxford University Press, New York.

Blassingame, John W. (editor)
1977   *Slave Testimony: Two Centuries of Letters, Speeches, Interviews, and Autobiographies.* Louisiana State University Press, Baton Rouge.
1979   *The Frederick Douglass Papers, Series One: Speeches, Debates, and Interviews: 1. 1841–46.* Yale University Press, New Haven, Connecticut.

Bonacich, Philip
1976   Secrecy and Solidarity. *Sociometry* 39: 200–208.

Borucki, Alex, David Eltis, and David Wheat
2015   Atlantic History and the Slave Trade to Spanish America. *American Historical Review* 120: 433–461.

Boyd, Mark F.
1937   Events at Prospect Bluff on the Apalachicola River, 1808–1818. *Florida Historical Quarterly* 16: 55–96.

Brackett, David
2012   Preaching Blues. *Black Music Research Journal* 32: 113–136.

Bradbury, John
1817   *Travels in the Interior of America, in the Years 1809, 1810, and 1811.* Sherwood, Neely, and Jones, London.
Breen, T. H.
1984   Creative Adaptations: Peoples and Cultures. In *Colonial British America: Essays in the New History of the Early Modern Era,* edited by Jack P. Greene and J. R. Pole, pp. 195–232. Johns Hopkins University Press, Baltimore.
Brinkman, Inge
2016   Kongo Interpreters, Traveling Priests, and Political Leaders in the Kongo Kingdom (15th–19th Century). *International Journal of African Historical Studies* 49: 255–276.
Brinton, Daniel G.
1890   *Races and Peoples: Lectures on the Science of Ethnography.* N.D.C. Hodges, New York.
Brown, Brittany
2016   Reexamining English Clay Pipes in Captive African Burials on the Island of Barbados. *Journal of African Diaspora Archaeology and Heritage* 5: 245–262.
Brown, David H.
1990   Conjure/Doctors: An Exploration of a Black Discourse in America, Antebellum to 1940. *Folklore Forum* 23: 3–46.
Brown, James A.
1976   The Southern Cult Reconsidered. *Midcontinental Journal of Archaeology* 1: 115–135.
1997   The Archaeology of Ancient Religion in the Eastern Woodlands. *Annual Review of Anthropology* 26: 465–485.
Brown, Kenneth L.
1994   Material Culture and Community Structure: The Slave and Tenant Community at Levi Jordan's Plantation, 1848–1892. In *Working Toward Freedom: Slave Society and Domestic Economy in the American South,* edited by Larry E. Hudson Jr., pp. 95–118. University of Rochester Press, Rochester, New York.
2004   Ethnographic Analogy, Archaeology, and the African Diaspora: Perspectives from a Tenant Community. *Historical Archaeology* 38(1): 79–89.
2011   BaKongo Cosmograms, Christian Crosses, or None of the Above: An Archaeology of African American Spiritual Adaptations into the 1920s. In *The Materiality of Freedom: Archaeologies of Postemancipation Life,* edited by Jodi A. Barnes, pp. 209–227. University of South Carolina Press, Columbia.
Brown, Kenneth L., and Doreen C. Cooper
1990   Structural Continuity in an African-American Slave and Tenant Community. *Historical Archaeology* 24(4): 7–19.
Brugis, Thomas
1648   *The Marrow of Physicke, or A Learned Discourse of the Severall Parts of a Mans Body.* T. H. and M. H., London.

Bryant, Vaughn M., Sarah M. Kampbell, and Jerome Lynn Hall
2012   Tobacco Pollen: Archaeological and Forensic Applications. *Palynology* 36: 208–223.
Buffalohead, W. Roger
1992   Reflections on Native American Cultural Rights and Resources. *American Indian Culture and Research Journal* 16: 197–200.
Bullen, Adelaide K., and Ripley P. Bullen
1945   Black Lucy's Garden. *Bulletin of the Massachusetts Archaeological Society* 6(2): 17–28.
Burnell, A. C. (editor)
1881   *Hippocrates on Airs, Waters, and Places*. Wyman, London.
Burroughs, Jeremiah
1652   *Two Treatises of Mr. Jeremiah Burroughs*. Peter Cole, London.
Cable, George W.
1886a   The Dance in Place Congo. *Century Magazine* 31: 517–532.
1886b   Creole Slave Songs. *Century Magazine* 31: 807–828.
Caldwell, Joseph, and Catherine McCann
1941   *Irene Mound Site, Chatham County, Georgia*. University of Georgia Press, Athens.
Campbell, Alec C.
1968   Some Notes on Ngwaketse Divination. *Botswana Notes and Records* 1: 9–13.
Canadian Correspondent (Toronto)
1834   Visit to an Indian Mound. September 20.
Cantwell, Anne-Marie, and Diana diZerega Wall
2015   Looking for Africans in Seventeenth-Century New Amsterdam. In *The Archaeology of Race in the Northeast*, edited by Christopher N. Matthews and Allison Manfra McGovern, pp. 29–55. University Press of Florida, Gainesville.
Carr, Gillian
2010   The Archaeology of Occupation and the V-Sign Campaign in the Occupied British Channel Islands. *International Journal of Historical Archaeology* 14: 575–592.
Carson, Cary, Norman F. Barka, William M. Kelso, Garry Wheeler Stone, and Dell Upton
1981   Impermanent Architecture in the Southern American Colonies. *Winterthur Portfolio* 16: 135–196.
Carson, Cary, Joanne Bowen, Willie Graham, Martha McCartney, and Lorena Walsh
2008   New World, Real World: Improvising English Culture in Seventeenth-Century Virginia. *Journal of Southern History* 74: 51–63.
Cartier, Jacques
1580   *A Shorte and Briefe Narration of the Two Nauigations and Discoueries to the Northwest Partes Called Newe Fraunce*. H. Bynneman, London.
Castañeda, Quetzil E., and Christopher N. Matthews (editors)
2008   *Ethnographic Archaeologies: Reflections on Stakeholders and Archaeological Practices*. AltaMira, Walnut Creek, California.

Castle, W. E.
1924 *Genetics and Eugenics: A Text-Book for Students of Biology and a Reference Book for Animal and Plant Breeders.* Harvard University Press, Cambridge, Massachusetts.

Chambers, Ephraim
1738 *Cyclopædia: Or, an Universal Dictionary of Arts and Sciences,* Vol. 1. D. Midwinter, London.

Cheves, Langdon (editor)
1897 The Shaftesbury Papers and Other Records Relating to Carolina. *Collections of the South Carolina Historical Society,* Vol. 5. South Carolina Historical Society, Charleston.

Child, Lydia Maria
1843 *Letters from New-York.* Charles S. Francis, New York.

Chireau, Yvonne
1997 Conjure and Christianity in the Nineteenth Century: Religious Elements of African American Magic. *Religion and American Culture* 7: 225–246.

Claassen, Cheryl
1993 Black and White Women at Irene Mound. *Southeastern Archaeology* 12: 137–147.

Claassen, Cheryl (editor)
1994 *Women in Archaeology.* University of Pennsylvania Press, Philadelphia.

Clar, Mimi
1960 Folk Belief and Custom in the Blues. *Western Folklore* 19: 173–189.

Clist, Bernard, Els Cranshof, Gilles-Mauriece de Schryver, Davy Herremans, Karlis Karklins, Igor Matonda, Fanny Steyaert, and Koen Bostoen
2015 African-European Contacts in the Kong Kingdom (Sixteenth-Eighteenth Centuries): New Archaeological Insights from Ngongo Mbata (Lower Congo, DRC). *International Journal of Historical Archaeology* 19: 464–501.

Cobb, Charles R., and Chester B. DePratter
2012 Multisited Research on Colonowares and the Paradox of Globalization. *American Anthropologist* 114: 446–461.

Cochran, Matthew D.
1999 Hoodoo's Fire: Interpreting Nineteenth-Century African-American Material Culture at the Brice House, Annapolis, Maryland. *Maryland Archaeology* 35(1): 25–33.

Cole, Herbert M., and Chike C. Aniakor
1984 *Igbo Arts: Community and Cosmos.* Museum of Cultural History, University of California, Los Angeles.

Collier, John
1948 *Indians of the Americas: The Long Hope.* Mentor, New York.

Conkey, Margaret W., and Joan M. Gero
1997 Programme to Practice: Gender and Feminism in Archaeology. *Annual Review of Anthropology* 26: 411–437.

Cookey, S.J.S.
2011   An Ethnohistorical Reconstruction of Traditional Igbo Society. In *West African Culture Dynamics: Archaeological and Historical Perspectives,* edited by B. K. Swartz Jr. and Raymond E. Dumett, pp. 327–348. De Gruyter Mouton, Berlin.

Coon, Diane Perrine
2005   Project Report 2.0, December 13, 2005; Historybyperrine.com/category/henry-bibb-archaeological-study/; accessed December 2019.

Cordell, Ann S.
2013   Continuity and Change in Early Eighteenth-Century Apalachee Colonowares. In *The Archaeology of Hybrid Material Culture,* edited by Jeb J. Card, pp. 80–99. Center for Archaeological Investigations, Southern Illinois University, Carbondale.

Cortland, Clarissa I., Maureen A. Craig, Jenessa R. Shapiro, Jennifer A. Richeson, Rebecca Neel, and Noah J. Goldstien
2017   Solidarity through Shared Disadvantage: Highlighting Shared Experiences of Discrimination Improves Relations between Stigmatized Groups. *Journal of Personality and Social Psychology* 113: 547–567.

Cotter, John L.
1993   Historical Archaeology before 1967. *Historical Archaeology* 27(1): 4–9.

Cowgill, George L.
1977   Albert Spaulding and Archaeological Method and Theory. *American Antiquity* 42: 325–329.

Crader, Diana C.
1990   Slave Diet at Monticello. *American Antiquity* 55: 690–717.

Das, Nandini, João Vicente Melo, Haig Z. Smith, and Lauren Working
2021   Blackamoor/Moor. In *Keywords of Identity, Race, and Human Mobility in Early Modern England,* pp. 40–50. Amsterdam University Press, Amsterdam.

Davidson, James M.
2021   The Subfloor-Pit Tradition in the United States: A Florida Case Study and Critical Reappraisal of Its Origins. *Historical Archaeology* 55: 353–377.

Davidson, James M., and Karen E. McIlvoy
2012   New Perspectives from Old Collections: Potential Artifacts of African Spirituality at Couper Plantation, Georgia. *Journal of African Diaspora Archaeology and Heritage* 1: 126–133.

Davis, Arthur P.
1962   E. Franklin Frazier (1894–1962): A Profile. *Journal of Negro Education* 31: 429–435.

Davis, Christopher G., Hannah Brazeau, Elisabeth Bailin Xie, and Kathleen McKee
2021   Secrets, Psychological Health, and the Fear of Discovery. *Personality and Social Psychology Bulletin* 47: 781–795.

De Jong, Gerald Francis
1971   The Dutch Reformed Church and Negro Slavery in Colonial America. *Church History* 40: 423–436.

De Laune, Thomas
1681   *Tropologia, or, A Key to Open Scripture Metaphors.* John Richardson and John Darby, London.
Deagan, Kathleen
1978   The Material Assemblage of 16th Century Spanish Florida. *Historical Archaeology* 12: 25–50.
DeBoer, William R.
1988   Subterranean Storage and the Organization of Surplus: The View from Eastern North America. *Southeastern Archaeology* 7: 1–20.
Deetz, James
1993   *Flowerdew Hundred: The Archaeology of a Virginia Plantation, 1619–1864.* University of Virginia Press, Charlottesville.
1996   *In Small Things Forgotten: An Archaeology of Early American Life.* Rev. ed. Doubleday, New York.
Delle, James A.
1988   *An Archaeology of Social Space: Analyzing Coffee Plantations in Jamaica's Blue Mountains.* Plenum, New York.
Denbow, James
1999   Heart and Soul: Glimpses of Ideology and Cosmology in the Iconography of Tombstones from the Loango Coast of Central Africa. *Journal of American Folklore* 112: 404–423.
Domingues da Silva, Daniel B.
2013   The Atlantic Slave Trade from Angola: A Port-by-Port Estimate of Slaves Embarked, 1701–1867. *International Journal of African Historical Studies* 46: 105–122.
Dorson, Richard M.
1963   Melville J. Herskovits, 1895 1963. *Journal of American Folklore* 76: 249–250.
Drew, Benjamin
1856   *The Refugee: Or the Narratives of Fugitive Slaves in Canada.* John P. Jewett, Boston.
Du Bois, W.E.B.
1896   *The Suppression of the African Slave-Trade to the United States of America, 1638–1870.* Longmans, Green, New York.
1903   *The Souls of Black Folk: Essays and Sketches.* A. C. McClurg, Chicago.
1924   *The Gift of Black Folk: The Negroes in the Making of America.* Stratford, Boston.
1936   Social Planning for the Negro, Past and Present. *Journal of Negro Education* 5: 110–125.
1939   *Black Folk Then and Now: An Essay in the History and Sociology of the Negro Race.* Henry Holt, New York.
1942   Review of *The Myth of the Negro Past* by Melville J. Herskovits. *Annals of the American Academy of Political and Social Science* 222: 226–227.
Du Bois, W.E.B. (editor)
1908   *The Negro American Family.* Atlanta University Press, Atlanta.

East India Company
1719 *The East-India Company Sale, September the Fifth, 1719.* D. Bridge, London.

Echo-Hawk, Roger, and Larry J. Zimmerman
2006 Beyond Racism: Some Opinions about Racialism and American Archaeology. *American Indian Quarterly* 30: 461–485.

Egboh, E. O.
1971 The Beginning of the End of Traditional Religion in Iboland, South-Eastern Nigeria. *Civilisations* 21: 269–279.

Ekman, Paul, Wallace V. Friesen, and Maureen O'Sullivan
1988 Smiles When Lying. *Journal of Personality and Social Psychology* 54: 414–420.

Eliot, Thomas
1538 *The Dictionary by Syr Thomas Eliot, Knyght.* N.p.

Emerson, Matthew C.
1986 A Unique Terra Cotta Pipebowl from Flowerdew Hundred. *Quarterly Bulletin of the Archaeological Society of Virginia* 41(3): 169–172.
1988 Decorated Clay Tobacco Pipes from the Chesapeake. PhD dissertation, Department of Anthropology, University of California, Berkeley.
1994 Decorated Clay Tobacco Pipes from the Chesapeake: An African Connection. In *Historical Archaeology of the Chesapeake,* edited by Paul A. Shackel and Barbara J. Little, pp. 35–49. Smithsonian Institution Press, Washington, DC.
1999 African Inspirations in a New World Art and Artifact: Decorated Tobacco Pipes from the Chesapeake. In *"I, Too, Am America": Archaeological Studies of African-American Life,* edited by Theresa A. Singleton, pp. 47–82. University of Virginia Press, Charlottesville.

Emerson Thomas E., and Timothy R. Pauketat
2008 Historical-Processual Archaeology and Culture Making: Unpacking the Southern Cult and Mississippian Religion. In *Belief in the Past: Theoretical Approaches to the Archaeology of Religion,* edited by David S. Whitley and Kelley Hays-Gilpin, pp. 167–188. Left Coast Press, Walnut Creek, California.

Equiano, Olaudah
1837 *The Life of Olaudah Equiano, or Gustavus Vassa, the African.* Isaac Knapp, Boston.

Evans, Clifford
1955 *A Ceramic Study of Virginia Archaeology.* Smithsonian Institution Bureau of American Ethnology Bulletin 160. Government Printing Office, Washington, DC.

Fabend, Firth Haring
2012 *New Netherland in a Nutshell: A Concise History of the Dutch Colony in North America.* New Netherland Institute, Albany, New York.

Fagette, Paul
1996 *Digging for Dollars: American Archaeology and the New Deal.* University of New Mexico Press, Albuquerque.

Fairbanks, Charles
1937   The Occurrence of Coiled Pottery in New York State. *American Antiquity* 2: 178–179.
1962   A Colono-Indian Ware Milk Pitcher. *Florida Anthropologist* 15: 103–106.
1974   The Kingsley Slave Cabins in Duval County, Florida, 1968. *Conference on Historic Site Archaeology Papers* 7: 62–93.
1984   The Plantation Archaeology of the Southeastern Coast. *Historical Archaeology* 18(1): 1–14.
1994   Path to Prelude: "What Is Past Is Prelude; Study the Past." In *Pioneers in Historical Archaeology: Breaking New Ground,* edited by Stanley South, pp. 197–217 Plenum, New York.

Falconer, William
1781   *Remarks on the Influence of Climate, Situation, Nature of Country, Population, Nature of Food, and Way of Life.* C. Dilly, London.

Fandrich, Ina J.
2005   The Birth of New Orleans' Voodoo Queen: A Long-Held Mystery Revealed. *Louisiana History* 46: 293–309.

Fauset, Arthur Huff
1927   Negro Folk Tales from the South. (Alabama, Mississippi, Louisiana). *Journal of American Folk-Lore* 40: 213–303.

FBI File
2020   E. Franklin Frazier https://archive.org/details/E.FranklinFrazierFBIFile/page/n27/mode/2up; accessed September 2020.

Fennell, Christopher C.
2007   *Crossroads and Cosmologies: Diasporas and Ethnogenesis in the New World.* University Press of Florida, Gainesville.

Ferguson, Leland G.
1975   Analysis of Ceramic Materials from Fort Watson, December 1780–April 1781. *Conference on Historic Site Archaeology Papers* 8: 2–28.
1978   Looking for the "Afro" in Colono-Indian Pottery. *Conference on Historic Site Archaeology Papers* 12: 68–86.
1991   Struggling with Pots in Colonial South Carolina. In *The Archaeology of Inequality,* edited by Randall H. McGuire and Robert Paynter, pp. 28–39. Blackwell, Oxford.
1992   *Uncommon Ground: Archaeology and Early African America, 1650–1800.* Smithsonian Institution Press, Washington, DC.
1999   "The Cross Is a Magic Sign": Marks on Eighteenth-Century Bowls from South Carolina. In *"I, too, Am America": Archaeological Studies of African-American Life,"* edited by Theresa A. Singleton, pp. 116–131. University of Virginia Press, Charlottesville.
2011   Crosses, Secrets, and Lies: A Response to J. W. Joseph's "All of Cross"—African Potters, Marks, and Meanings in the Folk Pottery of the Edgefield District, South Carolina. *Historical Archaeology* 45: 163–165.

Ferguson, Leland, and Kelly Goldberg
2019 From the Earth: Spirituality, Medicine Vessels, and Consecrated Bowls as Responses to Slavery in the South Carolina Lowcountry. *Journal of African Diaspora Archaeology and Heritage* 8: 173–201.

Ferguson, Leland G., and Stanton Green
1983 Recognizing the American Indian, African and European in the Archaeological Record of Colonial South Carolina. In *Forgotten Places and Things: Archaeological Perspectives on American History*, edited by Albert E. Ward, pp. 275–281. Center for Anthropological Studies, Albuquerque.
1984 South Appalachian Mississippians: Politics and Environment in the Old, Old South. *Southeastern Archaeology* 3: 139–143.

Fesler, Garrett Randall
2004 From Houses to Homes: An Archaeological Case Study of Household Formation at the Utopia Slave Quarter, ca. 1675 to 1775. PhD dissertation, Department of Anthropology, University of Virginia, Charlottesville.

Fleszar, Mark J.
2012 "My Laborers in Haiti Are Not Slaves": Proslavery Factions and a Black Colonization Experiment on the Northern Coast, 1835–1846. *Journal of the Civil War Era* 2: 478–510.
2013 The Atlantic Legacies of Zephaniah Kingsley: Benevolence, Bondage, and Proslavery Fictions in the Age of Emancipation. PhD dissertation, Department of History, Georgia State University, Atlanta.

Flewellen, Ayana Omilade
2017 Locating Marginalized Historical Narratives at Kingsley Plantation. *Historical Archaeology* 51: 71–87.

Flewellen, Ayana Omilade, Justin P. Dunnavant, Alicia Odewale, Alexandra Jones, Tsione Wolde-Michael, Zoë Crossland, and Maria Franklin
2021 The Future of Archaeology is Antiracist: Archaeology in the Time of Black Lives Matter. *American Antiquity* 86: 224–243.

Ford, Charles
1998 Robert Johnson's Rhythms. *Popular Music* 17: 71–93.

Ford, James A.
1937 An Archaeological Report on the Elizafield Ruins. In *Georgia's Disputed Ruins*, edited by E. Merton Coulter, pp. 193–205. University of North Carolina Press, Chapel Hill.

Ford, Richard I.
2002 James Bennett Griffin, 1905–97. *American Anthropologist* 104: 635–637.

Foster, John Wells
1873 *Pre-Historic Races of the United States of America*. S. C. Griggs, Chicago.

Fountain, Daniel L.
1996 The Ironic Career of Zephaniah Kingsley. *Southern Historian* 17: 34–44.

Fox, Aileen
1974 Prehistoric Maori Storage Pits: Problems in Interpretation. *Journal of the Polynesian Society* 83: 141–154.

Fox, Georgia L.
2015　*The Archaeology of Smoking and Tobacco.* University Press of Florida, Gainesville.

Franklin, John Hope
1969　*From Slavery to Freedom: A History of Negro Americans.* 3rd ed. Vintage, New York.

Franklin, Maria
1997　Out of Site, Out of Mind: The Archaeology of an Enslaved Virginian Household, ca. 1740–1778. PhD dissertation, Department of Anthropology University of California, Berkeley.
2004　*An Archaeological Study of the Rich Neck Slave Quarter and Enslaved Domestic Life.* Colonial Williamsburg Foundation, Williamsburg, Virginia.

Franklin, Maria, Justin P. Dunnavant, Ayana Omilade Flewellen, and Alicia Odewale
2020　The Future Is Now: Archaeology and the Eradication of Anti-Blackness. *International Journal of Historical Archaeology* 24: 753–766.

Frazier, E. Franklin
1928　The Negro Family. *Annals of the American Academy of Political and Social Science* 140: 44–51.
1932　*The Negro Family in Chicago.* University of Chicago Press, Chicago.
1939　*The Negro Family in the United States.* University of Chicago Press, Chicago.
1962　The Failure of the Negro Intellectual. *Negro Digest* 11(4): 26–36.

Freud, Sigmund
1963　*Dora: An Analysis of a Case of Hysteria.* Edited by Philip Rieff. Collier, New York.

Fry, Gladys-Marie
1975　*Night Riders in Black Folk History.* University of Tennessee Press, Knoxville.
1990　*Stitched from the Soul: Slave Quilts from the Ante-Bellum South.* Dutton Studios / Penguin, New York.

Furnivall, Frederick J.
1877　*Harrison's Description of England in Shakespere's Youth Being the Second and Third Books.* Shakespere Society, London.

Gaines, Kevin
2005　E. Franklin Frazier's Revenge: Anticolonialism, Nonalignment, and Black Intellectuals' Critiques of Western Culture. *American Literary History* 17: 506–529.

Galke, Laura J.
2000　Did the Gods of Africa Die? A Re-examination of a Carroll House Crystal Assemblage. *North American Archaeologist* 21: 19–33.
2009　Colonowhen, Colonowho, Colonowhere, Colonowhy: Exploring the Meaning behind the Use of Colonoware Ceramics in Nineteenth-Century Manassas, Virginia. *International Journal of Historical Archaeology* 13: 303–326.

Gall, Michael J., Adam Heinrich, Ilene Grossman-Bailey, Philip A. Hayden, and Justine McKnight
2020　The Place beyond the Fence: Slavery and Cultural Invention of a Delaware Tenant Farm. *Historical Archaeology* 54: 305–333.

Gaskins, Nettrice R.
2020 The Hidden Code of the Kongo Cosmogram in African American Art and Culture. In *African American Arts: Activism, Aesthetics, and Futurity*, edited by Sharrell D. Luckett, pp. 139–151. Bucknell University Press, Lewisburg, Pennsylvania.

Gately, Iain
2003 *Tobacco: A Cultural History of How an Exotic Plant Seduced Civilization*. Grove, New York.

Gates, Louis Henry, Jr.
1988 *The Signifying Monkey: A Theory of African-American Literary Criticism*. Oxford University Press, New York.

Genovese, Eugene D.
1970 The Influence of the Black Power Movement on Historical Scholarship: Reflections of a White Historian. *Daedalus* 99: 473–494.

Gero, Joan M.
1985 Socio-politics of Archaeology and the Woman-at-Home Ideology. *American Antiquity* 50: 342–350.

Godlaski, Theodore M.
2013 Holy Smoke: Tobacco Use Among Native American Tribes in North America. *Substance Use and Misuse* 48: 1–8.

Goggin, John M.
1968 *Spanish Majolica in the New World: Types of the Sixteenth to Eighteenth Centuries*. Department of Anthropology, Yale University, New Haven, Connecticut.

González-Tennant, Edward
2018 *The Rosewood Massacre: The Archaeology and History of Intersectional Violence*. University Press of Florida, Gainesville.

Gott, Suzanne
2003 Golden Emblems of Maternal Benevolence: Transformations of Form and Meaning in Akan Regalia. *African Arts* 36(1): 66–81, 93–96.

Griffin, John W.
1950 An Archaeologist at Fort Gadsden. *Florida Historical Quarterly* 28: 254–261.
1994 Missions and Mills. In *Pioneers in Historical Archaeology: Breaking New Ground*, edited by Stanley South, pp. 67–77. Plenum, New York.

Grinnell, George Bird
1922 The Medicine Wheel. *American Anthropologist* 24: 299–310.

Grossman, Joel W. (editor)
1985 *The Excavation of Augustine Hermans' Warehouse and Associated 17th century Dutch West India Company Deposits*, Vol. 2. Greenhouse Consultants, New York.

Gundaker, Grey
2011 The Kongo Cosmogram in Historical Archaeology and the Moral Compass of Dave the Potter. *Historical Archaeology* 45: 176–183.

Gundaker, Grey, and Judith McWillie
2005   *No Space Hidden: The Spirit of African-American Yard Work.* University of Tennessee Press, Knoxville.
Gutman, Herbert G.
1976   *The Black Family in Slavery and Freedom, 1750–1925.* Vintage, New York.
Hall, Robert L.
1985   Medicine Wheels, Sun Circles, and the Magic of World Center Shrines. *Plains Anthropologist* 30: 181–193.
Hally, David J. (editor)
2009   *Ocmulgee Archaeology, 1936–1986.* University of Georgia Press, Athens.
Hammil, Jan
1987   Cultural Imperialism: American Indian Remains in Cardboard Boxes. *World Archaeological Bulletin* 1: 34–36.
Hammon, Dorothy
1970   Magic: A Problem in Semantics. *American Anthropologist* 72: 1349–1356.
Hammond, John Craig
2003   "They Are Very Much Interested in Obtaining an Unlimited Slavery": Rethinking the Expansion of Slavery in the Louisiana Purchase Territories, 1803–1805. *Journal of the Early Republic* 23: 353–380.
Handler, Jerome S.
1983   An African Pipe from a Slave Cemetery in Barbados, West Indies. In *The Archaeology of the Clay Tobacco Pipe: 8. America,* edited by Peter Davey, pp. 245–254. British Archaeological Reports, Oxford.
1997   An African-Type Healer/Diviner and His Grave Goods: A Burial from a Plantation Slave Cemetery in Barbados, West Indies. *International Journal of Historical Archaeology* 1: 91–130.
2009   The Middle Passage and the Material Culture of Captive Africans. *Slavery and Abolition* 30: 1–26.
Handler, Jerome S., and Frederick W. Lange
1978   *Plantation Slavery in Barbados: An Archaeological and Historical Investigation.* Harvard University Press, Cambridge, Massachusetts.
Hanson, Lee H., Jr.
1971   Kaolin Pipe Stems: Boring in on a Fallacy. *Conference on Historic Site Archaeology Papers* 4: 2–15.
Hariot, Thomas
1590   *A Briefe and True Report of the New Found Land of Virginia, of the Commodities and of the Nature and Manners of the Naturall Inhabitants.* Johann Wechell, London.
Harrington, J. C.
1951   Tobacco Pipes from Jamestown. *Quarterly Bulletin of the Archaeological Society of Virginia* 5(4): n.p.
1954   Dating Stem Fragments of Seventeenth and Eighteenth Century Clay Tobacco Pipes. *Quarterly Bulletin of the Archaeological Society of Virginia* 9(1): 10–14.

Harrison, William Henry
1839 A Discourse on the Aborigines of the Valley of the Ohio. *Transactions of the Historical and Philosophical Society of Ohio* 1: 217–267.

Hatfield, April Lee
2011 Slavery, Trade, War, and the Purposes of Empire. *William and Mary Quarterly* 68: 405–408.

Haveman, Christopher D. (editor)
2018 *Bending Their Way Onward: Creek Indian Removal in Documents*. University of Nebraska Press, Lincoln.

Hawkes, Christopher
1954 Archaeology Theory and Method: Some Suggestions from the Old World. *American Anthropologist* 56: 155–168.

Heath, Barbara J.
2016 Cowrie Shells, Global Trade, and Local Exchange: Piecing Together the Evidence for Colonial Virginia. *Historical Archaeology* 50: 17–46.

Heath, Barbara J., and Amber Bennett
2000 "The Little Spots Allow'd Them": The Archaeological Study of African-American Yards. *Historical Archaeology* 34: 38–55.

Heighton, Robert F., and Kathleen A. Deagan
1972 A New Formula for Dating Kaolin Clay Pipestems. *Conference on Historic Site Archaeology Papers* 6: 220–229.

Henderson, Lawrence W.
1979 *Angola: Five Centuries of Conflict*. Cornell University Press, Ithaca, New York.

Hendon, Julia A.
2000 Having and Holding: Storage, Memory, Knowledge, and Social Relations. *American Anthropologist* 102: 42–53.

Hening, William Waller (editor)
1823 [1680] An Act for Preventing Negroes Insurrections. In *The Statutes at Large; Being a Collection of all the Laws of Virginia*, Vol. 2, pp. 481–482. R. & W. & G. Bartow, New York.

Henry, Susan L.
1979 Terra-Cotta Tobacco Pipes in 17th Century Maryland and Virginia: A Preliminary Study. *Historical Archaeology* 13: 14–37.

Herskovits, Melville J.
1930 The Negro in the New World: The Statement of a Problem. *American Anthropologist* 32: 145–155.
1933 On the Provenience of New World Negroes. *Social Forces* 12: 247–262.
1941 *The Myth of the Negro Past*. Harper and Brothers, New York.

Heywood, Linda M., and John K. Thornton
2007 *Central Africans, Atlantic Creoles, and the Foundation of the Americas, 1585–1660*. Cambridge University Press, Cambridge.
2019 In Search of the 1619 African Arrivals. *Virginia Magazine of History and Biography* 127: 200–211.

Hicks, Brian
2020   Slavery in Charleston: A Chronicle of Human Bondage in the Holy City. *Post and Courier,* April 20, 2020, https://www.postandcourier.com/news/special_reports/slavery-in-charleston-a-chronicle-of-human-bondage-in-the/article_54334e04-4834-50b7-990b-f81fa3c2804a.html, accessed August 2020.

Hill, Matthew H.
1987   Ethnicity Lost? Ethnicity Gained? Information Functions of "African Ceramics" in West Africa and North America. In *Ethnicity and Culture,* edited by Réginald Auger, Margaret F. Glass, Scott MacEachern, and Peter H. McCartney, pp. 135–139. University of Calgary Archaeological Association, Calgary.

Hodgen, Margaret T.
1931   The Doctrine of Survivals: The History of an Idea. *American Anthropologist* 33: 307–324.
1936   *The Doctrine of Survivals: A Chapter in the History of Scientific Method in the Study of Man.* Allenson, London.

Hoggard, Brian
2004   The Archaeology of Counter-Witchcraft and Popular Magic. In *Beyond the Witch Trials: Witchcraft and Magic in Enlightenment Europe,* edited by Owen Davies and Willem de Blécourt, pp. 167–186. Manchester University Press, Manchester.
2016   Witch Bottles: Their Contents, Contexts, and Uses. In *Physical Evidence for Ritual Acts, Sorcery and Witchcraft in Christian Britain: A Feeling for Magic,* edited by Ronald Hutton, pp. 91–105. Palgrave Macmillan, Basingstoke.

Hollander, Jocelyn A., and Rachel L. Einwohner
2004   Conceptualizing Resistance. *Sociological Forum* 19: 533–554.

hooks, bell
1990   *Yearning: Race, Gender, and Cultural Politics.* South End Books, Boston.

Huey, Paul R.
1974   Reworked Pipe Stems: A 17th Century Phenomenon from the Site of Fort Orange, Albany, New York. *Historical Archaeology* 8: 105–111.

Hume, David
1799   *Essays and Treatises on Several Subjects,* Vol. 1. J. Williams, Dublin.

Hurston, Zora Neale
1930   Dance Songs and Tales from the Bahamas. *Journal of American Folk-Lore* 43: 294–312.
1931   Hoodoo in America. *Journal of American Folk-Lore* 44: 317–417.
1945   Crazy for This Democracy. *Negro Digest* 4: 45–48.
1990   *Mules and Men.* HarperCollins, New York.

Hurston, Zora Neale, and John R. Lynch
1927   Communications. *Journal of Negro History* 12: 664–669.

Hutchinson, Margarite (editor)
1881   *A Report of the Kingdom of Congo and of the Surrounding Countries, Drawn out of the Writings and Discourses of the Portuguese Duarte Lopez, by Filippo Pigafetta.* John Murray, London.

Hutton, Ronald
2017   *The Witch: A History of Fear, from Ancient Times to the Present.* Yale University Press, New Haven, Connecticut.
Hutton, Ronald (editor)
2016   *Physical Evidence for Ritual Acts, Sorcery and Witchcraft in Christian Britain: A Feeling for Magic.* Palgrave Macmillan, Basingstoke.
Huysecom, E., M. Rasse, L. Lespez, K. Neumann, A. Fahmy, A. Ballouche, S. Ozainne, M. Maggetti, Ch. Tribolo, and S. Soriano
2009   The Emergence of Pottery in Africa During the Tenth Millennium cal BC: New Evidence from Ounjougou (Mali). *Antiquity* 83: 905–917.
Ibn Khaldun
1958   *The Muqaddimah: An Introduction to History,* Vol. 1. Translated by Franz Rosenthal. Pantheon, New York.
Isichei, Elizabeth
1997   *A History of African Societies to 1870.* Cambridge University Press, Cambridge.
Jackson, Antoinette T.
2004   African Communities in Southeast Coastal Plantation Spaces in America. PhD dissertation, Department of History, University of Florida, Gainesville.
Jackson, Gale P.
2020   *Put Your Hands on Your Hips and Act Like a Woman: Black History and Poetics in Performance.* University of Nebraska Press, Lincoln.
Jacobs, Claude F.
1989   Spirit Guides and Possession in the New Orleans Black Spiritual Churches. *Journal of American Folklore* 102: 45–56, 65–67.
James I
1604   *A Counterblaste to Tobacco.* R. B., London.
1619   *An Abstract of Some Branches of His Maiesties Late Charter Granted to the Tobacco-Pipe Makers of Westminster.* n.p., London.
James, C.L.R.
1989   *The Black Jacobins: Toussaint L'Ouverture and the San Domingo Revolution.* 2nd ed. Vintage, New York.
Janzen, John M., and Reinhild K. Janzen
1988   Nkisi. In *Expressions of Belief: Masterpieces of African, Oceanic, and Indonesian Art from the Museum Voor Volkenkunde, Rotterdam,* edited by Suzanne Greub, pp. 38–55. Rizzoli, New York.
Jefferson, Thomas
1832   *Notes on the State of Virginia.* Lilly and Wait, Boston.
Johnson, David Andrew, II
2018   Enslaved Native Americans and the Making of South Carolina, 1659–1739. PhD dissertation, Department of History, Rice University, Houston.
Johnson, Keith V., and Elwood D. Watson
2005   A Historical Chronology of the Plight of African Americans Gaining Recognition in Engineering and Technology. *Journal of Technology Studies* 31: 81–93.

Jones, Graham M.
2014 Secrecy. *Annual Review of Anthropology* 43: 53–69.
Jordán, Manuel
1998 *The Kongo Kingdom*. Franklin Watts, New York.
Joseph, J. W.
2011 "All of Cross": African Potters, Marks, and Meanings in the Folk Pottery of the Edgefield District, South Carolina. *Historical Archaeology* 45: 134–155.
Keel, Bennie C.
1970 Cyrus Thomas and the Mound Builders. *Southern Indian Studies* 22: 3–16.
Kelley, Sean M., and Henry B. Lovejoy
2016 The Origins of the African-Born Population of Antebellum Texas: A Research Note. *Southwestern Historical Quarterly* 120: 216–232.
Kelly, Kenneth G.
2017 J. C. Harrington Medal in Historical Archaeology: Leland Greer Ferguson. *Historical Archaeology* 51: 9–16.
Kelsey, R. W.
1922 Swiss Settlers in South Carolina. *South Carolina Historical and Genealogical Magazine* 23: 85–91.
Kelso, William M.
1971 *A Report on Exploratory Excavations at Carter's Grove Plantation*. Colonial Williamsburg Foundation Library, Williamsburg, Virginia.
1984 *Kingsmill Plantations, 1619–1800: Archaeology of Country Life in Colonial Virginia*. Academic Press, Orlando.
1986 Mulberry Row: Slave Life at Thomas Jefferson's Monticello. *Archaeology* 39(5): 28–35.
1992 J. C. Harrington Medal in Historical Archaeology: Ivor Noël Hume, 1991. *Historical Archaeology* 26(2): 1–2.
Kendi, Ibram X.
2017 *Stamped from the Beginning: The Definitive History of Racist Ideas in America*. Bold Type, New York.
Kennedy, Roger G.
1996 *Hidden Cities: The Discovery and Loss of Ancient North American Civilization*. Penguin, New York.
Kimmel, Richard H.
1993 Notes on the Cultural Origins and Functions of Sub-Floor Pits. *Historical Archaeology* 27(3): 102–113.
King, Charles
2019 *Gods of the Upper Air: How a Circle of Renegade Anthropologists Reinvented Race, Sex, and Gender in the Twentieth Century*. Doubleday, New York.
Kingsley, Zephaniah
1828 [An Inhabitant of Florida] *A Treatise on the Patriarchal or Co-operative System of Society as It Exists in Some Governments, and Colonies in America, and in the United States under the Name of Slavery, with Its Necessity and Advantages*. n.p.
1838 Hayti. *Colored American* (New York), August 11.

Kleinfeld, Rachel, and John Dickas
2020 *Resisting the Call of Nativism: What US Political Parties Can Learn from Other Democracies.* Carnegie Endowment for International Peace, Washington, DC.

Klingelhofer, Eric
1987 Aspects of Early Afro-American Material Culture: Artifacts from the Slave Quarters of Garrison Plantation, Maryland. *Historical Archaeology* 21(2): 112–119.

Knight, Vernon James, Jr.
2006 Farewell to the Southeastern Ceremonial Complex. *Southeastern Archaeology* 25: 1–5.

Kohrman, Matthew, and Peter Benson
2011 Tobacco. *Annual Review of Anthropology* 40: 329–344.

Koven, Edward L.
1996 *Smoking: The Story Behind the Haze.* Nova Science, New York.

Lane, Julie D., and Daniel M. Wegner
1995 The Cognitive Consequences of Secrecy. *Journal of Personality and Social Psychology* 69: 237–253.

Langley, J. Ayo
1969 Pan-Africanism in Paris, 1924–36. *Journal of Modern African Studies* 7: 69–94.

LaRoche, Cheryl, and Michael Blakey
1997 Seizing Intellectual Power: The Dialogue at the New York African Burial Ground. *Historical Archaeology* 31: 84–106.

Larson, Lewis H., Jr.
1958 Southern Cult Manifestations on the Georgia Coast. *American Antiquity* 23: 426–430.

Lehmer, Donald J.
1971 *Introduction to Middle Missouri Archaeology.* National Park Service, Washington, DC.

Leo, John [Leo Africanus]
1600 *A Geographical Historie of Africa, Written in Arabicke and Italian by John Leo, a More Borne in Granada and Brought Up in Barbarie.* John Pory, London.

Leone, Mark P.
1973a Why the Coalville Tabernacle Had to Be Razed. *Dialogue: A Journal of Mormon Thought* 8: 30–39.
1973b Archaeology as the Science of Technology: Mormon Town Plans and Fences. In *Research and Theory in Current Archaeology,* edited by Charles L. Redman, pp. 125–150. John Wiley and Sons, New York.
1977 The New Mormon Temple in Washington, DC. In *Historical Archaeology and the Importance of Material Things,* edited by Leland Ferguson, pp. 43–61. Society for Historical Archaeology, Germantown, Maryland.
2005 *The Archaeology of Liberty in an American Capital: Excavations in Annapolis.* University of California Press, Berkeley.
2010 *Critical Historical Archaeology.* Left Coast Press, Walnut Creek, California.

2020 The Problem: Religion within the World of Slaves. *Current Anthropology* 61: S276–S288.

Leone, Mark P. (editor)
1972 *Contemporary Archaeology: A Guide to Theory and Contributions.* Southern Illinois University Press, Carbondale.

Leone, Mark P., and Gladys-Marie Fry
1999 Conjuring in the Big House Kitchen: An Interpretation of African American Belief Systems Based on the Uses of Archaeology and Folklore Sources. *Journal of American Folklore* 112: 372–403.
2001 Spirit Management among Americans of African Descent. In *Race and the Archaeology of Identity,* edited by Charles E. Orser Jr., pp. 143–157. University of Utah Press, Salt Lake City.

Leone, Mark P., Jocelyn E. Knauf, and Amanda Tang
2014 Ritual Bundle in Colonial Annapolis. In *Materialities of Ritual in the Black Atlantic,* edited by Akinwumi Ogundiran and Paula Saunders, pp. 198–215. Indiana University Press, Bloomington.

Leone, Mark P., Parker B. Potter Jr., and Paul A. Shackel
1987 Toward a Critical Archaeology. *Current Anthropology* 28: 283–292.

Leone, Mark P., Elizabeth Pruitt, Benjamin A. Skolnik, Stenfan Wochlke, and Tracy Jenkins
2018 The Archaeology of Early African American Communities in Talbot County, Eastern Shore, Maryland, U.S.A., and Their Relationship to Slavery. *Historical Archaeology* 52: 753–772.

Lieffring, Christina
2019 Steamboat Travel Was Dirty and Dangerous, Especially on the Missouri River, https://www.kcur.org/post/steamboat-travel-was-dirty-and-dangerous-especially-missouri-river#stream/0; accessed December 2019.

Linebaugh, Donald W.
1994 All the Annoyances and Inconveniences of the Country: Environmental Factors in the Development of Outbuildings in the Colonial Chesapeake. *Winterthur Portfolio* 29: 1–18.

Lister, Martin
1684 An Ingenious Proposal for a New Sort of Maps of Countrys, Together with Tables of Sands and Clays. *Philosophical Transactions* 14(164): 739–746.

Littell, William, and Jacob Swigert
1822 *A Digest of the Statute Law of Kentucky,* Vol. 2. Kendall and Russell, Frankfort.

Little, Barbara J., and Paul A. Shackel (editors)
2007 *Archaeology as a Tool of Civic Engagement.* AltaMira, Lanham, Maryland.

Littlefield, Daniel C.
2000 The Slave Trade to Colonial South Carolina: A Profile. *South Carolina Historical Magazine* 101: 110–141.

Logan, George C., Thomas W. Bodor, Lynn D. Jones, and Marian C. Creveling
1992 *1991 Archaeological Excavations at the Charles Carroll House in Annapolis, Maryland, 18AP45.* Charles Carroll House of Annapolis, Annapolis.

Lowie, Robert H.
1917   Edward B. Tylor. *American Anthropologist* 19: 262–263.
1918   Survivals and the Historical Method. *American Journal of Sociology* 23: 529–535.
1954   *Indians of the Plains.* McGraw-Hill, New York.
Lucas, Michael T.
2014   Empowered Objects: Material Expressions of Spiritual Beliefs in the Colonial Chesapeake Region. *Historical Archaeology* 48: 106–124.
Luckenbach, Al
2004   The Swan Cove Kiln: Chesapeake Tobacco Pipe Production, circa 1650–1669. In *Ceramics in America,* edited by Robert Hunter, pp. 1–14. Chipstone Foundation, Milwaukee, Wisconsin.
Luckenbach, Al, and Taft Kiser
2006   Seventeenth-Century Tobacco Pipe Manufacturing in the Chesapeake Region: A Preliminary Delineation of Makers and Their Styles. In *Ceramics in America,* edited by Robert Hunter, pp. 161–177. Chipstone Foundation, Milwaukee, Wisconsin.
Lurie, Nancy Oestreich
1966   Women in Early American Anthropology. In *Pioneers of American Anthropology: The Uses of Biography,* edited by June Helm, pp. 29–81. University of Washington Press, Seattle.
Lyon, Edwin A.
1996   *A New Deal for Southeastern Archaeology.* University of Alabama Press, Tuscaloosa.
MacGaffey, Wyatt
1970   The Religious Commissions of the Bakongo. *Man* 5: 27–38.
1986   *Religion and Society in Central Africa: The BaKongo of Lower Zaire.* University of Chicago Press, Chicago.
MacGaffey, Wyatt, and John M. Janzen
1974   Nkisi Figures of the BaKongo. *African Arts* 7: 87–89.
MacMahon, Darcie, and Kathleen Deagan
1996   Legacy of Fort Mose. *Archaeology* 49(5): 54–58.
Maiklem, Lara
2019   *Mudlark: In Search of London's Past along the River Thames.* W. W. Norton, New York.
Mallios, Seth
2005   Back to the Bowl: Using English Tobacco Pipebowls to Calculate Mean Site-Occupation Dates. *Historical Archaeology* 39: 89–104.
Markham, Clements R. (editor)
1878   *The Hawkins' Voyages during the Reigns of Henry VIII, Queen Elizabeth, and James I.* Hakluyt Society, London.
Marrinan, Rochelle A.
2001   Best Supporting Actress? The Contributions of Adelaide K. Bullen. In *Grit-Tempered: Early Women Archaeologists in the Southeastern United States,* edited

by Nancy Marie White, Lynne P. Sullivan, and Rochelle A. Marrinan, pp. 148–162. University Press of Florida, Gainesville.

Marsh, A.
1682 *The Ten Pleasures of Marriage, Relating All the Delights and Contentments That Are Mask'd under the Bands of Matrimony.* N.p., London.

Mason, Otis T.
1877 Anthropology. *American Naturalist* 11: 624–627.

Mather, Increase
1684 *An Essay for the Recording of Illustrious Providences: Wherein an Account Is Given of Many Remarkable and Very Memorable Events, Which Have Hapned This Last Age, Especially in New-England.* Samuel Green, Boston.

Maxwell, William J.
2013 Editorial Federalism: The Hoover Raids, the New Negro Renaissance, and the Origins of FBI Literary Surveillance. In *Publishing Blackness: Textual Constructions of Race since 1850*, edited by George Hutchinson and John K. Young, pp. 136–159. University of Michigan Press, Ann Arbor.

May, Philip S.
1945 Zephaniah Kingsley, Nonconformist (1765–1843). *Florida Historical Quarterly* 23: 145–159.

McDavid, Carol
2007 Beyond Strategy and Good Intentions: Archaeology, Race, and White Privilege. In *Archaeology as a Tool of Civic Engagement*, edited by Barbara J. Little and Paul A. Shackel, pp. 67–88. AltaMira, Lanham, Maryland.

McIlvoy, Karen E.
2020 The Ceramic Assemblage from the Kingsley Plantation Slave Quarters. National Park Service, https://www.nps.gov/archeology/sites/npSites/kingsleyCeramics.htm; accessed August 2020.

McKee, Larry, and Brian W. Thomas
1998 Starting a Conversation: The Public Style of Archaeology at the Hermitage. *Southeastern Archaeology* 17: 133–139.

Mead, Margaret
1928 *Coming of Age in Samoa: A Psychological Study of Primitive Youth for Western Civilisation.* William Morris, New York.

Meek, C. K.
1943 The Religions of Nigeria. *Africa: Journal of the International African Institute* 14: 106–117.

Meltzer, David J.
1998 Introduction: Ephraim Squier, Edwin Davis, and the Making of an American Archaeological Classic. In *Ancient Monuments of the Mississippi Valley by Ephraim G. Squier and Edwin H. Davis*, edited by David J. Meltzer, pp. 1–95. Smithsonian Institution Press, Washington, DC.

Merriam, Alan P.
1964 Melville Jean Herskovits, 1895–1963. *American Anthropologist* 66: 83–109.

Merrifield, Ralph
1954 The Use of Bellarmines as Witch-Bottles. *Guildhall Miscellany* 3: 3–15.
1955 Witch Bottles and Magical Jugs. *Folklore* 66: 195–207.
1967 A Curious Object Seen on Motor-Cars. *Folklore* 78: 307–308.
1988 *The Archaeology of Ritual and Magic*. New Amsterdam, New York.
Merrifield, Ralph, and A. W. Smith
1956 Comment on Good Friday Skipping. *Folklore* 67: 246–248.
Miles
1842 *A Letter to Sir Robert Peel, Bart., on the Causes of the Success of the Non-Productive Classes*. J. Eve, London.
Milling, Chapman J. (editor).
1951 *Colonial South Carolina: Two Contemporary Descriptions*. University of South Carolina Press, Columbia.
M'Lennan, John Ferguson
1896 *Studies in Ancient History: The Second Series*. Macmillan, London.
Morgan, Kenneth
1998 Slaves Sales in Colonial Charleston. *English Historical Review* 113: 905–927.
Morlot, A.
1861 General Views on Archaeology. *Annual Report of the Board of Regents of the Smithsonian Institution . . . for the Year 1860*, pp. 284–343. George W. Bowman, Washington, DC.
Morrison, Toni
2015 *God Help the Child*. Alfred A. Knopf, New York.
Moses, Sharon K.
2018 Enslaved African Conjure and Ritual Deposits on the Hume Plantation, South Carolina. *North American Archaeologist* 39: 131–164.
Mouer, L. Daniel
1993 Chesapeake Creoles: The Creation of Folk Culture in Colonial Virginia. In *The Archaeology of 17th-Century Virginia*, edited by Theodore R. Reinhart and Dennis J. Pogue, pp. 105–166. Dietz, Richmond, Virginia.
Mouer, L. Daniel, Mary Ellen N. Hodges, Stephen R. Potter, Susan L. Henry Renaud, Ivor Noël Hume, Dennis J. Pogue, Martha W. McCartney, and Thomas E. Davidson
1999 Colonoware Pottery, Chesapeake Pipes, and "Uncritical Assumptions." In *"I, Too, Am America": Archaeological Studies of African-American Life*, edited by Theresa A. Singleton, 83–115. University of Virginia Press, Charlottesville.
Mrozowski, Stephen A., Maria Franklin, and Leslie Hunt
2008 Archaeobotanical Analysis and Interpretation of Enslaved Virginian Plant Use at Rich Neck Plantation (44WB52). *American Antiquity* 73: 699–728.
Mullins, Paul R.
2016 J. C. Harrington Medal in Historical Archaeology: Mark P. Leone. *Historical Archaeology* 50: 1–8.
Muys, John
1686 *A Rational Practice of Chyrurgery, or Chyrurigical Observations Resolved According to the Solid Fundamentals of True Philosophy*. Samuel Crouch, London.

Myer, William Edward
1928 Two Prehistoric Villages in Middle Tennessee. *Forty-First Annual Report of the Bureau of American Ethnology to the Secretary of the Smithsonian Institution, 1919–1924*, pp. 485–626. Government Printing Office, Washington, DC.

Nairne, Thomas
1710 *A Letter from South Carolina*. A. Baldwin, London.

Neiman, Fraser D.
1999 Dimensions of Ethnicity. In *Historical Archaeology, Identity Formation, and the Interpretation of Ethnicity*, edited by Maria Franklin and Garrett Fesler, pp. 139–149. Colonial Williamsburg Foundation, Williamsburg, Virginia.

Nelson, Alondra
2013 DNA Ethnicity as Black Social Action? *Cultural Anthropology* 28: 527–536.

Neuman, Robert W.
1984 *An Introduction to Louisiana Archaeology*. Louisiana State University Press, Baton Rouge.

Newby-Alexander, Cassandra
2019 The Arrival of the First Africans to English North America. *Virginia Magazine of History and Biography* 127: 186–199.

Newell, Margaret Ellen
2015 *Brethren by Nature: New England Indians, Colonists, and the Origins of American Slavery*. Cornell University Press, Ithaca, New York.

Ngai, Mae M.
1999 The Architecture of Race in American Immigration Law: A Reexamination of the Immigration Act of 1924. *Journal of American History* 86: 67–92.

Noël Hume, Ivor
1962 An Indian Ware of the Colonial Period. *Quarterly Bulletin of the Archaeological Society of Virginia* 17(1): 1–14.
1963 *Excavations at Rosewell in Gloucester County, Virginia, 1957–1959*. Contributions from the Museum of History and Technology Paper 18. Smithsonian Institution, Washington, DC.
1966 *Excavations at Tutter's Neck in James County, Virginia, 1960–1961*. Contributions from the Museum of History and Technology Paper 53. Smithsonian Institution, Washington, DC.
1972 *A Guide to Artifacts of Colonial America*. Alfred A. Knopf, New York.
1983 *Martin's Hundred: The Discovery of a Lost Colonial Virginia Settlement*. Delta, New York.
2001 *If These Pots Could Talk: Collecting 2,000 Years of British Household Pottery*. Chipstone Foundation, Milwaukee, Wisconsin.
2003–2004 Hunting for a Little Ladle: Tobacco Pipes. *Colonial Williamsburg Journal*, Winter, https://research.colonialwilliamsburg.org/Foundation/journal/Winter03-04/pipes.cfm; accessed November 2020.
2010 *A Passion for the Past: The Odyssey of a Transatlantic Archaeologist*. University of Virginia Press, Charlottesville.

Noël Hume, Ivor, and Henry M. Miller
2011   Ivor Noël Hume: Historical Archaeologist. *Public Historian* 33: 9–32.
Norton, Marcy
2008   *Sacred Gifts, Profane Pleasures: A History of Tobacco and Chocolate in the Atlantic World.* Cornell University Press, Ithaca, New York.
O'Callaghan, E. B. (editor)
1856   *Documents Relative to the Colonial History of the State of New-York.* Weed, Parsons, Albany.
Odum, Howard W.
1910   *Social and Mental Traits of the Negro: Research into the Conditions of the Negro Race in Southern Towns, A Study in Race Traits, Tendencies, and Prospects.* Columbia University Press, New York.
Ogundiran, Akinwumi
2002   Of Small Things Remembered: Beads, Cowries, and Cultural Translations of the Atlantic Experience in Yorubaland. *International Journal of African Historical Studies* 35: 427–457.
2014   Cowries and Rituals of Self-Realization in the Yoruba Region, ca. 1600–1860. In *Materialities of Ritual in the Black Atlantic,* edited by Akinwumi Ogundiran and Paula Saunders, pp. 68–86. Indiana University Press, Bloomington.
O'Hearn, Denis
2009   Repression and Solidary Cultures of Resistance: Irish Political Prisoners on Protest. *American Journal of Sociology* 115: 491–526.
O'Malley, Gregory E.
2017   Slavery's Converging Ground: Charleston's Slave Trade as the Black Heart of the Lowcountry. *William and Mary Quarterly* 74: 271–302.
O'Neill, Aaron
2021   Black and Slave Population in the United States, 1790-1880. *Statista,* March 19, 2021, https://www.statista.com/statistics/1010169/black-and-slave-population-us-1790-1880/; accessed November 2021.
Oriji, John N.
1989   Sacred Authority in Igbo Society. *Archives de Sciences Sociales des Religions* 68: 113–123.
Orser, Charles E., Jr.
1985   Artifacts, Documents, and Memories of the Black Tenant Farmer. *Archaeology* 39(4): 48–53.
1994   The Archaeology of African-American Slave Religion in the Antebellum South. *Cambridge Archaeological Journal* 4: 33–45.
2018   *An Archaeology of the English Atlantic World, 1600–1700.* Cambridge University Press, Cambridge.
2019   Rethinking "Bellarmine" Contexts in 17th-Century England. *Post-Medieval Archaeology* 53: 88–101.
Orser, Charles E., Jr., and Pedro P. A. Funari
2001   Archaeology of Slave Resistance and Rebellion. *World Archaeology* 33: 61–72.

O'Sullivan, John
1845   Annexation. *United States Magazine and Democratic Review* 17(1): 5–10.
Oswald, Adrian
1969   Marked Clay Pipes from Plymouth, Devon. *Post-Medieval Archaeology* 3: 122–142.
Overholtzer, Lisa, and Catherine L. Jalbert
2021   A "Leaky" Pipeline and Chilly Climate in Archaeology in Canada. *American Antiquity* 86: 261–282.
Ozanne, Paul
1962   Notes on the Early Historic Archaeology of Accra. *Transactions of the Historical Society of Ghana* 6: 54–60.
Palmer, Robert
1981   *Deep Blues*. Penguin, New York.
Papadopoulos, John K.
1994   Early Iron Age Potter's Marks in the Aegean. *Hesperia: The Journal of the American School of Classical Studies at Athens* 63: 441–445.
Paper, Jordan
1987   Cosmological Implications of Pan-Indian Sacred Pipe Ritual. *Canadian Journal of Native Studies* 7: 297–306.
Park, Robert E.
1919   The Conflict and Fusion of Cultures with Special Reference to the Negro. *Journal of Negro History* 4: 111–133.
Patten, Drake
1992   Mankala and Minkisi: Possible Evidence of African American Folk Beliefs and Practices. *African American Archaeology* 6: 5–7.
Paterson, David A.
1993   It Took a Community to Save Burial Ground. *New York Times*, August 21: 18.
Patterson, Thomas C.
1995   *Toward a Social History of Archaeology in the United States*. Harcourt Brace College, Fort Worth, Texas.
Pavan, Alexia, Agnese Fusaro, Chiara Visconti, Alessandro Ghidoni, and Arturo Annuci
2018   Archaeological Works at the Fortified Castle of Al Baleed (Husn al Baleed), Southern Oman. *Egitto e Vicino Oriente* 41: 211–234.
Pawson, Michael
1969   Clay Tobacco Pipes in the Knowles Collection. *Quarterly Bulletin of the Archaeological Society of Virginia* 23(3): 115–147.
Paynter, Robert
1992   W.E.B. Du Bois and the Material World of African-Americans in Great Barrington, Massachusetts. *Critique of Anthropology* 12: 277–291.
Peña, J. Theodore, and Myles McCallum
2009   The Production and Distribution of Pottery at Pompeii: A Review of the Evidence, Part 2: The Material Basis for Production and Distribution. *American Journal of Archaeology* 113: 165–201.

Penn Museum
2020 Montroville Wilson Dickeson Collection. PU-Mu. 1080. https://www.penn.museum/collections/archives/findingaid/552853; accessed October 2020.

Perdue, Charles L.
1976 *Weevils in the Wheat: Interviews with Virginia Ex-Slaves.* University of Virginia Press, Charlottesville.

Perry, Warren R., Jean Howson, and Barbara A. Bianco (editors)
2009 *The Archaeology of the New York African Burial Ground, Part 2: Descriptions of Burials.* Howard University Press, Washington, DC.

Pettigrew, William A.
2016 *Freedom's Debt: The Royal African Company and the Politics of the Atlantic Slave Trade, 1672–1752.* University of North Carolina Press, Chapel Hill.

Piwonka, Ruth
2008 "... and I Have Made Good Friends with Them": Plants and the New Netherland Experience. *New York History* 89: 397–425.

Platt, Tony
1989 E. Franklin Frazier Reconsidered. *Social Justice* 16: 186–195.

Pollard, John Garland
1894 *The Pemunkey Indians of Virginia.* Government Printing Office, Washington, DC.

Porter, John A.
1965 *The Vertical Mosaic: An Analysis of Social Class and Power in Canada.* University of Toronto Press, Toronto.

Puckett, Newbell Niles
1926 *Folk Beliefs of the Southern Negro.* University of North Carolina, Chapel Hill.

Purnell, Brian
2010 The African Burial Ground National Monument. *Journal of American History* 97: 735–740.

Quaife, Milo M. (editor)
1916 *The Journals of Captain Meriwether Lewis and Sergeant John Ordway Kept on the Expedition of Western Exploration, 1803–1806.* State Historical Society of Wisconsin, Madison.

Quimby, George I., Jr.
1938 Dated Indian Burials in Michigan. *Papers of the Michigan Academy of Science, Arts, and Letters* 23: 63–72.

Rafferty, Sean M.
2006 Evidence of Early Tobacco in Northeastern North America? *Journal of Archaeological Science* 33: 453–458.

Rawick, George (editor)
1972–1978 *The American Slave: A Composite Autobiography,* 31 vols. Greenwood, Westport, Connecticut.

R. B.
1708 *The English Acquisitions in Guinea & East-India.* Nathaniel Crouch, London.

Redpath, James
1859   *The Roving Editor, Or, Talks with Slaves in the Southern States.* A. B. Burdick, New York.

Reeves, Matthew
2014   Mundane or Spiritual? The Interpretation of Glass Bottle Containers Found on Two Sites of the African Diaspora. In *Materialities of Ritual in the Black Atlantic,* edited by Akinwumi Ogundiran and Paula Saunders, pp. 176–197. Indiana University Press, Bloomington.

Reid, L. Chardé
2022   "It's Not About Us": Exploring White-Public Heritage Space, Community, and Commemoration on Jamestown Island, Virginia. *International Journal of Historical Archaeology* 26: 22–52.

Rivers, W.H.R.
1913   Survival in Sociology. *Sociological Review* 6: 293–305.

Rodriguez, Junius P. (editor)
2006   *Encyclopedia of Slave Resistance and Rebellion.* 2 vols. Greenwood, Westport, Connecticut.

Rouse, Irving
1964   John Mann Goggin, 1916–1963. *American Antiquity* 29: 369–375.

Royal Adventurers
1667   *The Several Declarations of the Company of Royal Adventurers of England Trading into Africa.* N.p., London.

Rucker, Walter
2001   Conjure, Magic, and Power: The Influence of Afro-Atlantic Religious Practices on Slave Resistance and Rebellion. *Journal of Black Studies* 32: 84–103.

Ruppel, Timothy, Jessica Neuwirth, Mark P. Leone, and Gladys-Marie Fry
2003   Hidden in View: African Spiritual Spaces in North American Landscapes. *Antiquity* 77: 321–335.

Ryan, Joanne, Donald G. Hunter, Bryan Haley, and David B. Kelley
2022   *Archaeological Investigations at the Levi Jordan Plantation (41BO165) State Historic Site, Brazoria County, Texas.* Coastal Environments, Houston.

Sagee, Alona
2007   Bessie Smith: "Down Hearted Blues" and "Gulf Coast Blues" Revisited. *Popular Music* 26: 117–127.

Samford, Patricia
1988   *Carter's Grove Slave Quarter's Archaeological Report, Block 50.* Colonial Williamsburg Foundation Library, Williamsburg, Virginia.
1999   "Strong Is the Bond of Kinship": West African-Style Ancestor Shrines and Subfloor Pits on African-American Quarters. In *Historical Archaeology, Identity Formation, and the Interpretation of Ethnicity,* edited by Maria Franklin and Garrett Fesler, pp. 71–91. Colonial Williamsburg Foundation, Williamsburg, Virginia.
2000   Power Runs in Many Channels: Subfloor Pits and West African-Based Spiritual

Traditions in Colonial Virginia. PhD dissertation, Department of Anthropology, University of North Carolina, Chapel Hill.
2007 *Subfloor Pits and the Archaeology of Slavery in Colonial Virginia.* University of Alabama Press, Tuscaloosa.

Sansevere, Keri J.
2017 Colonoware in the Upper Mid-Atlantic and Northeast. In *Archaeologies of African American Life in the Upper Mid-Atlantic,* edited by Michael J. Gall and Richard F. Veit, pp. 37–54. University of Alabama Press, Tuscaloosa.

Sassaman, Kenneth E.
1993 *Early Pottery in the Southeast: Tradition and Innovation in Cooking Technology.* University of Alabama Press, Tuscaloosa.

Sattes, Corey A. H., Jon Bernard Marcoux, Sarah E. Platte, Martha Zierden, and Ronald W. Anthony
2020 Preliminary Identification of African-Style Rouletted Colonoware in the Colonial South Carolina Lowcountry. *Journal of African Diaspora Archaeology and Heritage* 9: 1–36.

Saunders, Rebecca
2012 Deep Surfaces: Pottery Decoration and Identity in the Mission Period. *Historical Archaeology* 46(1): 94–107.

Sayers, Daniel O.
2014 *A Desolate Place for a Defiant People: The Archaeology of Maroons, Indigenous Americans, and Enslaves Laborers in the Great Dismal Swamp.* University Press of Florida, Gainesville.

Schablitsky, Julie M.
2011 Meanings and Motivations behind the Use of West African Spirit Practices. In *Historical Archaeology and the Importance of Material Things II,* edited by Julie M. Schablitsky and Mark P. Leone, pp. 45–67. Society for Historical Archaeology, Rockville, Maryland.
2016 Belvoir's Legacy: The Highly Personal Archaeology of Enslavement on a Tobacco Plantation. *Archaeology* 69(6): 55–56, 58, 62–63.

Schablitsky, Julie M., Kelsey E. Witt, Jazmín Ramos Madrigal, Martin R. Ellegaard, Ripan S. Malhi, and Hannes Schroeder
2019 Ancient DNA Analysis of a Nineteenth Century Tobacco Pipe from a Maryland Slave Quarter. *Journal of Archaeological Science* 105: 11–18.

Schafer, Daniel L.
2003 *Anna Madgigine Jai Kingsley: African Princess, Florida Slave, Plantation Slaveowner.* University Press of Florida, Gainesville.
2013 *Zephaniah Kingsley Jr. and the Atlantic World: Slave Trader, Plantation Owner, Emancipator.* University Press of Florida, Gainesville.

Schiffer, Michael B.
1987 *Formation Processes of the Archaeological Record.* University of New Mexico Press, Albuquerque.

Schouler, James
1882   *History of the United States of America Under the Constitution: 2. 1801–1817.* William H. Morrison, Washington, DC.
Schneider, Tsim D., and Lee M. Panich (editors)
2022   *Archaeologies of Indigenous Presence.* University of Florida Press, Gainesville.
Schroeder, Patricia R.
2015   Neo-Hoodoo Dramaturgy: Robert Johnson on Stage. *African American Review* 48: 83–96.
Schuyler, Robert
1976   Images of America: The Contribution of Historical Archaeology to National Identity. *Southwestern Lore* 42(4): 27–39.
Scott, Elizabeth M.
2001   Food and Social Relations at Nina Plantation. *American Anthropologist* 103: 671–691.
Seguin, Charles, and David Rigby
2019   National Crimes: A New National Data Set of Lynchings in the United States, 1883 to 1945. *Socius: Sociological Research for a Dynamic World* 5: 1–9.
Shackel, Paul A.
2011   *New Philadelphia: An Archaeology of Race in the Heartland.* University of California Press, Berkeley.
Shadwell, Thomas
1689   *Bury-Fair: A Comedy, as it is Acted by His Majesty's Servants.* James Knapton, London.
Shepherd, Samuel (editor)
1835 [1795]   An Act to Reduce into One, the Several Acts concerning Slaves, Free Negroes, and Mulattoes. In *The Statutes at Large of Virginia,* Vol. 1, pp. 122–130. Samuel Shepherd, Richmond.
Shorto, Russell
2004   *The Island at the Center of the World: The Epic Story of Dutch Manhattan and the Forgotten Colony that Shaped America.* Random House, New York.
Shott, Michael J.
2012   Toward Settlement Occupation Span from Dispersion of Tobacco-Pipe Stem-Bore Diameter Values. *Historical Archaeology* 46: 16–38.
Sikes, Kathryn
2008   Stars as Social Space? Contextualizing 17th-Century Chesapeake Star-Motif Pipes. *Post-Medieval Archaeology* 42: 75–103.
Silverberg, Robert
1970   *The Mound Builders.* Ohio University Press, Athens.
Simms, William Gilmore
1853   *The Wigwam and the Cabin: or, Tales of the South, Second Series.* Lippincott, Grambo, Philadelphia.
Singleton, Theresa A.
1980   The Archaeology of Afro-American Slavery in Coastal Georgia: A Regional Per-

ception of Slave Households and Community Patterns. PhD dissertation, Department of Anthropology, University of Florida, Gainesville.
1995   The Archaeology of Slavery in North America. *Annual Review of Anthropology* 24: 119-140.

Singleton, Theresa A., and Mark Bograd
2000   Breaking Typological Barriers: Looking into the Colono in Colonoware. In *Lines That Divide: Historical Archaeologies of Race, Class, and Gender*, edited by James A. Delle, Stephen A. Mrozowski, and Robert Paynter, pp. 3-21. University of Tennessee Press, Knoxville.

Slepian, Michael L., Jinseok S. Chun, and Malia F. Mason
2017   The Experience of Secrecy. *Journal of Personality and Social Psychology* 113: 1-33.

Slepian, Michael L., Nir Halevy, and Adam D. Galinsky
2019   The Solitude of Secrecy: Thinking About Secrets Evokes Goal Conflict and Feelings of Fatigue. *Personality and Social Psychology Bulletin* 45: 1129-1151.

Slepian, Michael L., E. J. Masicampo, and Adam D. Galinsky
2016   The Hidden Effect of Recalling Secrets: Assimilation, Contrast, and the Burdens of Secrecy. *Journal of Experimental Psychology* 145: e27-e48.

Smith, Ayana
2005   Blues, Criticism, and the Signifying Trickster. *Popular Music* 24: 179-191.

Smith, Hale G.
1948   Two Historical Archaeological Periods in Florida. *American Antiquity* 13: 313-319.

Smith, J. M. Powis
1926   Archaeology and the Old Testament During the First Quarter of the Twentieth Century. *Journal of Religion* 6: 284-301.

Smith, Thomas T.
1996   U.S. Army Combat Operations in the Indian Wars of Texas, 1849-1881. *Southwestern Historical Quarterly* 99: 501-531.

Smyth, J.F.D.
1784   *A Tour in the United States of America*, Vol. 1. G. Robinson, London.

Soper, Robert
1985   Roulette Decoration on African Pottery: Technical Considerations, Dating, and Distributions. *African Archaeological Review* 3: 29-51.

South, Stanley
1964   Preface. *Florida Anthropologist* 17(2): 34.
1974   *Palmetto Parapets*. Anthropological Studies 1. South Carolina Institute of Archaeology and Anthropology, Columbia.
1979   Historic Site Content, Structure, and Function. *American Antiquity* 44: 213-237.

Speck, Frank G.
1928   *Chapters on the Ethnology of the Powhatan Tribes of Virginia*. Museum of the American Indian, Heye Foundation, New York.

Spivey, Ashley Layne Atkins
2019   Knowing the River, Working the Land, and Digging for Clay: Pamunkey Indian

Subsistence Practices and the Market Economy, 1800–1900. PhD dissertation, Department of Anthropology, College of William and Mary, Williamsburg, Virginia.

St. Jean, Wendy
2003 Trading Paths: Mapping Chickasaw History in the Eighteenth Century. *American Indian Quarterly* 27: 758–780.

Stanton, Susan Marion
2001 "Voice of the Fugitive": Henry Bibb and "Racial Uplift" in Canada West, 1851–1852. PhD dissertation, Department of History, University of Victoria, Victoria, BC.

Stanwood, Owen
2006 Captives and Slaves: Indian Labor, Cultural Conversion, and the Plantation Revolution in Virginia. *Virginia Magazine of History and Biography* 114: 435–463.

Steen, Carl
2011 Cosmograms, Crosses, and Xs: Context and Inference. *Historical Archaeology* 45: 166–175.

Steinbauer, M.
1862 *Catalogue of a Collection of Ancient and Modern Stone Implements and Other Weapons, Tools, and Utensils of the Aborigines of Various Countries in the Possession of Henry Christy.* Taylor and Francis, London.

Steinmetz, Paul B.
1984 The Sacred Pipe in American Indian Religions. *American Indian Culture and Research Journal* 8: 27–80.

Steponaitis, Vincas P., and David T. Dockery III
2011 Mississippian Effigy Pipes and the Glendon Limestone. *American Antiquity* 76: 345–354.

Stowell, Daniel W. (editor)
2000 *Balancing Evils Judiciously: The Proslavery Writings of Zephaniah Kingsley.* University Press of Florida, Gainesville.

Sturtevant, William C.
1964 John Mann Goggin, 1916–1963. *American Anthropologist* 66: 385–394.

Sundiata, Tiki
1970 A Portrait of Marcus Garvey. *Black Scholar* 2: 7–19.

Sweet, James H.
1997 The Iberian Roots of American Racist Thought. *William and Mary Quarterly* 54: 143–166.

Talbot, Steve
1981 *Roots of Oppression: The American Indian Question.* International, New York.

Talley, Thomas W.
1922 *Negro Folk Rhymes: Wise and Otherwise.* Macmillan, New York.

Tatler
1850 Management of Negroes. *Southern Cultivator* 8(11): 62.

Tax, Thomas Gilbert
1973 The Development of American Archaeology, 1800–1879. PhD dissertation, Department of History, University of Chicago, Chicago.
Taylor, Walter W.
1948 *A Study of Archeology*. American Anthropological Association, Washington, DC.
Thackeray, Frank W., and John E. Findling (editors)
2001 *Events That Changed the World Through the Sixteenth Century*. Greenwood, Westport, Connecticut.
Thomas, Cyrus
1884 Who Were the Mound Builders? *American Antiquarian and Oriental Journal* 69(2): 90–99.
1894 Report on the Mound Explorations of the Bureau of Ethnology. *Twelfth Annual Report of the Bureau of American Ethnology to the Secretary of the Smithsonian Institution, 1890–91*. Government Printing Office, Washington, DC.
Thomas, Keith
1975 An Anthropology of Religion and Magic, II. *Journal of Interdisciplinary History* 6: 91–109.
1991 *Religion and the Decline of Magic*. Penguin, London.
Thompson, Edgar T.
1940 The Planter in the Pattern of Race Relations in the South. *Social Forces* 19: 244–252.
1959 The Plantation as Social System. *Revista Geográfica* 25(51): 41–56.
2010 *The Plantation*. Edited by Sidney W. Mintz and George Baca. University of South Carolina Press, Columbia.
Thompson, L. O'Brien
1982 Franklin Frazier: Mainstream or Black Sociologist? An Appraisal. *Sociological Focus* 15: 219–229.
Thompson, Robert Ferris
1978 The Grand Detroit "N'Kondi." *Bulletin of the Detroit Institute of Arts* 56: 206–221.
1983 *Flash of the Spirit: African and Afro-American Art and Philosophy*. Random House, New York.
2005 Kongo Influences on African-American Artistic Culture. In *Africanisms in American Culture*, 2nd ed., edited by Joseph E. Holloway, pp. 288–294. Indiana University Press, Bloomington.
Thornton, John K.
1977 Demography and History in the Kingdom of Kongo, 1550–1750. *Journal of African History* 18: 507–530.
1998 The African Experience of the "20. and Odd Negroes" Arriving in Virginia in 1619. *William and Mary Quarterly* 55: 421–434.
2006 Elite Women in the Kingdom of Kongo: Historical Perspectives on Women's Political Power. *Journal of African History* 47: 437–460.

2013   Afro-Christian Syncretism in the Kingdom of Kongo. *Journal of African History* 54: 53–77.
2016   The Kingdom of Kongo and the Thirty Year's War. *Journal of World History* 27: 189–213.
Tilford, Kathy
1997   Anna Kingsley: A Free Woman. *OAH Magazine of History* 12: 35–37.
Trigger, Bruce G.
1984   Alternative Archaeologies: Nationalist, Colonialist, Imperialist. *Man* 19: 355–370.
Turner, Frederick Jackson
1893   The Significance of the Frontier in American History. *Proceedings of the State Historical Society of Wisconsin at Its Forty-First Annual Meeting,* pp. 79–112. Democrat Printing, Madison.
Tylor, Edward B.
1861   *Anahuac: Or, Mexico and the Mexicans, Ancient and Modern.* Longmans, Green, Reader, and Dyer, London.
1871   *Primitive Culture: Researches into the Development of Mythology, Philosophy, Religion, Art, and Custom,* Vol. 1. John Murray, London.
Veit, Richard
1997   A Case of Archaeological Amnesia: A Contextual Biography of Montroville Wilson Dickeson (1810–1882), Early American Archaeologist. *Archaeology of Eastern North America* 25: 97–123.
1999   Mastodons, Mound Builders, and Montroville Wilson Dickeson: Pioneering American Archaeologist. *Expedition* [Penn Museum] 41(3): 20–31.
Vermillion, Stephanie
2021   Georgia's Ocmulgee Mounds May be America's Next National Park. *Condé Nast Traveler,* September 22, https://www.cntraveler.com/story/georgias-ocmulgee-mounds-may-be-americas-next-national-park; accessed November 2021.
Vernon, Richard
1988   17th Century Apalachee Colono-Ware as a Reflection of Demography, Economics, and Acculturation. *Historical Archaeology* 22(1): 76–82.
Vince, Alan, and Allan Peacey
2006   Pipemakers and Their Workshops: The Use of Geochemical Analysis in the Study of the Clay Tobacco Pipe Industry. In *Between Dirt and Discussion: Methods, Methodology, and Interpretation in Historical Archaeology,* edited by Steven N. Archer and Kevin M. Bartoy, pp. 11–31. Springer, New York.
Vines, Richard
1656   *Sermons Preached upon Several Publike and Eminent Occasions.* Abel Roper, London.
Voorhies, Barbara
1992   Albert C. Spaulding, 1914–1990. *American Antiquity* 57: 197–201.
Voss, Barbara
2021   Documenting Cultures of Harassment in Archaeology: A Review and Analysis

of Quantitative and Qualitative Research Studies. *American Antiquity* 86: 244–260.

Walker, Iain C.
1977   *Tobacco Pipes, with Particular Reference to the Bristol Industry.* National Historic Parks and Sites Branch, Parks Canada, Ottawa.

Walker, Karen Jo
1988   *Kingsley and His Slaves: Anthropological Interpretations and Evaluations.* South Carolina Institute of Archaeology and Anthropology, Columbia.

Wallace, Dale
2015   Rethinking Religion, Magic, and Witchcraft in South Africa: From Colonial Coherence to Postcolonial Conundrum. *Journal for the Study of Religion* 28: 23–51.

Walters, Kerry
2015   *American Slave Revolts and Conspiracies: A Reference Guide.* ABC-CLIO, Santa Barbara.

Waring, A. J., Jr., and Preston Holder
1945   A Prehistoric Ceremonial Complex in the Southeastern United States. *American Anthropologist* 47: 1–34.

Washington, Booker T.
1910   The Negro's Part in Southern Development. *Annals of the American Academy of Political and Social Science* 35: 124–133.

Watkins, Rachel
2020   Science and Freedom. *Washington History* 32: 51–53.

Wehmeyer, Stephen C.
2000   Indian Altars of the Spiritual Church: Kongo Echoes in New Orleans. *African Arts* 33(4): 62–69, 95–96.
2007   Indians at the Door: Power and Placement on New Orleans Spiritual Church Altars. *Western Folklore* 66: 15.

Weik, Terrance M.
2012   *The Archaeology of Antislavery Resistance.* University Press of Florida, Gainesville.

West, Cornel
1989   *The American Evasion of Philosophy: A Genealogy of Pragmatism.* University of Wisconsin Press, Madison.

Westmacott, Richard
1992   *African-American Gardens and Yards in the Rural South.* University of Tennessee Press, Knoxville.

White, John
1585   A Young Woman of Aquascogoc. British Museum, Department of Prints and Drawings, SL,5270.6, www.britishmuseum.org/collection/object/P_SL-5270-6; accessed November 2020.

White, Marilyn M.
2017   Gladys-Marie Fry (1931–2015). *Journal of American Folklore* 130: 473–474.

Wilkerson, S. Jeffrey K.
1978   Ripley Pierce Bullen, 1902–1976. *American Antiquity* 43: 622–631.

Wilkie, Laurie A.
1995   Magic and Empowerment on the Plantation: An Archaeological Consideration of African-American World View. *Southeastern Archaeology* 14: 136–148.
Willey, Gordon R.
1969   James A. Ford, 1911–1968. *American Antiquity* 34: 62–71.
Willey, Gordon R., and Jeremy A. Sabloff
1993   *A History of American Archaeology,* 3rd ed. W. H. Freeman, New York.
Wingfield, Chris
2009   Is the Heart at Home? E. B. Tylor's Collections from Somerset. *Journal of Museum Ethnography* 22: 22–38.
Winter, Joseph C.
2000   Introduction to the North American Tobacco Species. In *Tobacco Use by Native North Americans: Sacred Smoke and Silent Killer,* edited by Joseph C. Winter, pp. 3–8. University of Oklahoma Press, Norman.
Wolf, Eric R.
1963   Melville J. Herskovits. *Comparative Studies in Society and History* 5: 480–481.
Wood, Peter H.
1974   *Black Majority: Negroes in Colonial South Carolina from 1670 through the Stono Rebellion.* Alfred A. Knopf, New York.
Yetter, George Humphrey
1988   *Williamsburg Before and After: The Rebirth of Virginia's Colonial Capital.* Colonial Williamsburg Foundation, Williamsburg, Virginia.
Young, Amy L.
1996   Archaeological Evidence of African-Style Ritual and Healing Practices in the Upland South. *Tennessee Anthropologist* 21: 139–155.
Zedeño, María Nieves
2008   Bundled Worlds: The Roles and Interactions of Complex Objects from the North American Plains. *Journal of Archaeological Method and Theory* 15: 362–378.
Zimmerman, Larry J.
2006   Sharing Control of the Past. In *Archaeological Ethics,* 2nd ed., edited by Karen D. Vitelli and Chip Colwell-Chanthaphonh, pp. 170–174. Rowman and Littlefield, Lanham, Maryland.

Index

Aegean Sea, 83
African American: archaeologists, 44–45, 70–71; artifacts of, 156–58, 160, 162–63, 168–71, 174; charms, 164; Charter Generation, 1, 97–98, 159, 203; crossroads, importance to, 101; dance, 26; diet, 140–41, 185–86; dress, 26; emancipated, 155; family, 27–28, 31–33; folklore, 161, 166; hoodoo, 164–67; housing, 125, 130–31, 138–39, 141, 150 155–57, 158; magician/curer, conjurer, 157; music, 5, 101, 165; pits of, 129, 131–32, 139–40, 151 191, 196; Plantation Generation, 98; pottery, 77–81, 201, 203–4; quilting, 161, 204; racism against, 2, 26, 35, 47–48, 50, 79, 97, 130–31, 192–93, 200, 203; resistance of, 191–93, 196; ritual bundles of, 151, 163–64, 167–72, 191, 197, 201, 203–4; shrines of, 144–48, 150; Spiritual churches, 170–71; terrorism of, 161; yards of, 204
African Burial Ground (New York), 144, 200–201
Africanisms, 32, 77, 115–16, 124, 148, 155, 156, 172, 175, 199, 203; Fairbanks and, 19–21; Frazier on, 31–33; Herskovits on, 34–35; Park on, 32
Afro-American Life Insurance Company, 202
Agar, Ben, 106
Agbe-Davies, Anna, 119–23
Alexandria (Virginia) Archaeology, 138
Alexandria (Virginia) Archaeology Research Center, 112
American Antiquarian Society, 46
American Ethnological Society, 46
Amherst College, 114

Anderson, Leafy, 170–71
Anglo-Saxons, 61
Angola, 91–95; Luanda, 1
Apalachicola National Forest (Florida), 53
Apalachicola River (Florida), 54
Archaeology, text-aided, 91
Aryans, 48
Assimilation, 62–63
Association for the Study of Negro Life and History, 166
Atlanta University Negro Conference, 27, 31
Atwater, Caleb, 40
Aztecs, 41, 172

Babylonians, 48
Bacon, Francis, 30
Bahamas, 166
Baker, Stephen, 64–65
BaKongo, 82, 91, 93, 95–96, 97, 159; religion of, 98–100
Ball, Charles, 197
Banking, American, 180–81
Bantu, languages, 98
Barbados, 114–15, 144, 146
Bartmann jugs. *See* Bellarmine jugs
Basden, G. T., 147–48
Bastille, 196
Bearded-man jugs. *See* Bellarmine jugs
Bellarmine, Robert (Roberto Bellarmino), 154
Bellarmine jugs, 153–54
Belvoir Plantation (Maryland), 124–25
Beverly, Robert, 132
Bibb, George, 177
Bibb, Granville, 177

Bibb, Henry, 176, 200; attends prayer meeting, 186–87; befriends Irish, 189; capture (first), 182–83, (second), 184; creates *Voice of the Fugitive*, 190; early years, 177–78; escape (first), 179–80, (second), 183, (third), 187–88; jailed, 182, 184–85; marriage (to Malinda), 178–79, (to Mary E. Miles), 190; punishment of, 187; purchases family, 181; resistance of (overt/covert), 193–94; sold, (to Garrison), 184, (to Whitfield), 185; test of account of, 191; tries conjuring, 197
Bibb, James, 177
Bibb, Malinda, 178–79, 181–82, 183–84, 186–87
Bibb, Mary Francis, 179, 181, 183
Bibb, Milldred, 177, 183, 191
Binford, Lewis, 110–11
Black Hawk, 170–71
Blakey, Michael, 200–201
Blassingame, John, 2
Blues (music), 5, 101, 165
Bluff Plantation (South Carolina), 67
Boas, Franz, 30–31, 35, 50, 63, 166; lectures at Howard University, 31
Bradbury, John, 128
Brice House (Maryland), 168
Brinton, Daniel G., 50–51
Brown, Kenneth, 155–60, 162, 163
Brugis, Thomas, 133
Bullen, Adelaide K., 52–53, 55
Bullen, Ripley P., 52–53, 55
Bulow Plantation (Florida), 149–50
Bundles, ritual, 151, 163–64, 167–72, 201, 203–4
Bureau of (American) Ethnology, 49, 73, 77
Butler, William, 177

Cahokia Mounds (Illinois), 49, 66, 190
Canada, 3, 178, 179, 185, 190
Caribbean, 1, 3, 78, 104, 183, 189
Carroll, Charles (of Annapolis), 162
Carroll, Charles (of Carrollton), 162
Carroll, Charles (settler), 162
Carter's Grove Plantation (Virginia), 129–30, 141
Cartier, Jacques, 105
Castle, William E., 79–80

Catholicism, 93, 154, 162, 167, 170
Cellars, English, 127, 132–34
Central America, 104
Chaco Canyon (New Mexico), 52
Chad, 120
Charles Carroll House (Maryland), 162–63, 172
Charleston, South Carolina, 12–13, 63, 65, 96, 97, 100
Charlevoix, Pierre, 129
Charter Generation, 1, 97–98, 159, 203
Chicago Academy of Science, 47
Child, Lydia Maria, 12
China, 48, 156, 167, 173; Ming Dynasty, 83; Neolithic, 87; porcelain, 83; seafarers of, 41
Christianity, 89–90, 94–96, 133, 146–49, 158. *See also* Catholicism; Pentecostalism; Protestantism
Christy, Henry, 22, 25
Church of Latter-Day Saints, 162
Cincinnati, Ohio, 29–30, 40
Civil Rights Movement, 55, 69, 122
Clapton, Eric, 101
Coe, Joffre, 66, 91
Cole, Johnetta Betsch, 202
Colono-Indian ware, 62–70, 123. *See also* Colonoware
Colonoware, 57, 72–81, 82–84, 86, 89–90, 102, 114, 117, 126, 131, 158, 196
Columbia University, 30–31, 52
Combahee River (South Carolina), 67, 68, 72
Confederate Army, 54
Conference on Historic Site Archaeology, 10
Congo, Belgian, 35
Congo River, 92
Coolidge, Calvin, 79
Couper Plantation (Georgia), 172
Cowrie shells, 143–44, 148, 160
Cream (rock band), 101
Creek (Muscogee), removal, 6
Crossroads, importance of, 101
Cultural retentions: Thucydides on, 21; Tylor on, 24–26. *See also* Africanisms
Cunning folk, 152

Dahomey, 35, 38
Darwin, Charles, 22

Davidson, James, 148–50
Davis, Edwin H., 45–46, 87
Deagan, Kathleen, 72
Declaration of Independence, 162
Deetz, James, 70, 73
Democratic Republic of Congo, 91
Descartes, René, 30
Dickeson, Montroville Wilson, 42–45, 48, 66, 70
Dikenga, 92, 99–101
Douglass, Frederick, 11
Drake, Francis, 105
Drayton, Mary Henrietta, 84
Drayton Hall Plantation (South Carolina), 84, 97
Drue, Emanuel, 113–14
Du Bois, W.E.B., 27, 31–32, 50, 79, 80, 90, 122, 150, 200; on African American family, 27–28, 203; connection between U.S. and Africa, 27; on healers, 197; and NAACP, 55
Dundy, John, 179–80
Dutch, colonial, 1, 109, 112, 134, 165, 172–73

East India Company, 144, 173
Egan, John J., 43–44
Egypt, 23, 39
Eliot, Thomas, 132
Elizafield Plantation (Georgia), 51–52
Emerson, Matthew, 114–16, 119, 120, 151, 171
English, colonial, 96–97, 112–13, 116–17, 143–45, 165
Equiano, Olaudah, 145–46, 147, 148
Europe, 39, 83, 87, 153; artifacts of, 58, 61, 64
Evans, Clifford, 62
Evolution, cultural, 24–25

Fairbanks, Charles H., 3, 5–6, 26–28, 56, 57, 63–64, 69, 70, 72, 74, 76, 91, 121, 129, 149, 150, 172, 175, 199–200, 203; Africanisms and, 19–21; at Kingsley Plantation, 18–20; at University of Michigan, 7, 9
Fairbanks, Evelyn, 7
Falconer, William, on race, 16
Fauset, Arthur, 26
Ferguson, Leland, 65–70, 72, 74, 79, 81, 82, 91, 114, 120, 131, 148, 151, 171

Fesler, Garrett, 135, 138–40
First World War, 28–29, 30
Flowerdew Hundred Plantation (Virginia), 118
Folklore, 161, 163–64, 166, 200; British, 153
Ford, James A., 51–52
Fort Ancient Aspect, 7
Fort Gadsden (Florida), 53–55, 58
Fort George Island (Florida), 5, 14, 54–55
Fort Mose (Florida), 166
Fort Moultrie (South Carolina), 65
Fort Orange (New York), 109
Fort Watson (South Carolina), 66–67, 68
Foster, John Wells, 47–48; racial types of, 48
Foster, Lucy, 53
Franklin, John Hope, 2
Franklin, Maria, 135–38
Frazier, E. Franklin, 21, 28–29, 62, 64, 122, 203; on Africanisms, 31; and Chicago Urban League, 31; at Howard University, 28; on integration, 37; views on *Brown v. Board of Education*, 37
French, colonial, 1, 105, 165; housing, 190
Fry, Gladys-Marie, 160–61, 163, 164, 167, 170

Gallatin, Albert, 46
Garrison, Madison, 184–85
Garvey, Marcus, 55
Gaskins, Nettrice R., 102
Gatewood, William H., 182–83, 194
Germany, 153
Ghana, 35, 67, 82, 115, 145
Goggin, John, 9–10
Great Awakening, 164–65
Great Depression, 6
Great Serpent Mound (Ohio), 7
Greeks, 42, 118
Greenfield, Richard, 105
Green Spring Plantation (Virginia), 115–16
Greybeard jugs. *See* Bellarmine jugs
Griffin, James B., 7–9, 52, 57, 66, 76
Griffin, John, 53–55, 58
Guatemala, 155
Guildhall Museum (London), 60, 62, 85, 110, 152

Haiti, 35, 166, 167
Harlem Renaissance, 165

Harrington, J. C., 61, 85; and clay pipes, 110–11, 112
Harrison, William, 105
Harrison, William Henry, 40–41
Harvard University, 52, 192
Hawkes, Christopher, 85–86, 90–91, 102
Hawkins, John, 105
Hayden Geological Survey, 49
Hebrew Union College (Cincinnati, Ohio), 30
Henry, Susan, 112–13, 114, 119
Heriot, Thomas, 105
Herodotus, 42
Herskovits, Melville J., 21, 29–30, 64, 122, 166, 199; on Africanisms, 34–35; Boas and, 30–31; fieldwork of, 35; overlooks material culture, 37–38
Hippocrates: climatic theory of race, 23; on race, 16
Holmes, Sherlock, 113
Holy Land, 86
Hoodoo, 151, 164–67
Howard University, 28, 31, 200
Hudson, Henry, 173
Hudson River, 174
Hume, David, 97
Hurston, Zora Neale, 26, 165–67, 200, 202

Ibn Khaldun, climatic theory of race, 23
Igbo, 145, 149; religion of, 146–48
Illinois Natural History Society, 49
Immigration Act of 1924, 79
India, 23, 48
Indian Ocean, 143
Indigenous Americans, 1, 40–41, 57, 132, 135, 151, 203; Apalachee, 72; archaeology of, 7–9; Arikara, 128; artifacts of, 8, 58, 169; Catawba, 63–65, 77; charms of, 170; Chickahominy, 74; Chickasaw, 87; clay pipes, 107, 112, 116–17, 126; Dakota, 128; Great Lakes, 129; Guale, 73; Hidatsa, 128; Mandan, 128; Mattapony, 73, 74; Medicine Wheel (Wyoming), 87; mounds of, 40–50, 87; Natchez, 48; Onondaga Haudenosaunee (Iroquois), 6; Pamunkey, 65, 73, 74, 77; pits, 128–29; Plains, 52, 87, 128, 129, 134; pottery, 7–8, 57, 61–63, 72–74, 76, 83; Powhatan, 63, 73, 118; Puebloans, 52, 87; Rappahannock, 118; Southeastern Ceremonial Complex, 87–89; symbolic motifs of, 88–89; Thakiwaki (Sauk/Sac), 170; use of tobacco, 104–5, 114, 116
Innocent IX (Pope), 93
Irene Mounds (Georgia), 89
Irish, 189–90; monks, 41
Iron Age, 83

Jack (enslaved), 187–88
Jackson, Andrew, 54
Jackson, Antoinette T., 201–2
Jai, Anta Madgigine. *See* Kingsley, Anna H.
Jamaica, 97, 166
James, William, 121
James Fort (Virginia), 129
James I, 106, 107
James River, 129, 138
Jamestown, Virginia, 61, 70, 91, 110, 114, 115, 123, 129
Jefferson, Thomas, 41–42, 45–46, 73, 125, 143
Jim Crow, 36, 70, 80, 122, 165–66
Johnson, Charles, 153, 154
Johnson, Robert, 101
Jordon, Levi, 155, 159

Kelso, William, 129–30, 143
Key, Francis Scott, 124
Kingsley, Anna H. (Anta Madgigine Jai), 14, 149, 150, 202
Kingsley, George, 17
Kingsley, Zephaniah, Jr., 11–12, 199, 202; climatic theory of race, 16; Danish citizenship, 13; early life, 12; in Haiti, 17; purchase of enslaved, 15–16; Spanish citizenship, 13; views on enslavement, 13–14; views on White Americans, 15
Kingsley, Zephaniah, Sr., 12–13
Kingsley Plantation (Florida), 5, 6, 129, 149, 172, 175, 199–200, 201, 202, 204. *See also* Kingsley, Zephaniah, Jr.
Kingsmill Plantation (Virginia), 141
Kongo, Kingdom of, 92, 93
Ku Klux Klan, 79, 161

Lane, Ralph, 105
Latifundia, 11

Latin America, 78
Laurel Grove Plantation (Florida), 14
Led Zeppelin (rock band), 101
Lehman College, 200
Leo, John [Leo Africanus], 92
Leone, Mark P., 160, 161–64, 167, 170, 172
Leveau (Leveaux), Marie, 167
Levi Jordan Plantation (Texas), 155–58, 175
Lewis, Abraham Lincoln, 202
Lewis, Mary Sammis, 202
Lewis and Clark Expedition, 128
Ligue universelle pour le défense de la race negro, 55
Lincoln Golf and Country Club, 202
Liverpool, England, 103
London (England), 58–60, 62, 103, 106, 107, 116, 146, 152, 172
Lopez, Duarte, 93
Lost Tribes of Israel, 41
Louisiana Purchase, 47
Lying, 191
Lynching, 79, 203

Magic, 24, 151–52, 154
Malays, 41
Manifest Destiny, 46–47, 50
Māori, 128
Martin's Hundred Plantation (Virginia), 134, 137
Maryland Department of Transportation, 124
Mason, Otis T., 73
Massachusetts Archaeological Society, 52
Maumee River, 180
Mead, Margaret, 30
Medicine Wheel (Wyoming), 87
Mende, 125
Merrifield, Ralph, 152–54
Mexicans, 22–23, 48
Mexico, 22–23, 104; Mexico City, 41, 172; Vera Cruz, 1
Middle Ages, 153
Middle East, 23
Middle Tennessee State University, 117
Miles, Mary E., 190
Ming Dynasty (China), 83
Minkisi (nkisi), 159–60, 163

Mississippi Department of Archives and History, 51
Mississippi River, 43–44, 66, 75, 128
Mississippi Valley, 1, 43–44, 52
Mojo bag, 164
Monticello Plantation (Virginia), 143
Montserrat, 146
Mooney, James, 77
Morehouse College, 29
Morgan, Lewis Henry, 194
Morocco, 96
Morrison, Toni, 87
Mound Builders, 40–50
Mudlarks, 59, 153
Museum of London (England), 152

Nairne, Thomas, 31
National Association for the Advancement of Colored People (NAACP), 55
National Museum of African Art, 202
National Negro Business League, 55
National Pipe Archive, 103
Ndongo, Kingdom of, 92, 94
Near East, 39
Negro Fort (Florida), 54
Negros Burial Ground (New York). *See* African Burial Ground
New Amsterdam, 173–74
Newton Plantation (Barbados), 114–15, 144
New York City Landmarks Preservation Commission, 172, 174
New Zealand, 128
Nicot, Jean, 104
Nicotiana, 104
Nigeria, 35, 120, 145, 148
Noël Hume, Ivor, 59–64, 67, 69, 74, 103, 110, 116, 123, 129, 134, 137, 152; and Colono-Indian pottery, 62–64; at Rosewell Plantation (Virginia), 63
Noël Hume (Baines), Audrey, 60–61, 85, 129
North Africa, 23
North Pole, 146
Northwestern University, 31

Ocmulgee National Monument, Georgia, 6–7, 9
Ohio River, 177, 179, 181, 190

Ordway (John), Sergeant, 128
Oswald, Adrian, 60, 109

Park, Robert E., 26, 31–32, 62; Africanisms and, 32
Parrish, Joseph, 42
Peabody Foundation for Archaeology, 52
Peirce, Charles S., 121
Pentecostalism, 170
Phillips Academy, 52
Phoenicians, 41
Pigafetta, Filippo, 93
Pipes, clay tobacco, 60, 103, 153, 158, 171, 191, 196, 201, 203–4; African, 115–17, 125–26; clay used in, 106–8; formula for dating, 111–12; Indigenous, 107, 112, 116–17, 126; infilling on, 115; initial European names for, 105; manufacture of, 106–9; styles of, 108–9, 112; terra cotta, 112–13
Pits, 129, 131–32, 139–40, 151 191, 196, 201, 203–4
Plantation, definition of, 11
Point Comfort, Virginia, 1
Poitiers, University of, 30
Polhemus, Richard, 67, 82
Pollard, John Garland, 77
Pompeii, 83
Portuguese, colonial, 92–94, 104
Pottery, 56, 171; Indigenous, 7–8, 57, 61–63, 72–74, 76, 83; makers' marks, 83–84
Powell, John Wesley, 49, 73
Pragmatism, 121–23
Pre-Adamites, 41
Protestantism, 154, 164, 170

Race: Falconer, William, on, 16; Hippocrates, on, 16; Ibn Khaldun on, 23; theory of, 16–17, 23
Racism, 2, 26, 35, 47–48, 50, 79, 97, 130–31, 192–93, 200, 203
Radcliffe College, 52
Raleigh, Walter, 105, 116
Reconquista, Spanish, 23
Red River, 187
Religion, 151–52
Republic of Congo, 91
Revolutionary War, 66, 80, 103, 124

Rich Neck Plantation (Virginia), 137, 141
Roanoke (North Carolina), 105, 116
Rochambeau, Comte de, 124–25
Rolling Stones (rock band) 101
Romano-British, 62
Romans, 59, 61, 118, 152, 172
Roosevelt, Franklin, 165
Rosewell Plantation (Virginia), 63
Royal African Company, 96, 143–44
Ruppel, Timothy, 163

Sahara Desert, 143
Samford, Patricia, 135–37, 140–43
San Marcos (pottery), 72–74
Schablitsky, Julie, 124–26
Schouler, James, 192
Scythians, 48
Second World War, 7, 52, 55, 59, 70, 196
Secrecy, 177, 191, 194–96, 198
Seven Years' War, 146
Shadwell, Thomas, 133
Sibley, Albert, 178–79
Sibley, John, 177
Sierra Leone, 125
Sikes, Kathryn, 117–19
Simms, William Gilmore, 63, 64
Singleton, Theresa, 11, 150, 163
Slave hunters, 181, 188
Slayton House (Maryland), 168
Smith, Bessie, 5
Smith, J. W., 190
Smithsonian Institution, 46, 163, 202
Smyth, John Ferdinand Dalziel, 64
Social Darwinism, 79–80
South, Stanley, 65, 67, 69, 82
South Africa, 23
South America, 1, 3, 104
South Carolina Institute for Archaeology and Anthropology, 66, 67
Southeastern Ceremonial Complex, 87–89
Southern Illinois Normal University (Carbondale), 49
Spanish, colonial, 1, 72, 74, 96, 104, 166
Spaulding, Albert C., 7–9
Speck, Frank G., 63, 73, 77
Spiritualism, 170
Squier, Ephraim, 45–46, 87

Subterfuge, 177, 191
Supremacy, White, 11, 191
Suriname, 35
Survivals. *See* Africanisms; Cultural retentions
Syracuse University, 150

Talley, Thomas W., 26
Tatler, 139
Taylor, Walter, 55–56, 86
Thames River (London), 59–60, 153
Thomas, Cyrus, 48–50, 51, 55
Thucydides, on cultural retentions, 21
Tobacco, 103–4; English views of, 105–6; Indigenous use of, 104–5, 114, 116
Travel, steamboat, 189
Trinidad, 35
Turner, Frederick Jackson, 50
Tuskegee Institute, 31
Tylor, Edward B., 21, 152; early life, 22; ethnocentrism of, 22–23, 26; in Mexico, 22–23

Underground Railroad, 179
Universal Negro Improvement and Conservation Association and African Communities League, 55
University of Arizona, 161
University of Chicago, 29, 30, 53
University of Florida, 5, 149
University of Houston, 155
University of Michigan, 7, 9, 52
University of New Mexico, 52
University of North Carolina, 66
University of South Carolina, 64, 65, 82

University of Texas, Austin, 135
US Civil War, 103
US Entomological Commission, 49
Utopia Plantation (Virginia), 138, 141, 142, 144, 148

Van Hooghvelt, Elysabeth Croon, 173
Van Tienhoven, Cornelius, 173–74, 175
Vassa, Gustavus, 146
Vikings, 41
Vires, Mr., 178
Voodoo, 170

War of 1812, 54
Washington, Booker T., 31, 55
Waters, Muddy (McKinley Morganfield), 165
West, Cornel, 122
West Africa, 65, 67–68, 72, 76, 101, 114, 115–16, 118, 126, 143, 145, 148–50, 163, 169
West India Company, 173
West Indies, 26, 104, 105
White, John, 116–17, 120
Whiteness, 40
Whitfield, Francis, 185–87
Williamsburg, Virginia, 17, 61, 67, 70, 114, 137
Wilson, Woodrow, 28
Witch bottles, 154
Witchcraft, 24, 197
Witches, 152, 154

Yorkshire, England, 107
Yorktown, Virginia, 124
Yoruba, 38, 78

Charles E. Orser Jr. is an anthropological historical archaeologist who investigates the modern world as it was created after about 1492. He received his PhD in 1980 and has conducted excavations in the United States (Midwest and South), Europe (Ireland and England), and South America (Brazil). He has lectured throughout the United States and in Ireland, England, Sweden, Portugal, Brazil, Colombia, Italy, Canada, Iceland, New Zealand, and Australia. He is a retired Distinguished Professor at Illinois State University and Research Professor at Arizona State University and the University of Western Ontario. He is the author of 100 professional articles and several books, including *Historical Archaeology* (now in its third edition); *A Historical Archaeology of the Modern World; The Archaeology of Race and Racialization in Historic America; Race and Practice in Archaeological Interpretation; Unearthing Hidden Ireland: Historical Archaeology at Ballykilcline, County Roscommon; A Primer on Modern-World Archaeology; Archaeological Thinking* (2nd edition); and *An Archaeology of the English Atlantic World, 1600–1700*. He is the founder and editor of the *International Journal of Historical Archaeology*. In 2019 he received the J. C. Harrington Medal from the Society for Historical Archaeology.

www.ingramcontent.com/pod-product-compliance
Lightning Source LLC
Chambersburg PA
CBHW070304240426
43661CB00057B/2637